Student Companion

Accelerated Grade 7
Volume 1

PEARSON

Boston, Massachusetts • Chandler, Arizona • Glenview, Illinois • Upper Saddle River, New Jersey

Acknowledgments for illustrations and composition: Rory Hensley, David Jackson, Jim Mariano, Rich McMahon, Lorie Park, Ted Smykal, Ralph Voltz, and Laserwords

PEARSON

ISBN-13: 978-0-13-330640-8
ISBN-10: 0-13-330640-2
2 3 4 5 6 7 8 9 10 V001 17 16 15 14

digits™ System Requirements

Supported System Configurations

	Operating System (32-bit only)	Web Browser* (32-bit only)	Java® Version**
PC	Windows® XP (SP3) Windows Vista (SP1) Windows 7	Internet Explorer® 7 Internet Explorer 8 Internet Explorer 9 Mozilla Firefox® 11 Google Chrome™	1.4.2 1.5 [5.0 Update 11 or higher] 1.6 [6.0 through Update 18]
Mac	Macintosh® OS 10.6.x, 10.7.x	Safari® 5.0 Safari 5.1 Google Chrome™	1.5 [5.0 Update 16 or higher]

* Pop-up blockers must be disabled in the browser.
** Java (JRE) plug-in must be installed and JavaScript® must be enabled in the browser.

Additional Requirements

Software	Version
Adobe® Flash®	Version 10.4 or higher
Adobe Reader® (required for PC*)	Version 8 or higher
Word processing software	Microsoft® Word®, Open Office, or similar application to open ".doc" files

* Macintosh® OS 10.6 has a built-in PDF reader, Preview.

Screen Resolution

PC
Minimum: 1024 x 768*
Maximum: 1280 x 1024
Mac
Minimum: 1024 x 768*
Maximum: 1280 x 960
*recommended for interactive whiteboards

Internet Connection

Broadband (cable/DSL) or greater is recommended.

AOL® and AT&T™ Yahoo!® Users

You cannot use the AOL or AT&T Yahoo! browsers. However, you can use AOL or AT&T as your Internet Service Provider to access the Internet, and then open a supported browser.

For *digits*™ Support

go to **http://support.pearsonschool.com/index.cfm/digits**

digits™ Learning Team

My Name: ______________________________

My Teacher's Name: ______________________________

My School: ______________________________

Visit **www.digitsmath.com** to learn more about the **digits** authors and advisors.

Francis (Skip) Fennell
***digits* Author**
Approaches to mathematics content and curriculum, educational policy, and support for intervention

Eric Milou
***digits* Author**
Approaches to mathematical content and the use of technology in middle grades classrooms

Art Johnson
***digits* Author**
Approaches to mathematical content and support for English language learners

William F. Tate
***digits* Author**
Approaches to intervention, and use of efficacy and research

Helene Sherman
***digits* Author**
Teacher education and support for struggling students

Grant Wiggins
***digits* Consulting Author**
Understanding by Design

Stuart J. Murphy
***digits* Author**
Visual learning and student engagement

Randall I. Charles
***digits* Advisor**

Janie Schielack
***digits* Author**
Approaches to mathematical content, building problem solvers, and support for intervention

Jim Cummins
***digits* Advisor**
Supporting English Language Learners

Jacquie Moen
***digits* Advisor**
Digital Technology

Go online for all your cool digits™ stuff!

Be sure to save your login information by writing it here.

My Username: ______________________________

My Password: ______________________________

First, go to **MyMathUniverse.com**. From there you can explore the **Channel List**, which includes fun and interactive games and videos, or select your program and log in.

Play some cool math **games!**

Complete your **homework** online!

Discover math **tricks** and **tips!**

Check out fun **videos!**

ACTIVe-book

No more pencils! No more books! Why? Because the Student Companion you have in front of you can also be found online in ACTIVe-book format. You can access your ACTIVe-book on a tablet or on a computer, so any questions you can answer in your Student Companion you can also master online.

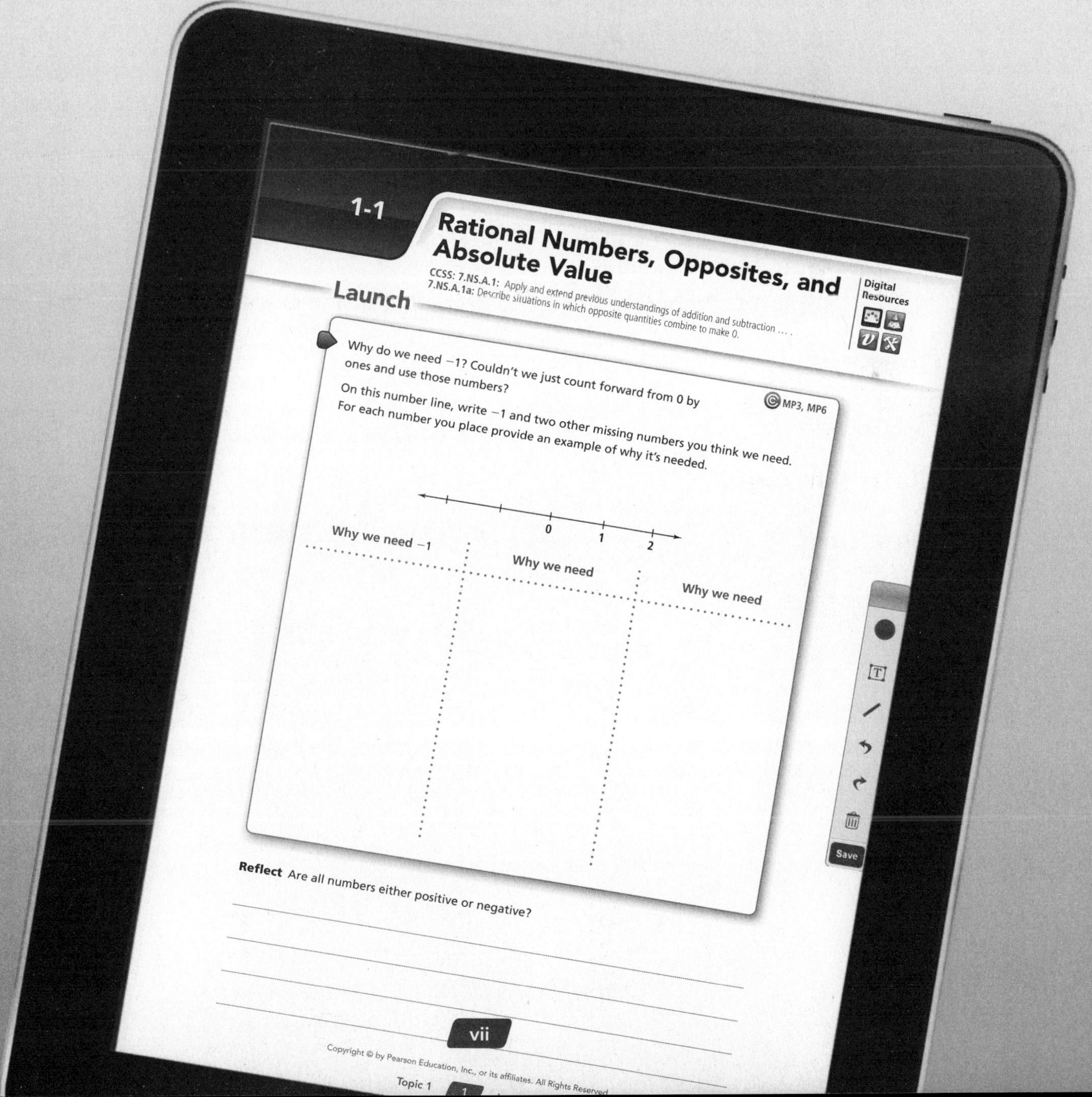

Contents

Welcome to digits™

Using the Student Companion

digits is designed to help you master mathematics skills and concepts in a way that's relevant to you. As the title ***digits*** suggests, this program takes a digital approach. The Student Companion supports your work on ***digits*** by providing a place to demonstrate your understanding of lesson skills and concepts in writing.

Your companion supports your work on ***digits*** in so many ways!

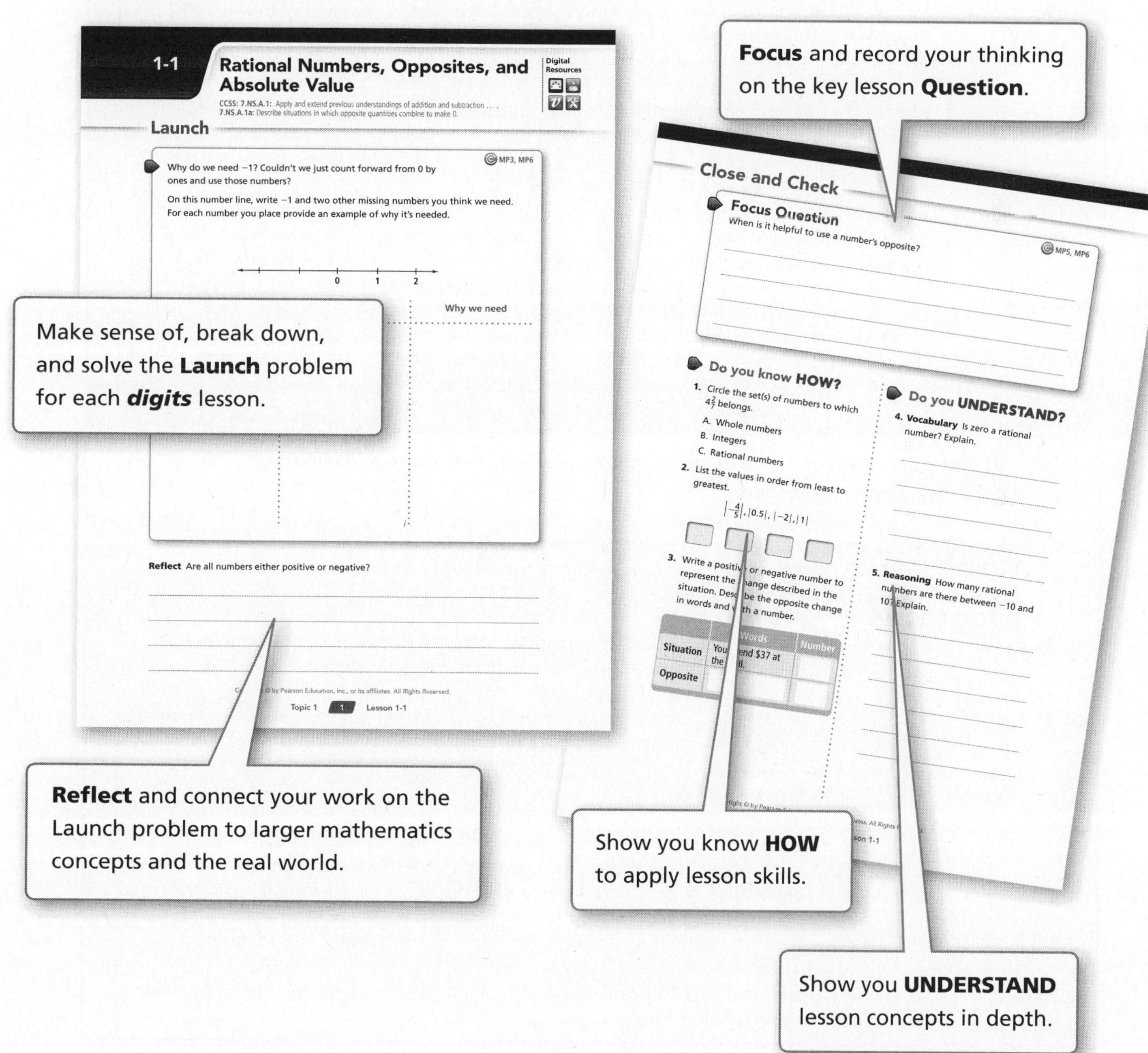

Number	Standard for Mathematical Content
7.RP Ratios and Proportional Relationships	
Analyze proportional relationships and use them to solve real-world and mathematical problems.	
7.RP.A.1	Compute unit rates associated with ratios of fractions, including ratios of lengths, areas and other quantities measured in like or different units.
7.RP.A.2	Recognize and represent proportional relationships between quantities.
7.RP.A.2a	Decide whether two quantities are in a proportional relationship, e.g., by testing for equivalent ratios in a table or graphing on a coordinate plane and observing whether the graph is a straight line through the origin.
7.RP.A.2b	Identify the constant of proportionality (unit rate) in tables, graphs, equations, diagrams, and verbal descriptions of proportional relationships.
7.RP.A.2c	Represent proportional relationships by equations.
7.RP.A.2d	Explain what a point (x, y) on the graph of a proportional relationship means in terms of the situation, with special attention to the points (0, 0) and $(1, r)$ where r is the unit rate.
7.RP.A.3	Use proportional relationships to solve multistep ratio and percent problems. Examples: simple interest, tax, markups and markdowns, gratuities and commissions, fees, percent increase and decrease, percent error.
7.NS The Number System	
Apply and extend previous understandings of operations with fractions to add, subtract, multiply, and divide rational numbers.	
7.NS.A.1	Apply and extend previous understandings of addition and subtraction to add and subtract rational numbers; represent addition and subtraction on a horizontal or vertical number line diagram.
7.NS.A.1a	Describe situations in which opposite quantities combine to make 0. For example, a hydrogen atom has 0 charge because its two constituents are oppositely charged.
7.NS.A.1b	Understand $p + q$ as the number located a distance $\|q\|$ from p, in the positive or negative direction depending on whether q is positive or negative. Show that a number and its opposite have a sum of 0 (are additive inverses). Interpret sums of rational numbers by describing real-world contexts.
7.NS.A.1c	Understand subtraction of rational numbers as adding the additive inverse, $p - q = p + (-q)$. Show that the distance between two rational numbers on the number line is the absolute value of their difference, and apply this principle in real-world contexts.
7.NS.A.1d	Apply properties of operations as strategies to add and subtract rational numbers.
7.NS.A.2	Apply and extend previous understandings of multiplication and division and of fractions to multiply and divide rational numbers.

Number	Standard for Mathematical Content

7.NS The Number System *(continued)*

Apply and extend previous understandings of operations with fractions to add, subtract, multiply, and divide rational numbers.

Number	Standard for Mathematical Content
7.NS.A.2a	Understand that multiplication is extended from fractions to rational numbers by requiring that operations continue to satisfy the properties of operations, particularly the distributive property, leading to products such as $(-1)(-1) = 1$ and the rules for multiplying signed numbers. Interpret products of rational numbers by describing real-world contexts.
7.NS.A.2b	Understand that integers can be divided, provided that the divisor is not zero, and every quotient of integers (with non-zero divisor) is a rational number. If p and q are integers, then $\left(\frac{p}{q}\right) = \frac{(-p)}{q} = \frac{p}{(-q)}$. Interpret quotients of rational numbers by describing real- world contexts.
7.NS.A.2c	Apply properties of operations as strategies to multiply and divide rational numbers.
7.NS.A.2d	Convert a rational number to a decimal using long division; know that the decimal form of a rational number terminates in 0s or eventually repeats.
7.NS.A.3	Solve real-world and mathematical problems involving the four operations with rational numbers.

7.EE Expressions and Equations

Use properties of operations to generate equivalent expressions.

Number	Standard for Mathematical Content
7.EE.A.1	Apply properties of operations as strategies to add, subtract, factor, and expand linear expressions with rational coefficients.
7.EE.A.2	Understand that rewriting an expression in different forms in a problem context can shed light on the problem and how the quantities in it are related. For example, $a + 0.05a = 1.05a$ means that "increase by 5%" is the same as "multiply by 1.05."

Solve real-life and mathematical problems using numerical and algebraic expressions and equations.

Number	Standard for Mathematical Content
7.EE.B.3	Solve multi-step real-life and mathematical problems posed with positive and negative rational numbers in any form (whole numbers, fractions, and decimals), using tools strategically. Apply properties of operations to calculate with numbers in any form; convert between forms as appropriate; and assess the reasonableness of answers using mental computation and estimation strategies.
7.EE.B.4	Use variables to represent quantities in a real-world or mathematical problem, and construct simple equations and inequalities to solve problems by reasoning about the quantities.
7.EE.B.4a	Solve word problems leading to equations of the form $px + q = r$ and $p(x + q) = r$, where p, q, and r are specific rational numbers. Solve equations of these forms fluently. Compare an algebraic solution to an arithmetic solution, identifying the sequence of the operations used in each approach.
7.EE.B.4b	Solve word problems leading to inequalities of the form $px + q > r$ or $px + q < r$, where p, q, and r are specific rational numbers. Graph the solution set of the inequality and interpret it in the context of the problem.

Grade 7 Common Core State Standards *continued*

Number	Standard for Mathematical Content
7.G Geometry	
Draw construct, and describe geometrical figures and describe the relationships between them.	
7.G.A.1	Solve problems involving scale drawings of geometric figures, including computing actual lengths and areas from a scale drawing and reproducing a scale drawing at a different scale.
7.G.A.2	Draw (freehand, with ruler and protractor, and with technology) geometric shapes with given conditions. Focus on constructing triangles from three measures of angles or sides, noticing when the conditions determine a unique triangle, more than one triangle, or no triangle.
7.G.A.3	Describe the two-dimensional figures that result from slicing three- dimensional figures, as in plane sections of right rectangular prisms and right rectangular pyramids.
Solve real-life and mathematical problems involving angle measure, area, surface area, and volume.	
7.G.B.4	Know the formulas for the area and circumference of a circle and use them to solve problems; give an informal derivation of the relationship between the circumference and area of a circle.
7.G.B.5	Use facts about supplementary, complementary, vertical, and adjacent angles in a multi-step problem to write and solve simple equations for an unknown angle in a figure.
7.G.B.6	Solve real-world and mathematical problems involving area, volume and surface area of two- and three-dimensional objects composed of triangles, quadrilaterals, polygons, cubes, and right prisms.
7.SP Statistics and Probability	
Use random sampling to draw inferences about a population.	
7.SP.A.1	Understand that statistics can be used to gain information about a population by examining a sample of the population; generalizations about a population from a sample are valid only if the sample is representative of that population. Understand that random sampling tends to produce representative samples and support valid inferences.
7.SP.A.2	Use data from a random sample to draw inferences about a population with an unknown characteristic of interest. Generate multiple samples (or simulated samples) of the same size to gauge the variation in estimates or predictions.
Draw informal comparative inferences about two populations.	
7.SP.B.3	Informally assess the degree of visual overlap of two numerical data distributions with similar variabilities, measuring the difference between the centers by expressing it as a multiple of a measure of variability.
7.SP.B.4	Use measures of center and measures of variability for numerical data from random samples to draw informal comparative inferences about two populations.
Investigate chance processes and develop, use, and evaluate probability models.	
7.SP.C.5	Understand that the probability of a chance event is a number between 0 and 1 that expresses the likelihood of the event occurring. Larger numbers indicate greater likelihood. A probability near 0 indicates an unlikely event, a probability around $\frac{1}{2}$ indicates an event that is neither unlikely nor likely, and a probability near 1 indicates a likely event.

Number	Standard for Mathematical Content
7.SP Statistics and Probability *(continued)*	
Investigate chance processes and develop, use, and evaluate probability models.	
7.SP.C.6	Approximate the probability of a chance event by collecting data on the chance process that produces it and observing its long-run relative frequency, and predict the approximate relative frequency given the probability.
7.SP.C.7	Develop a probability model and use it to find probabilities of events. Compare probabilities from a model to observed frequencies; if the agreement is not good, explain possible sources of the discrepancy.
7.SP.C.7a	Develop a uniform probability model by assigning equal probability to all outcomes, and use the model to determine probabilities of events.
7.SP.C.7b	Develop a probability model (which may not be uniform) by observing frequencies in data generated from a chance process.
7.SP.C.8	Find probabilities of compound events using organized lists, tables, tree diagrams, and simulation.
7.SP.C.8a	Understand that, just as with simple events, the probability of a compound event is the fraction of outcomes in the sample space for which the compound event occurs.
7.SP.C.8b	Represent sample spaces for compound events using methods such as organized lists, tables and tree diagrams. For an event described in everyday language (e.g., "rolling double sixes"), identify the outcomes in the sample space which compose the event.
7.SP.C.8c	Design and use a simulation to generate frequencies for compound events. For example, use random digits as a simulation tool to approximate the answer to the question: If 40% of donors have type A blood, what is the probability that it will take at least 4 donors to find one with type A blood?

Number	Standard for Mathematical Practice
MP1	Make sense of problems and persevere in solving them.
MP2	Reason abstractly and quantitatively.
MP3	Construct viable arguments and critique the reasoning of others.
MP4	Model with mathematics.
MP5	Use appropriate tools strategically.
MP6	Attend to precision.
MP7	Look for and make use of structure.
MP8	Look for and express regularity in repeated reasoning.

Gr 8 | Common Core State Standards

Number	Standard for Mathematical Content
8.NS The Number System	
Know that there are numbers that are not rational, and approximate them by rational numbers.	
8.NS.A.1	Know that numbers that are not rational are called irrational. Understand informally that every number has a decimal expansion; for rational numbers show that the decimal expansion repeats eventually, and convert a decimal expansion which repeats eventually into a rational number.
8.NS.A.2	Use rational approximations of irrational numbers to compare the size of irrational numbers, locate them approximately on a number line diagram, and estimate the value of expressions (e.g., π^2). For example, by truncating the decimal expansion of $\sqrt{2}$, show that $\sqrt{2}$ is between 1 and 2, then between 1.4 and 1.5, and explain how to continue on to get better approximations.
8.EE Expressions and Equations	
Work with radicals and integer exponents.	
8.EE.A.1	Know and apply the properties of integer exponents to generate equivalent numerical expressions. For example, $3^2 \times 3^{(-5)} = 3^{(-3)} = \frac{1}{(3^3)} = \frac{1}{27}$.
8.EE.A.2	Use square root and cube root symbols to represent solutions to equations of the form $x^2 = p$ and $x^3 = p$, where p is a positive rational number. Evaluate square roots of small perfect squares and cube roots of small perfect cubes. Know that $\sqrt{2}$ is irrational.
8.EE.A.3	Use numbers expressed in the form of a single digit times an integer power of 10 to estimate very large or very small quantities, and to express how many times as much one is than the other. For example, estimate the population of the United States as 3×10^8 and the population of the world as 7×10^9, and determine that the world population is more than 20 times larger.
8.EE.A.4	Perform operations with numbers expressed in scientific notation, including problems where both decimal and scientific notation are used. Use scientific notation and choose units of appropriate size for measurements of very large or very small quantities (e.g., use millimeters per year for seafloor spreading). Interpret scientific notation that has been generated by technology.
Understand the connections between proportional relationships, lines, and linear equations.	
8.EE.B.5	Graph proportional relationships, interpreting the unit rate as the slope of the graph. Compare two different proportional relationships represented in different ways. For example, compare a distance-time graph to a distance-time equation to determine which of two moving objects has greater speed.
8.EE.B.6	Use similar triangles to explain why the slope m is the same between any two distinct points on a non-vertical line in the coordinate plane; derive the equation $y = mx$ for a line through the origin and the equation $y = mx + b$ for a line intercepting the vertical axis at b.

Number	Standard for Mathematical Content
8.EE Expressions and Equations *(continued)*	
Analyze and solve linear equations and pairs of simultaneous linear equations.	
8.EE.C.7	Solve linear equations in one variable.
8.EE.C.7a	Give examples of linear equations in one variable with one solution, infinitely many solutions, or no solutions. Show which of these possibilities is the case by successively transforming the given equation into simpler forms, until an equivalent equation of the form $x = a$, $a = a$, or $a = b$ results (where a and b are different numbers).
8.EE.C.7b	Solve linear equations with rational number coefficients, including equations whose solutions require expanding expressions using the distributive property and collecting like terms.
8.G Geometry	
Understand congruence and similarity using physical models, transparencies, or geometry software.	
8.G.A.1	Verify experimentally the properties of rotations, reflections, and translations:
8.G.A.1a	Verify experimentally the properties of rotations, reflections, and translations: Lines are taken to lines, and line segments to line segments of the same length.
8.G.A.1b	Verify experimentally the properties of rotations, reflections, and translations: Angles are taken to angles of the same measure.
8.G.A.1c	Verify experimentally the properties of rotations, reflections, and translations: Parallel lines are taken to parallel lines.
8.G.A.2	Understand that a two-dimensional figure is congruent to another if the second can be obtained from the first by a sequence of rotations, reflections, and translations; given two congruent figures, describe a sequence that exhibits the congruence between them.
8.G.A.3	Describe the effect of dilations, translations, rotations, and reflections on two-dimensional figures using coordinates.
8.G.A.4	Understand that a two-dimensional figure is similar to another if the second can be obtained from the first by a sequence of rotations, reflections, translations, and dilations; given two similar two- dimensional figures, describe a sequence that exhibits the similarity between them.
8.G.A.5	Use informal arguments to establish facts about the angle sum and exterior angle of triangles, about the angles created when parallel lines are cut by a transversal, and the angle-angle criterion for similarity of triangles.
Solve real-world and mathematical problems involving volume of cylinders, cones, and spheres.	
8.G.C.9	Know the formulas for the volumes of cones, cylinders, and spheres and use them to solve real-world and mathematical problems.

Grade 8 Common Core State Standards *continued*

Number	Standard for Mathematical Practice
MP1	Make sense of problems and persevere in solving them.
MP2	Reason abstractly and quantitatively.
MP3	Construct viable arguments and critique the reasoning of others.
MP4	Model with mathematics.
MP5	Use appropriate tools strategically.
MP6	Attend to precision.
MP7	Look for and make use of structure.
MP8	Look for and express regularity in repeated reasoning.

Vocabulary

Language of Math for Topic 1

Lesson	Vocabulary	
	New	Review
1-1 Rational Numbers, Opposites, and Absolute Value	absolute value opposites rational numbers	integers whole numbers
1-2 Adding Integers		integers opposites
1-3 Adding Rational Numbers		absolute value rational numbers
1-4 Subtracting Integers		integers opposites
1-5 Subtracting Rational Numbers		opposites rational numbers
1-6 Distance on a Number Line		absolute value distance
1-7 Problem Solving		interquartile range range
Topic 1 Topic Review	absolute value additive inverse Inverse Property of Addition opposites rational numbers	distance integers whole numbers

Vocabulary

Language of Math for Topic 2

Lesson	Vocabulary	
	New	Review
2-1 Multiplying Integers		integers
2-2 Multiplying Rational Numbers		rational numbers
2-3 Dividing Integers		integers quotient unit rate
2-4 Dividing Rational Numbers	reciprocals	denominator numerator quotient rational numbers
2-5 Operations With Rational Numbers	complex fraction	Distributive Property order of operations
2-6 Problem Solving		constant of proportionality mean proportional relationship
Topic 2 Topic Review	complex fraction reciprocals	denominator Distributive Property integers numerator order of operations quotient rational numbers unit rate

Vocabulary

Language of Math for Topic 3

Lesson	Vocabulary	
	New	**Review**
3-1 Repeating Decimals	repeating decimal	decimal rational number
3-2 Terminating Decimals	terminating decimal	decimal
3-3 Percents Greater Than 100		percent
3-4 Percents Less Than 1		percent
3-5 Fractions, Decimals, and Percents		decimal fraction percent ratio rational number
3-6 Percent Error	accuracy percent error	dot plot
3-7 Problem Solving		percent percent error
Topic 3 Topic Review	accuracy percent error repeating decimal terminating decimal	decimal fraction percent ratio rational number

Vocabulary

Language of Math for Topic 4

Lesson	Vocabulary	
	New	Review
4-1 Expressing Rational Numbers with Decimal Expansions	repeating decimal terminating decimal	rational numbers
4-2 Exploring Irrational Numbers	irrational numbers perfect square real numbers square root	integer natural numbers whole numbers
4-3 Approximating Irrational Numbers		estimate
4-4 Comparing and Ordering Rational and Irrational Numbers		order
4-5 Problem Solving		natural numbers rational numbers repeating decimal
Topic 4 Topic Review	irrational numbers perfect square real numbers repeating decimal square root terminating decimal	integer natural numbers rational numbers whole numbers

Vocabulary

Language of Math for Topic 5

Lesson	Vocabulary	
	New	Review
5-1 Perfect Squares, Square Roots, and Equations of the form $x^2 = p$		inverse operations perfect square square root
5-2 Perfect Cubes, Cube Roots, and Equations of the form $x^3 = p$	cube root perfect cube	inverse operations
5-3 Exponents and Multiplication		base exponent power
5-4 Exponents and Division		base exponent power
5-5 Zero and Negative Exponents	Negative Exponent Property Zero Exponent Property	base exponent
5-6 Comparing Expressions with Exponents		base equivalent expressions exponent
5-7 Problem Solving		algebraic expression
Topic 5 Topic Review	cube root Negative Exponent Property perfect cube Zero Exponent Property	base exponent inverse operations perfect square power square root

Vocabulary

Language of Math for Topic 6

Lesson	Vocabulary	
	New	Review
6-1 Exploring Scientific Notation	scientific notation	base exponent power standard form
6-2 Using Scientific Notation to Describe Very Large Quantities		base exponent power scientific notation standard form
6-3 Using Scientific Notation to Describe Very Small Quantities		base exponent power scientific notation standard form
6-4 Operating with Numbers Expressed in Scientific Notation		base exponent power scientific notation
6-5 Problem Solving		scientific notation
Topic 6 Topic Review	scientific notation	base exponent power standard form

Vocabulary

Language of Math for Topic 7

Lesson	Vocabulary	
	New	Review
7-1 Equivalent Ratios	equivalent ratios ratio terms of a ratio	greatest common factor simplest form
7-2 Unit Rates	rate unit price unit rate	ratio
7-3 Ratios With Fractions		least common multiple ratio simplest form
7-4 Unit Rates With Fractions		unit rate
7-5 Problem Solving		ratio
Topic 7 Topic Review	equivalent ratios rate ratio terms of a ratio unit price unit rate	greatest common factor least common multiple simplest form

Vocabulary

Language of Math for Topic 8

Lesson	Vocabulary	
	New	**Review**
8-1 Proportional Relationships and Tables	proportional relationship	equivalent ratios
8-2 Proportional Relationships and Graphs		proportional relationship
8-3 Constant of Proportionality	constant of proportionality	proportional relationship
8-4 Proportional Relationships and Equations	proportion	constant of proportionality proportional relationship
8-5 Maps and Scale Drawings	scale scale drawing	constant of proportionality proportional relationship
8-6 Problem Solving		proportional relationship
Topic 8 Topic Review	constant of proportionality proportion proportional relationship scale scale drawing	equivalent ratios

Vocabulary

Language of Math for Topic 9

Lesson	Vocabulary	
	New	Review
9-1 The Percent Equation	percent equation	percent ratio
9-2 Using the Percent Equation		percent equation
9-3 Simple Interest	balance interest interest rate principal simple interest	explain identify
9-4 Compound Interest	compound interest interest period	balance principal simple interest
9-5 Percent Increase and Decrease	percent decrease percent increase percent of change	percent
9-6 Markups and Markdowns	markdown markup	percent decrease percent increase
9-7 Problem Solving		percent percent decrease percent increase
Topic 9 Topic Review	balance compound interest interest interest period interest rate markdown markup percent decrease percent equation percent increase percent of change principal simple interest	percent ratio

Vocabulary

Language of Math for Topic 10

Lesson	Vocabulary	
	New	Review
10-1 Expanding Algebraic Expressions	expand an algebraic expression	algebraic expression Distributive Property
10-2 Factoring Algebraic Expressions	factor an algebraic expression like terms	algebraic expression Distributive Property greatest common factor (GCF)
10-3 Adding Algebraic Expressions	coefficient constant simplify an algebraic expression	algebraic expression like terms terms
10-4 Subtracting Algebraic Expressions		algebraic expression
10-5 Problem Solving		equivalent expression
Topic 10 Topic Review	coefficient constant expand an algebraic expression factor an algebraic expression like terms simplify an algebraic expression	algebraic expression Distributive Property greatest common factor (GCF)

Vocabulary

Language of Math for Topic 11

<table>
<tr><th rowspan="2">Lesson</th><th colspan="2">Vocabulary</th></tr>
<tr><th>New</th><th>Review</th></tr>
<tr><td>11-1 Solving Simple Equations</td><td>Addition Property of Equality
Division Property of Equality
isolate a variable
Multiplication Property of Equality
Subtraction Property of Equality</td><td>equation</td></tr>
<tr><td>11-2 Writing Two-Step Equations</td><td></td><td>two-step equation</td></tr>
<tr><td>11-3 Solving Two-Step Equations</td><td></td><td>isolate a variable
two-step equation</td></tr>
<tr><td>11-4 Solving Equations Using the Distributive Property</td><td></td><td>Distributive Property</td></tr>
<tr><td>11-5 Problem Solving</td><td></td><td>isolate a variable</td></tr>
<tr><td>Topic 11 Topic Review</td><td>Addition Property of Equality
Division Property of Equality
isolate a variable
Multiplication Property of Equality
Subtraction Property of Equality</td><td>Distributive Property
Equation
two-step equation</td></tr>
</table>

Vocabulary

Language of Math for Topic 12

Lesson	Vocabulary	
	New	Review
12-1 Solving Two-Step Equations		Commutative Property Distributive Property isolate the variable order of operations
12-2 Solving Equations with Variables on Both Sides		solution of an equation
12-3 Solving Equations Using the Distributive Property		Distributive Property least common multiple
12-4 Solutions – One, None, or Infinitely Many	infinitely many solutions no solution	solution of an equation
12-5 Problem Solving		equation
Topic 12 Topic Review	infinitely many solutions no solution	Commutative Property Distributive Property least common multiple order of operations solution of an equation

Vocabulary

Language of Math for Topic 13

Lesson	Vocabulary	
	New	**Review**
13-1 Solving Inequalities Using Addition or Subtraction	Addition Property of Inequality inequality solution of an inequality solution set Subtraction Property of Inequality	isolate a variable
13-2 Solving Inequalities Using Multiplication or Division	Division Property of Inequality Multiplication Property of Inequality	negative number positive number
13-3 Solving Two-Step Inequalities	equivalent inequalities	solution of an inequality
13-4 Solving Multi-Step Inequalities		Distributive Property
13-5 Problem Solving		inequality
Topic 13 Topic Review	equivalent inequalities inequality solution of an inequality	Distributive Property isolate a variable negative number positive number

Vocabulary

Language of Math for Topic 14

Lesson	Vocabulary	
	New	Review
14-1 Graphing Proportional Relationships		constant of proportionality proportional relationship
14-2 Linear Equations: $y = mx$	linear equation	proportional relationship
14-3 The Slope of a Line	slope slope of a line	*x*-coordinate *y*-coordinate
14-4 Unit Rates and Slope		rate slope unite rate
14-5 The *y*-intercept of a Line	*y*-intercept	*y*-axis
14-6 Linear Equations: $y = mx + b$		slope slope-intercept form *y*-intercept
14-7 Problem Solving		equation proportional relationship
Topic 14 Topic Review	linear equation slope *y*-intercept	constant of proportionality proportional relationship rate unit rate

1-1

Rational Numbers, Opposites, and Absolute Value

Digital Resources

CCSS: 7.NS.A.1: Apply and extend previous understandings of addition and subtraction … .
7.NS.A.1a: Describe situations in which opposite quantities combine to make 0.

Launch

MP3, MP6

Why do we need −1? Couldn't we just count forward from 0 by ones and use those numbers?

On this number line, write −1 and two other missing numbers you think we need. For each number you place provide an example of why it's needed.

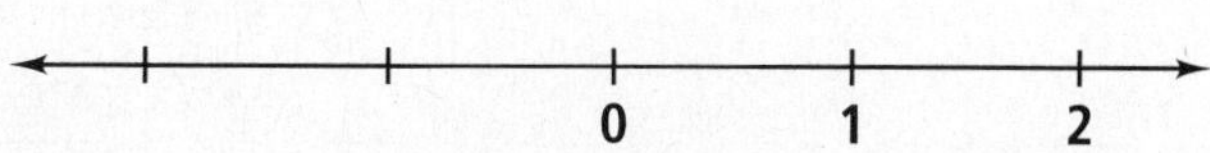

Why we need −1	Why we need	Why we need

Reflect Are all numbers either positive or negative?

Got It?

PART 1 Got It (1 of 2)

To which sets of numbers does $-1\frac{3}{5}$ belong?

I. Whole numbers
II. Integers
III. Rational numbers

PART 1 Got It (2 of 2)

One of your friends says the number $\frac{4}{4}$ belongs only in the category *Rational Numbers*. Another friend says it belongs in each category: *Whole Numbers*, *Integers*, and *Rational Numbers*. Who is correct? Explain.

Discuss with a classmate
Read each other's explanation to the problem.
Check for the following:
Is the explanation clear?
Are the key words, such as rational number, used correctly in the explanation? If not, discuss how to improve the explanation.

Got It?

PART 2 Got It

Which list of numbers is in order from least to greatest?

I. $\left|\frac{1}{2}\right|, \left|\frac{3}{4}\right|, |-3|$

II. $|-1|, |-0.8|, \left|\frac{1}{5}\right|$

PART 3 Got It

Write a positive or negative number to represent the change described in the situation. Describe the opposite change in words and with a number.

Situations and Their Opposites

	Words	Number
Situation	You win 50 tokens at the arcade.	
Opposite		

Close and Check

Focus Question

MP5, MP6

When is it helpful to use a number's opposite?

Do you know HOW?

1. Circle the set(s) of numbers to which $4\frac{2}{7}$ belongs.

A. Whole numbers

B. Integers

C. Rational numbers

2. List the values in order from least to greatest.

$$\left|-\frac{4}{5}\right|, |0.5|, |-2|, |1|$$

3. Write a positive or negative number to represent the change described in the situation. Describe the opposite change in words and with a number.

	Words	Number
Situation	You spend $37 at the mall.	
Opposite		

Do you UNDERSTAND?

4. Vocabulary Is zero a rational number? Explain.

5. Reasoning How many rational numbers are there between −10 and 10? Explain.

1-2 Adding Integers

Digital Resources

CCSS: 7.NS.A.1b: Understand $p + q$ as the number located a distance $|q|$ from p, in the positive or negative direction . . . . Show that a number and its opposite have a sum of 0 . . . . Interpret sums of rational numbers by describing real-world contexts. Also, **7.NS.A.1.**

Launch

MP1, MP4

Two rounds remain in a friendly video game of Zombie Pretzel Attack 2! Each zombie pretzel cheesed scores 100 points. Each player cheeses three zombie pretzels.

Write each player's new score. Tell how you found each score.

Player	Current Score	New Score
1	200 points	
2	−400 points	
3	−200 points	

Reflect Did any player's score change from negative to positive? Explain why.

Got It?

PART 1 Got It

$-5 + (-6)$ is ______ units from -5, in the ______ direction.

$-5 + (-6) =$ ______

PART 2 Got It

Is the value of the expression $-52 + (-52)$ *less than zero, equal to zero,* or *greater than zero*?

Got It?

PART 3 Got It

Write and simplify an addition expression for the model.

Close and Check

Focus Question

MP3, MP6

What does it mean to add less than nothing to something?

Do you know HOW?

1. Complete the statement. Then find the sum.

$-8 + 5$ is [5] units from -8 in the

[positive] direction.

$-8 + 5 =$ [-3]

2. Is the value of the expression $75 + (-75)$ *less than zero, equal to zero,* or *greater than zero*?

3. Write and simplify an addition expression for the model.

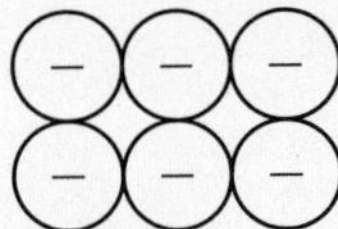

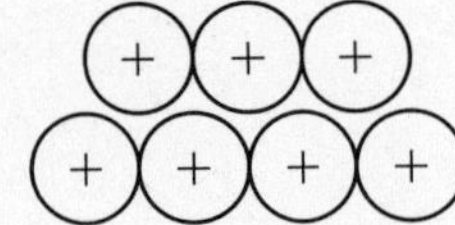

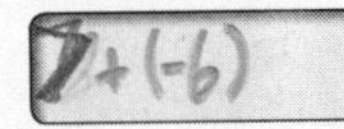

Do you UNDERSTAND?

4. Reasoning Does every rational number have an additive inverse? Explain.

5. Error Analysis A classmate says that the additive inverse of any rational number is negative. Is he correct? Explain.

1-3 Adding Rational Numbers

Digital Resources

CCSS: 7.NS.A.1b: Understand $p + q$ as the number located a distance $|q|$ from p, in the positive or negative direction . . . . Interpret sums of rational numbers by describing real-world contexts. **7.NS.A.1d:** Apply properties of operations . . . to add . . . rational numbers.

Launch

MP5, MP6

Without adding, tell whether $A + B$, $B + C$, and $A + C$ would result in a negative or positive sum.

Tell how you know.

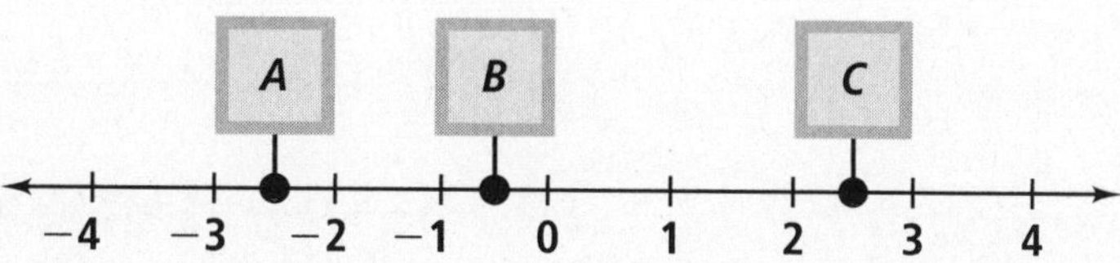

Reflect Would you solve the problem differently if *A*, *B*, and *C* were integers? Explain.

Got It?

PART 1 Got It

What property can you use to write the step "$[9.3 + (-9.3)] + (-3.4)$" in this addition problem?

$$\begin{aligned} 9.3 + (-12.7) &= 9.3 + [-9.3 + (-3.4)] \\ &= [9.3 + (-9.3)] + (-3.4) \\ &= 0 + (-3.4) \\ &= -3.4 \end{aligned}$$

PART 2 Got It

What is the sum $-2.7 + 3.2$?

Discuss with a classmate
Circle the key word in the problem statement.
Read the word out loud.
Give a definition of the word.
What symbol used in the problem is a clue about what the key word means?

Got It?

PART 3 Got It

The diagram shows the changes in the water level after the 6:49 A.M. high tide. Which expression represents the water level, in feet, at the 7:15 P.M. high tide?

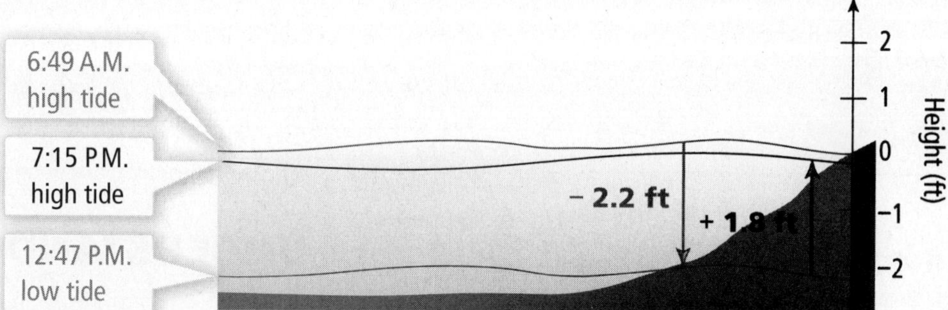

Close and Check

Focus Question

How is adding rational numbers different than adding whole numbers?

Do you know HOW?

1. Identify the property of addition used to complete the 2nd step of the equation: *Commutative, Associative, Inverse, Identity,* or *Zero*.

$-\frac{7}{9} + \frac{2}{3} = \left(-\frac{1}{9}\right) + \left(-\frac{2}{3} + \frac{2}{3}\right)$

$-\frac{7}{9} + \frac{2}{3} = \left(-\frac{1}{9}\right) + 0$

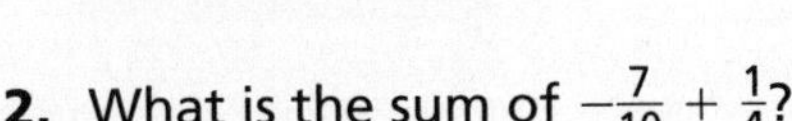

2. What is the sum of $-\frac{7}{10} + \frac{1}{4}$?

3. What is the sum of $-4\frac{5}{6} + \left(-2\frac{5}{9}\right)$?

4. A homeowner owes the electric company \$72.45. She pays \$57.50. Write and simplify an expression to model this situation.

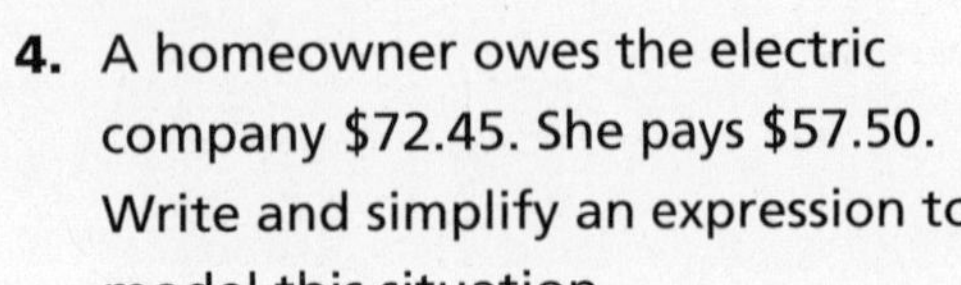

Do you UNDERSTAND?

5. **Writing** Describe a strategy you can use to find the sum of a positive and a negative integer.

6. **Reasoning** How can you tell without solving whether the sum or difference of a positive number and a negative number will be less than zero, equal to zero, or greater than zero?

Subtracting Integers

Digital Resources

CCSS: 7.NS.A.1: Apply and extend previous understandings of … subtraction to … subtract rational numbers; represent … subtraction on a … number line diagram. **7.NS.A.1c:** Understand subtraction of rational numbers as adding the additive inverse, $p - q = p + (-q)$ …

Launch

MP1, MP4

Player 3 goes last in the final round of Zombie Pretzel Attack 2! She loses 500 points when caught by two zombie pretzels.

What's her new score? How many points does she need to catch Player 1? Tell how you found out.

Player	Current Score	New Score
1	500 points	300 points
2	−100 points	−200 points
3	100 points	

Reflect How could the Zombie Pretzel Attack 2! game work without negative numbers? Would the game be as good? Explain.

Got It?

PART 1 Got It

Which expression(s) does the number line model represent?

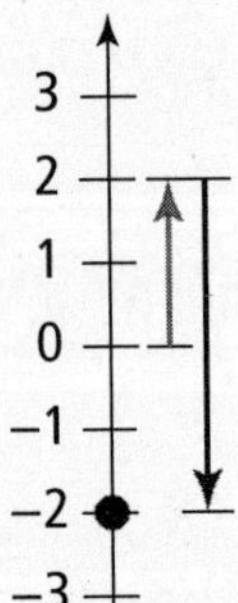

I. $2 - 4$

II. $2 - 2$

III. $2 + (-4)$

IV. $2 + (-2)$

PART 2 Got It

The map shows the highest temperature ever recorded in the United States. The lowest temperature ever recorded in the United States was 214°F lower than this temperature.

Write and simplify a subtraction expression to represent the lowest temperature ever recorded in the United States.

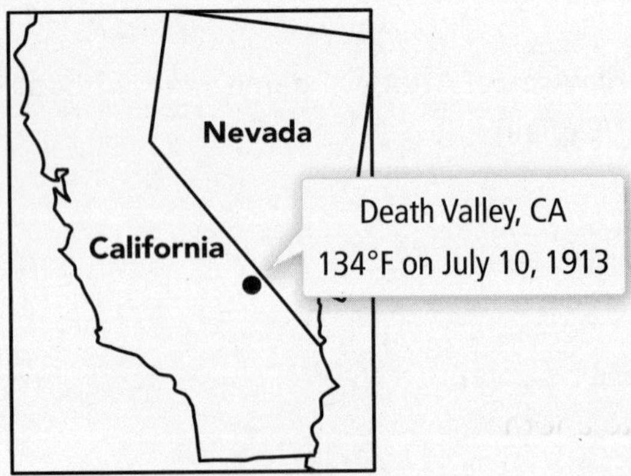

Got It?

PART 3 Got It

Which expressions are equivalent to $4 + (-9)$?

I. $-9 + 4$

II. $4 - 9$

III. $-9 - (-4)$

Discuss with a classmate

What key words or phrases do you need to use in order to explain whether one expression is equivalent to another expression?
After discussing the key words, choose one of the three answer choices.
Take turns explaining why the answer choice you selected is or is not equivalent to the given expression in the problem statement.

Close and Check

Focus Question

MP3, MP6

What does it mean to subtract less than nothing from something?

Do you know HOW?

1. Write equivalent subtraction and addition expressions for the number line model.

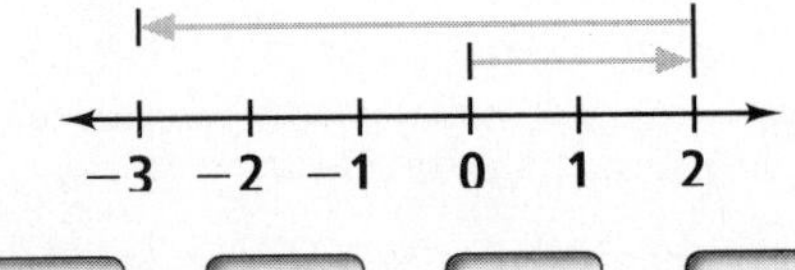

2. The highest point in California is Mt. Whitney at 14,494 ft above sea level. The lowest point in the state is Death Valley, which is 14,776 ft lower than Mt. Whitney. Write and simplify a subtraction expression to represent the lowest point in California.

3. Write and simplify an equivalent expression.

$-12 - (-8)$

Do you UNDERSTAND?

4. **Compare and Contrast** How is adding two negative integers the same as and different from subtracting two positive integers?

5. **Writing** Explain why subtracting a positive number and adding a negative number result in the same solution.

1-5

Subtracting Rational Numbers

Digital Resources

CCSS: 7.NS.A.1: Apply … previous understandings of addition and subtraction to … subtract rational numbers; represent … subtraction on a … number line diagram. **7.NS.A.1b:** … Interpret sums of rational numbers by describing real-world contexts.

Launch

MP5, MP6

Without subtracting, tell whether $A - C$, $A - B$, and $B - A$ would result in a negative or positive difference.

Tell how you know.

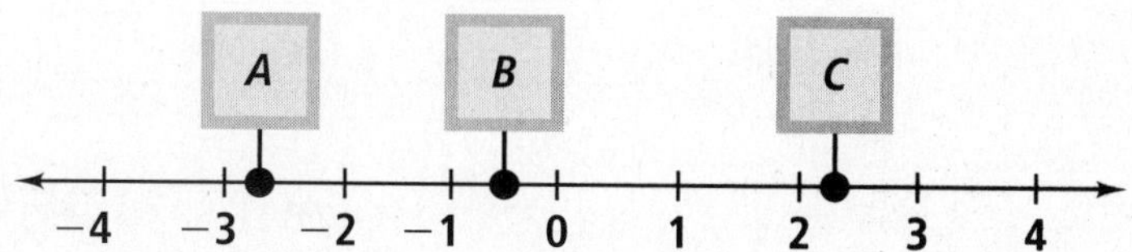

Reflect Would you solve the problem differently if *A*, *B*, and *C* were integers? Explain.

Got It?

PART 1 Got It

Is $-\frac{1}{5} - \left(-\frac{1}{5}\right)$ *less than zero, equal to zero,* or *greater than zero*?

PART 2 Got It

Which number line model represents the subtraction expression $1\frac{3}{4} - \left(-\frac{3}{8}\right)$?

I.

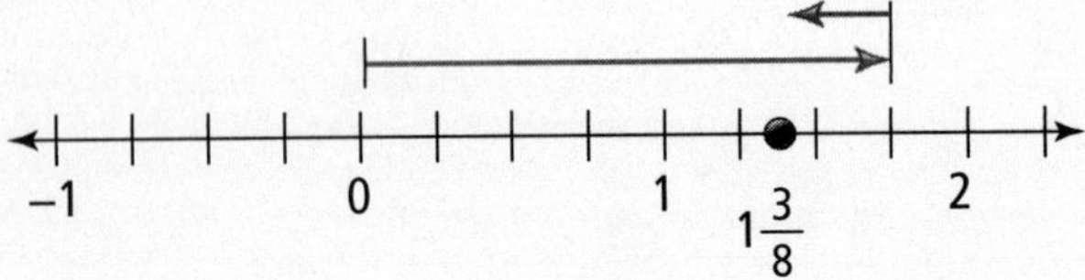

II.

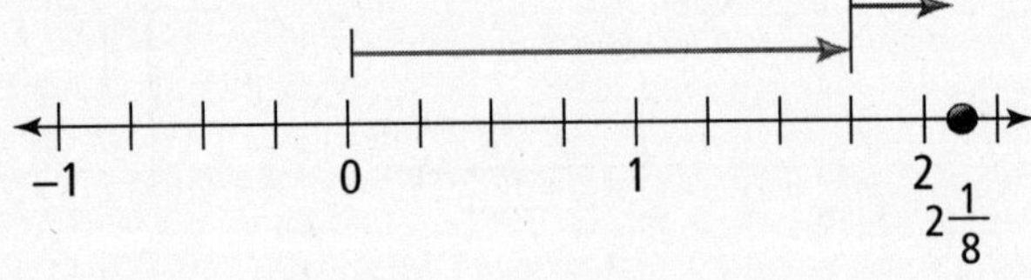

Got It?

PART 3 Got It

The temperature at which a liquid turns to gas is its boiling point. The temperature at which a liquid turns to a solid is its freezing point.

Liquid nitrogen's boiling point is **–195.79° C.**	Liquid nitrogen's freezing point is **–210°C.**

What is $-210 - (-195.79)$? What does the difference mean?

Close and Check

Focus Question

MP2, MP7

How is subtracting rational numbers different than subtracting whole numbers?

HW

Do you know HOW?

1. Is $-\frac{5}{9} + \left(+\frac{7}{9}\right)$ *less than zero, equal to zero, or greater than zero?*

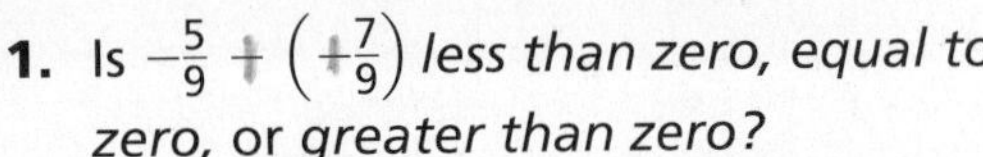

greater than 0

2. Write and simplify a subtraction expression for the number line model.

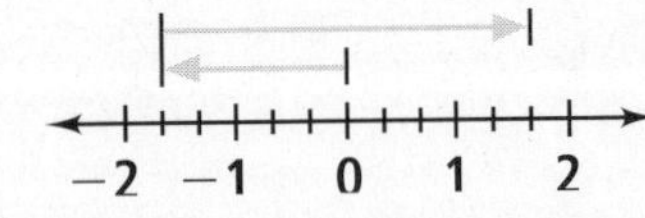

$-1\frac{2}{3} - (-3\frac{1}{3})$

3. The lowest point in the United States is Death Valley with an elevation of −282 ft in relation to sea level. The lowest point on land in the world is the shore of the Dead Sea at −1,385 ft. What is the difference between the two elevations?

1,103 ft

$$\begin{array}{r} 1385 \\ -\ 282 \\ \hline 1103 \end{array}$$

Do you UNDERSTAND?

4. **Writing** How would you explain the meaning of subtracting negative numbers to someone who had never heard of it?

Subtracting negatives will cancel each other out.

5. **Error Analysis** The record high temperature in the United States is 134°F and the record low temperature is −80°F. A classmate writes an equation to find the difference between the two temperatures. Explain her error and give the correct answer.

$$134 - 80 = 54$$

You would need to add them because 80 is negative. The answer is 214.

1-6 Distance on a Number Line

Digital Resources

CCSS: 7.NS.A.1c: Understand subtraction of rational numbers as adding the additive inverse . . . . Show that the distance between two rational numbers on the number line is the absolute value of their difference, and apply this principle in real-world contexts.

Launch

MP3, MP4

A family of runners position themselves near the starting line of a race to make the race fair.

Which runner has the greatest head start over another runner? Which runner has the least head start over another runner?

Reflect What number did you always use to make all the comparisons of head starts? Why?

Got It?

PART 1 Got It

What is the distance between the top and the bottom of this group of clouds?

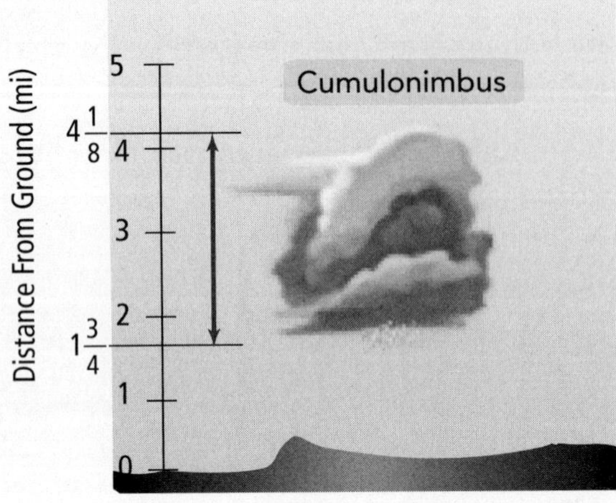

PART 2 Got It

A whale dives from the Twilight Zone into the Midnight Zone. How far does the whale dive?

Got It?

PART 3 Got It

Which expression(s) represent the distance between −2 and 4 on the number line?

I. $|4 - 2|$ **II.** $|-2 + 4|$

III. $|-2 - 4|$ **IV.** $|4 + 2|$

Close and Check

Focus Question

MP6, MP7

Subtraction is not commutative. In what situations does the order in which you subtract two numbers not matter?

Do you know HOW?

1. A space shuttle can orbit the earth at 330 mi above sea level. The average commercial airplane can fly at 5.7 mi above sea level. What is the distance between the two aircraft?

2. The lowest point on Earth is in the Mariana Trench in the Pacific Ocean. It is −10,924 m from sea level. The highest point on Earth is Mount Everest in the Himalaya Mountains at 8,850 m from sea level. What is the distance between the highest and lowest points on Earth?

3. Write an expression using absolute value to represent the distance between −12 and 12 on the number line.

Do you UNDERSTAND?

4. **Writing** Explain when to use absolute value in solving integer equations and when not to use it.

5. **Error Analysis** The Roman Empire lasted from 27 BC to 476 AD. Using 0 as the division between BC and AD, a classmate says he can find the total length of the Roman Empire using the equation $-27 + 476 = x$. Is he correct? Explain.

1-7

Problem Solving

Digital Resources

CCSS: 7.EE.B.3: Solve multi-step real-life and mathematical problems posed with positive and negative rational numbers in any form (whole numbers, fraction, and decimals), using tools strategically. Also, **7.NS.A.1b, 7.NS.A.1c.**

Launch

MP1, MP6

In the game of golf, players try to get negative scores, not positive scores, on each hole. Draw lines to order the players from 1st to 4th place. Then write how many shots each player was behind the winner. Explain your work.

Player A +6 | Player B −2 | Player C −7 | Player D +2

1st | 2nd | 3rd | 4th

Shots Behind: ☐ ☐ ☐

Reflect Can a player in any game be −5 points behind the lead player? Explain why or why not.

Got It?

PART 1 Got It

Paul lives $1\frac{3}{4}$ blocks east of Michele. What is the coordinate of Paul's house?

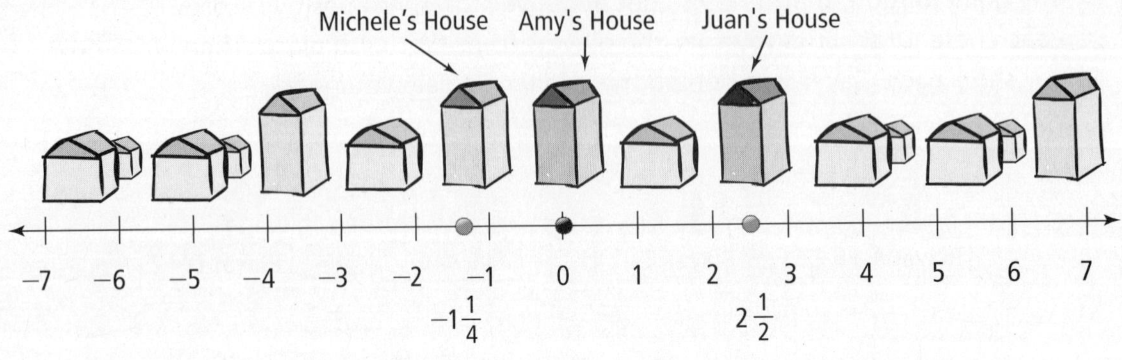

PART 2 Got It

Use the equation $V = R - N$, where
V = Variation From Normal,
R = Recorded Temperature, and
N = Normal Temperature.
If $V = -2.6$ and $N = 5.3$. what is R?

Got It?

PART 3 Got It

What is the range of the temperature data set?

Daily Low Temperature (°F), February 1 to February 14

13, 12, 15, 8, −1, −2, 0, 5, 3, −1, 9, 12, 14, 10

Close and Check

Focus Question

MP1, MP7

What kinds of problems can you solve by adding the different types of rational numbers? What kinds of problems can you solve by subtracting the different types of rational numbers?

Do you know HOW?

1. One cat weighs $5\frac{1}{4}$ lbs. Another cat's weight differs by $1\frac{5}{8}$ lbs. Place points on the number line to represent the possible weights of the second cat. Write the weights.

or

2. Find the value of x.

$$x + 17.3 = -5.2$$

Use the data set for Exercises 3 and 4.

−2, 6, −15, 0, 11, −9, 17, 9

3. Find the range of the data.

4. Find the interquartile range of the data.

Do you UNDERSTAND?

5. Reasoning The elevation of the basement floor of an office building is −18 ft. The height of the building above ground is 216 ft. To find the total distance between the basement floor and the top of the building, would you add or subtract the integers? Explain.

6. Writing Write another integer word problem about the office building that uses subtraction. Write the expression and solve the problem.

Topic Review

New Vocabulary: absolute value, additive inverse, Inverse Property of Addition, opposites, rational number
Review Vocabulary: distance, integers, whole numbers

Vocabulary Review

Identify two challenging vocabulary terms from this topic. Write one vocabulary term in the center oval, and fill in the surrounding boxes with details that will help you better understand the term.

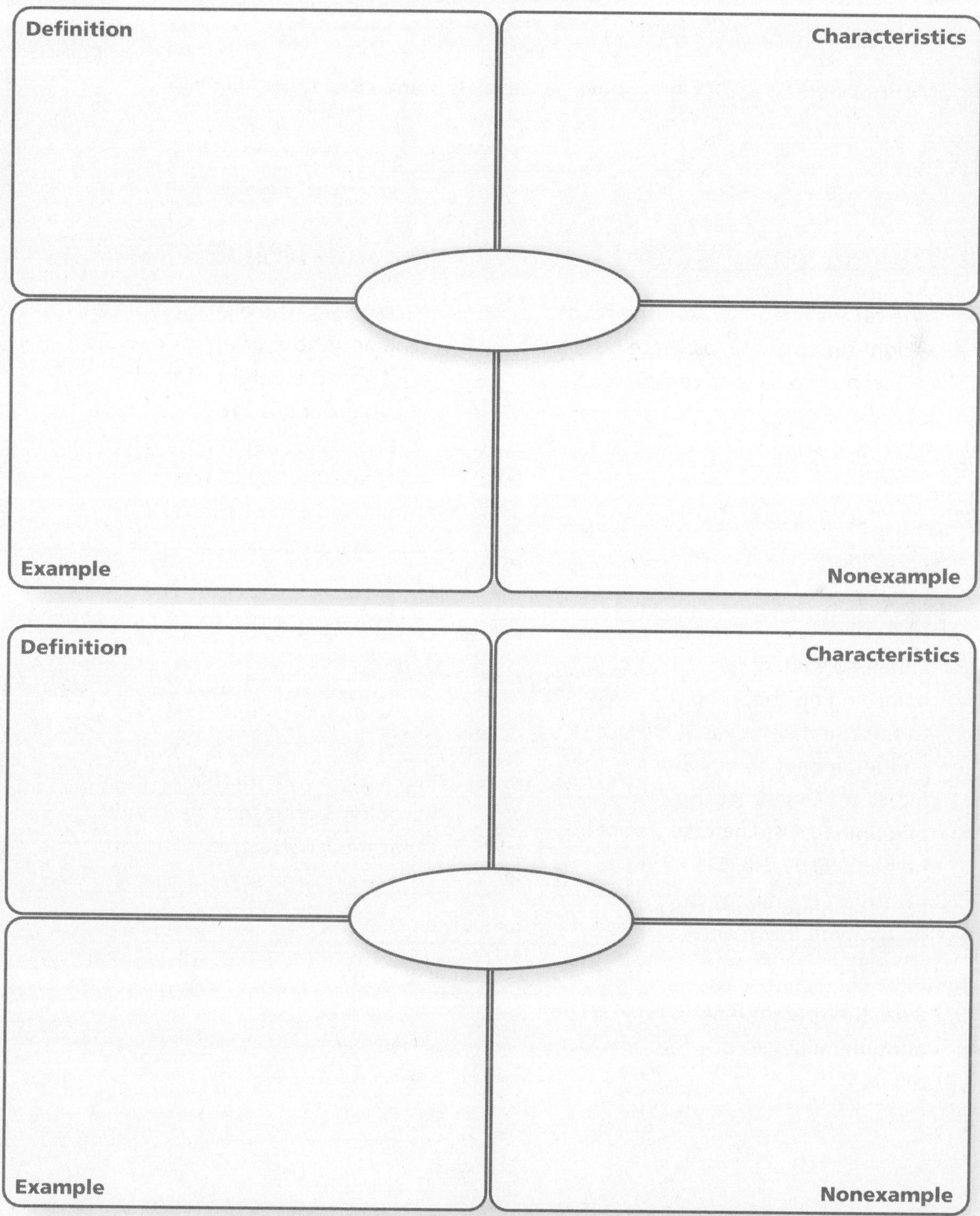

Pull It All Together

TASK 1

Mauna Kea is a mountain in Hawaii with an elevation of 13,796 feet above sea level. The base of the mountain is actually deep in the ocean, about 19,204 feet below sea level.

What is the height of Mauna Kea from base to peak?

Mount Everest is 29,029 feet above sea level. Is Mauna Kea taller? Explain.

TASK 1

A college student is balancing his checkbook to see whether he has enough money to buy a movie for $14.98. At the beginning of the month, he had $50.99. He is recording the money that he has withdrawn and deposited since then.

Does the student have enough money to buy the movie?

Date	Category	Deposit	Withdrawal	Balance
Oct. 1				$50.99
Oct. 3	Groceries		$33.54	
Oct. 8	Work			$47.45
Oct. 15	Books			$5.32
Oct. 17	Computer game		$11.05	
Oct. 20	Bank charge		$10.00	
Oct. 21	Work	$30.00		

2-1

Multiplying Integers

Digital Resources

CCSS: 7.NS.A.2a: Understand that multiplication is extended ... to rational numbers by requiring that operations ... satisfy ... the distributive property, leading to ... rules for multiplying signed numbers. Interpret products of rational numbers .... Also, **7.NS.A.2, 7.NS.A.2c.**

Launch

MP2, MP5, MP8

Complete the multiplication table. Describe at least one rule for multiplying integers based on what you see in the table.

x	−3	−2	−1	0	1	2	3
3							9
2							6
1							3
0							0
−1							−3
−2	6	4	2	0	−2	−4	−6
−3							−9

Reflect What do you notice about the signs of the products in the four shaded sections of the grid?

Got It?

PART 1 Got It (1 of 2)

What is the product −8(3)?

PART 1 Got It (2 of 2)

Write −20 as the product of a negative and a positive integer in at least three different ways.

Got It?

PART 2 Got It

What is the product $-11(-7)$?

PART 3 Got It (1 of 2)

Which products are equivalent to 36?

I. $-6 \times (-2) \times 3$ II. $-1 \cdot 18 \cdot (-2)$ III. $-2(-18)(-1)$

PART 3 Got It (2 of 2)

Suppose p and q are nonzero integers with different signs. Is the product $p(-q)$ *positive* or *negative*? Explain.

Close and Check

Focus Question

MP1, MP8

How does knowing how to add positive and negative integers help you multiply positive and negative integers? How do properties of addition and multiplication help you multiply positive and negative integers?

Do you know HOW?

1. Find the product of −5(8).

2. Find the product of −9(−9).

3. Circle the products that are equivalent to −100.

   A. $-5 \cdot 2(-10)$

   B. $-1(25 \cdot 4)$

   C. $-4 \cdot 5^2$

   D. $(-2)(25)(-2)$

4. Suppose a and b are nonzero integers with the same signs. Is the product of a and b positive or negative?

Do you UNDERSTAND?

5. **Writing** Draw a model to show the product of a and b, where $a < 0 < b$. Explain your model.

6. **Compare and Contrast** How does the sign of the product of a positive and a negative number compare with the sign of the sum of a positive and a negative number?

2-2

Multiplying Rational Numbers

Digital Resources

CCSS: 7.NS.A.2: Apply and extend previous understandings of multiplication and division of fractions to multiply and divide rational numbers. **7.NS.A.2a:** Understand … the rules for multiplying signed numbers. Interpret products … by describing real-world contexts.

Launch

MP3, MP7, MP8

Sort the tiles into two groups. Describe each group.

$1.5 \cdot 3$	$1.5 \cdot (-3)$	$3 \cdot 1.5$	$-3 \cdot 1.5$
$-1.5 \cdot 3$	$-1.5 \cdot (-3)$	$3 \cdot (-1.5)$	$-3 \cdot (-1.5)$

Group 1	Group 2

Reflect How would solving this problem be different if both factors of each expression were integers? Explain.

Got It?

PART 1 Got It (1 of 2)

Is the product $-8.1 \cdot 3$ positive or negative?

PART 1 Got It (2 of 2)

If a is negative and b is positive, is a^2b positive or negative? Explain.

Got It?

PART 2 Got It

Find the product.

$\frac{3}{8}\left(-2\frac{1}{8}\right)$

PART 3 Got It

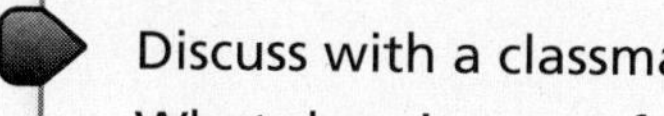

Discuss with a classmate

What does it mean for the value of a stock to drop?

You own 57.08 shares of stock. The value of a share drops \$.20. What is the total change in the value of your stocks?

Close and Check

Focus Question

How is multiplying rational numbers like multiplying fractions and multiplying decimals? How is it different?

HW 1-4

Do you know HOW?

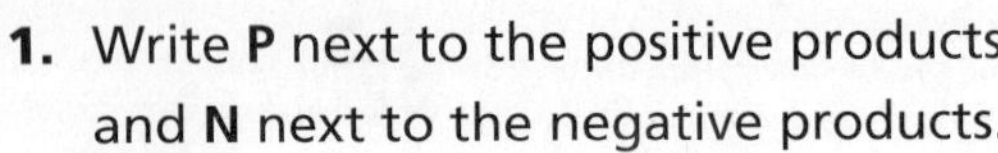

1. Write **P** next to the positive products and **N** next to the negative products.

$\frac{5}{9} \cdot \left(-\frac{3}{7}\right)$

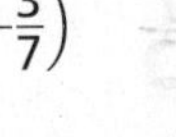

$(-4.8)(-0.2)$

$\left(-3\frac{2}{5}\right)\left(6\frac{1}{3}\right)\left(-1\frac{1}{9}\right)$

$14.2 \cdot (-2)\left(-5\frac{2}{7}\right)(-0.25)$

2. Find the product of $-5.8(3)(-2.2)$.

3. In 1911, the temperature in Rapid City, South Dakota, dropped at an amazing rate of about 3.1°F per minute. This remarkable temperature change took place in a span of 15 minutes. Write the change in temperature.

Do you UNDERSTAND?

4. **Reasoning** Will the product of -3^{17} be positive or negative? Explain.

If it is odd, the product is negative.

5. **Error Analysis** A classmate says that you can tell the sign of a product by comparing the number of positive and negative factors. If there are more negative factors, then the product will be negative. If there are more positive factors, then the product will be positive. Do you agree? Explain.

2-3

Dividing Integers

Digital Resources

CCSS: 7.NS.A.2b: Understand that integers can be divided, provided that the divisor is not zero, and every quotient of integers (with non-zero divisor) is a rational number. If p and q are integers, then $-\left(\frac{p}{q}\right) = \frac{(-p)}{q} = \frac{p}{(-q)}$ . . . . Also, **7.NS.A.2.**

Launch

MP2, MP3, MP5

Draw arrows to show how to redistribute the integer chips equally among the bags. Then write two equations, one using multiplication and one using division, to describe your distribution.

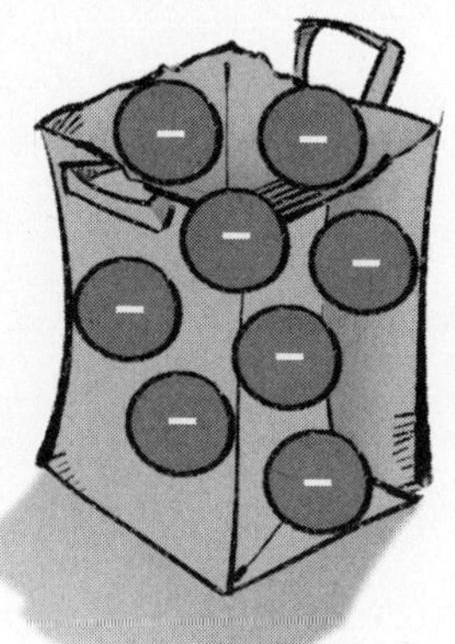
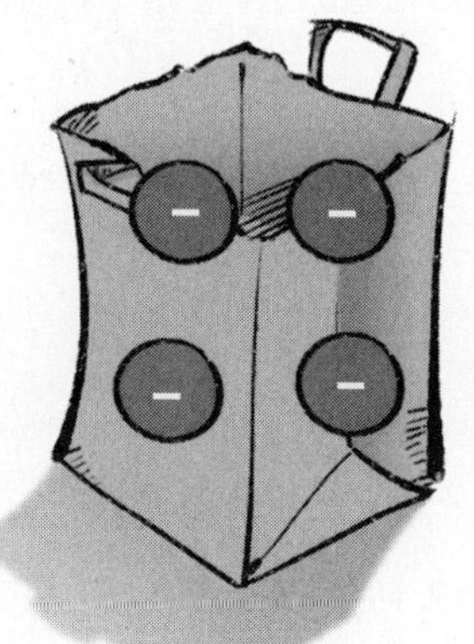

Reflect How is dividing integers similar to and different from dividing whole numbers?

Got It?

PART 1 Got It (1 of 2)

Find the quotient.

$-125 \div (-5)$

PART 1 Got It (2 of 2)

If possible, find a counterexample for one or both of these conjectures.

Conjecture 1
The quotient of any two nonzero integers is an integer.

Conjecture 2
For all whole numbers *a* and *b*, where $b \neq 0$:
$-\frac{a}{b} = \frac{-a}{b} = \frac{a}{-b}$

Got It?

PART 2 Got It

What is the value of *a*?

$\frac{8}{a} = -2$

PART 3 Got It

An elevator descends 1,000 feet in 8 seconds. Express the movement of the elevator as a unit rate.

Close and Check

Focus Question

MP2, MP7

How does the relationship between multiplication and division help you divide integers? When does division of integers not have meaning and why?

Do you know HOW?

1. Write **P** next to the positive quotients, **N** next to the negative quotients, and **U** next to the quotients that are undefined.

 $-3 \div (-7)$

 $-4 \div 0$

 $-12 \div 2$

 $14 \div 7$

2. Solve $-\frac{75}{a} = -25$.

$\frac{-75}{-25}$

3. The stock market lost 7,695 points in a 17-month period. Express the change in the stock market as a unit rate. Round your answer to the nearest integer.

Do you UNDERSTAND?

4. **Reasoning** Show that the quotient of two negative numbers is a positive number. Use multiplication to support your reasoning.

5. **Writing** Explain why division by 0 is undefined. Use an example.

2-4

Dividing Rational Numbers

Digital Resources

CCSS: 7.NS.A.2: Apply and extend previous understandings of multiplication and division of fractions to multiply and divide rational numbers. **7.NS.A.2b:** ... Interpret quotients of rational numbers by describing real-world contexts.

Launch

MP3, MP7, MP8

Sort the tiles into two groups. Describe your groups.

$7\frac{1}{2} \div 3$ $-7\frac{1}{2} \div 3$ $7\frac{1}{2} \div (-3)$ $-7\frac{1}{2} \div (-3)$

Group 1	Group 2

Reflect How would solving this problem be different if the dividend and divisors were always integers? Explain.

Got It?

PART 1 Got It (1 of 2)

What is the reciprocal of $-\frac{7}{21}$?

PART 1 Got It (2 of 2)

Does zero have a reciprocal? Explain.

Got It?

PART 2 Got It

Write $-\frac{9}{2} \div \frac{7}{5}$ as a multiplication expression.

PART 3 Got It

The equation $e = -\frac{1}{2}t$ describes the change in elevation, e, in miles, of a hiker t hours after beginning her descent into a canyon. The bottom of the canyon is $1\frac{1}{3}$ miles below the rim of the canyon. How long does it take the hiker to reach the bottom of the canyon?

Close and Check

Focus Question

MP6, MP7

How does the relationship between multiplication and division help you divide rational numbers?

Do you know HOW?

1. Write the reciprocal of each number.

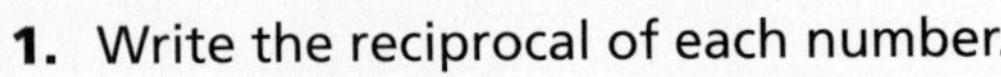

-30 

$\frac{1}{12}$ 

6 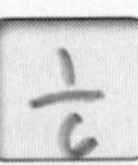

$-\frac{6}{11}$ 

2. Write $-\frac{7}{8} \div \frac{3}{5}$ as a multiplication expression.

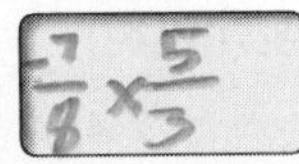

3. The equation $d = -\frac{3}{5}t$ describes the change in degrees Fahrenheit d after t hours. The temperature falls a total of $7\frac{1}{2}$ degrees. How long does it take the temperature to fall?

Do you UNDERSTAND?

4. Reasoning Can the product of reciprocals ever be equal to -1? Explain.

5. Writing Explain why multiplying by the reciprocal of a number is the same as dividing by that number. Use the equation in your explanation.

$$-\frac{7}{9} \div \frac{3}{8} = -\frac{7}{9} \cdot \frac{8}{3}$$

2-5 Operations with Rational Numbers

Digital Resources

CCSS: 7.NS.A.2c: Apply properties of operations as strategies to multiply and divide rational numbers. **7.NS.A.3:** Solve real-world and mathematical problems involving the four operations with rational numbers. Also, **7.NS.A.2.**

Launch

MP1, MP2

Is the value of this expression *positive* or *negative*? Show how to change the expression so that its value switches to the other sign. Do not change or move any numbers or operation symbols.

$$2 + \frac{1}{2} \cdot 1\frac{3}{4} - 3$$

Positive	Negative

Reflect How are the expression as shown and the expression after your change alike? How are they different?

Got It?

PART 1 Got It

Which expression is equivalent to $-10(5.8 - 6.2)$?
What is the value of the expression?

$-10(5.8) - 10(6.2)$ $\qquad$ $-10(5.8) - (-10)(6.2)$

PART 2 Got It

You can use the formula $C = \frac{5}{9}(F - 32)$ to convert a temperature given in degrees Fahrenheit to degrees Celsius. Convert the temperature shown on the thermometer to degrees Celsius.

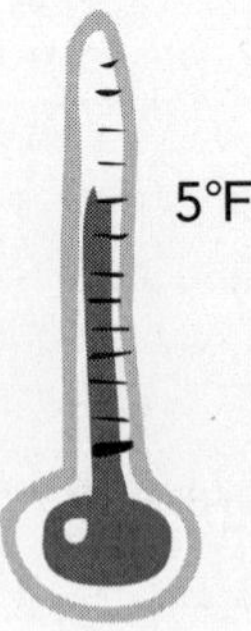

Got It?

PART 3 Got It (1 of 2)

What is the simplified form of the complex fraction $\frac{-\frac{5}{6}}{\frac{15}{2}}$?

PART 3 Got It (2 of 2)

A fraction bar is a grouping symbol as well as a division symbol. In the expression $\frac{2 + 4}{3}$, the fraction bar groups (2 + 4) and indicates that you add 2 to 4 before you divide by 3.

$$\begin{aligned}\frac{2 + 4}{3} &= (2 + 4) \div 3\\ &= 6 \div 3\\ &= 2\end{aligned}$$

Use this idea to simplify the complex fraction $\frac{-\frac{5}{6}}{\frac{1}{3} - 1}$.

Close and Check

Focus Question

MP6, MP7

Many problems involve more than one operation with rational numbers. How do you decide the order in which to carry out the operations?

Do you know HOW?

1. Write and simplify an equivalent expression by using the Distributive Property.

$$-7\left(\frac{5}{7} - \frac{12}{21}\right)$$

2. Antarctica holds the record for the lowest recorded temperature of $-129°$F. Use the formula to find the equivalent temperature in °C.

$$C = \frac{5}{9}(F - 32)$$

3. Simplify the complex fraction.

$$\frac{-\frac{3}{8}}{\frac{5}{7} - 2}$$

Do you UNDERSTAND?

4. Writing Describe another method for solving the expression in Exercise 1. Does this method always work? Explain.

5. Error Analysis Explain the error and find the correct answer.

$$\frac{\frac{7}{15}}{\frac{1}{6} - 1} = \frac{\frac{7}{15}}{-\frac{5}{6}} = \frac{7}{15} \cdot -\frac{5}{6} = -\frac{7}{18}$$

2-6 Problem Solving

Digital Resources

CCSS: 7.NS.A.3: Solve real-world and mathematical problems involving the four operations with rational numbers. **7.EE.B.3:** Solve multi-step real life and mathematical problems posed with positive and negative rational numbers in any form . . . .

Launch

MP1, MP4

A not-so-jazzed New Orleans dog forgets where she buries her favorite bone. She picks a spot and digs at a rate of 0.4 ft every 10 minutes for an hour to find it.

Write and evaluate an expression to represent the dog's elevation in relation to sea level after digging for one hour.

Reflect Is there one right expression to represent the dog's situation? Explain.

Got It?

PART 1 Got It

Find the median daily high temperature in Montreal during the last two weeks of February.

Montreal, Daily High Temperatures: February 15–28

Temperature	−8°C	−5°C	−3°C	1°C	5°C
Frequency	4	2	1	3	4

PART 2 Got It (1 of 2)

Renee's work contains an error. What did Renee do incorrectly? What is the value of the expression?

Renee's Work

$-8 \div \frac{1}{2} - \frac{1}{4}$

$-8 \times 2 - \frac{1}{4}$

$16 - \frac{1}{4}$

$15\frac{3}{4}$

Got It?

PART 2 Got It (2 of 2)

Paula's error when simplifying the expression $-2 - 4(5 - 1)$ was to subtract 4 from -2 before working inside parentheses and multiplying the result by 4.

Insert a pair of parentheses in the expression $-2 - 4(5 - 1)$ in order to make subtracting 4 from -2 the correct first step.

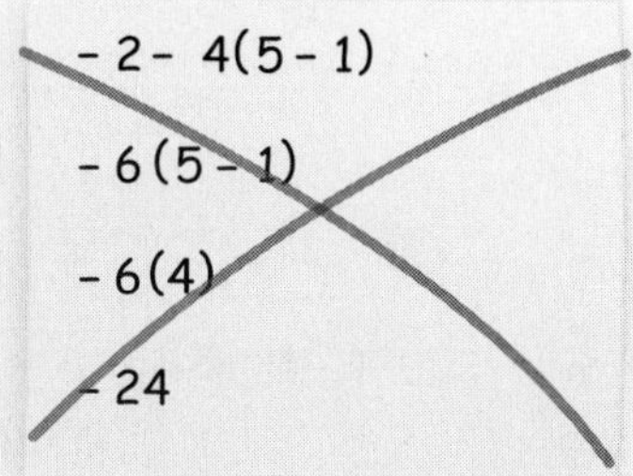

PART 3 Got It

The table shows the change in one bear's weight over 84 days of hibernation. Suppose the relationship between days of hibernation and change in weight is a proportional relationship.

What is the bear's change in weight over 112 days of hibernation?

Bear Hibernation

Days of Hibernation	Change in Weight (kg)
84	−7.56
112	

Close and Check

Focus Question

What types of problems can you solve using operations with rational numbers?

Do you know HOW?

1. Many places on land are located below sea level. The table shows the altitude of various locations. Find the mean altitude in relation to sea level. Round your answer to the nearest tenth.

Position Relative to Sea Level					
Altitude (ft)	−11	−13	−16	−20	−23
Frequency	2	4	6	2	4

2. Insert a pair of parentheses to make the expression true.

$6 - 5 + 4 + 9 = 6$

3. Complete the table to show the change in the water table levels during a severe drought. Assume the relationship is proportional.

Months of drought	3	5	8
Change in water level (cm)		−130	

Do you UNDERSTAND?

4. **Writing** An airplane descends from 35,000 ft at a rate of 33 feet per second. Explain how to use this information to find the altitude of the airplane after 12 minutes.

5. **Error Analysis** A classmate says that simplifying the expression is the same with or without parentheses. Do you agree? Explain.

$-9 \times (6 + 3) + 8$

2-R Topic Review

New Vocabulary: complex fraction, reciprocals
Review Vocabulary: denominator, Distributive Property, integers, numerator, order of operations, quotient, rational numbers, unit rate

Vocabulary Review

Identify two challenging vocabulary terms from this topic. Write one vocabulary term in the center oval, and fill in the surrounding boxes with details that will help you better understand the term.

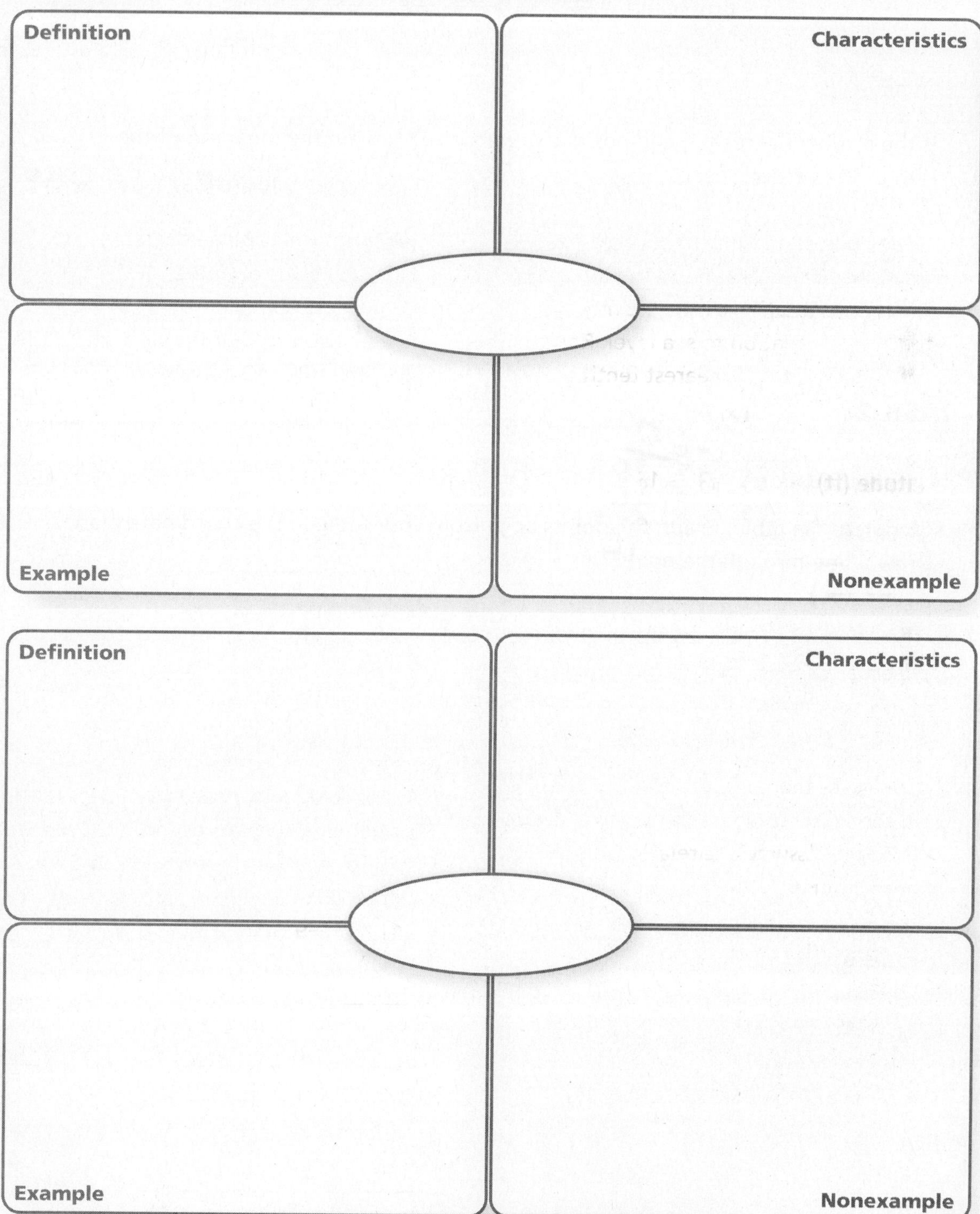

Pull It All Together

TASK 1

A rock climber is at an elevation of 10,000 feet. Four and a half hours later, she is at 7,751 feet.

Use the formula below to find the climber's vertical speed.

$$\text{vertical speed} = \frac{\text{final elevation} - \text{initial elevation}}{\text{time}}$$

Is the climber's vertical speed *positive* or *negative*? Explain the meaning of the sign of the vertical speed.

TASK 2

Use the equation $y = -\frac{1}{2}x - 3$.

Complete the table. Graph the points (x, y) from your table in the coordinate plane. Draw a line through the points.

x	-5	-4	-3	-2	-1	0	1	2
y	$-\frac{1}{2}$							

3-1 Repeating Decimals

Digital Resources

CCSS: 7.NS.A.2b: Understand that integers can be divided, provided that the divisor is not zero … .
7.NS.A.2d: Convert a rational number to a decimal using long division; know that the decimal form of a rational number terminates in 0s or eventually repeats.

Launch

MP3, MP4

Use a picture, words, and a number to represent the quantity 2 out of 3 in three other ways. Tell which of these ways may be best for problem solving and why.

A Picture	Words	A Number
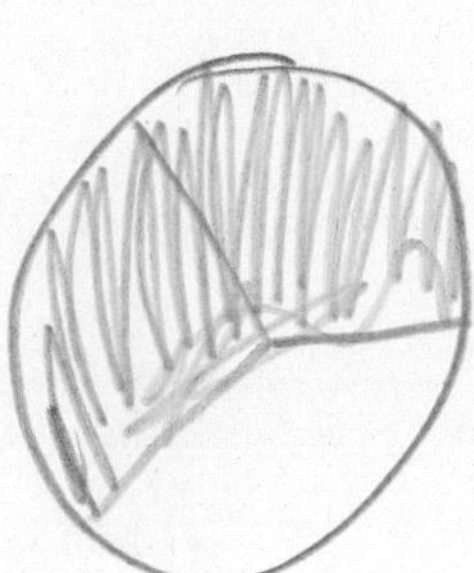	two-thirds exs of 111111 0.0 0.454545 $0.\overline{45}$ 0.199494 $0.1\overline{9}$	$\frac{2}{3}$ $0.\overline{6}$ $3\overline{)2.000}$ = 0.666 −18 20 −18 20

Writing a number would be easiest because it takes up less time. However, you can use whichever supports your needs.

Reflect When have you represented quantities in different ways in your past mathematics work? How was that helpful?

Got It?

PART 1 Got It

Identify the repeating decimal(s).

I. $3.9\overline{85}$ II. 0.404004   III. 1.72...

PART 2 Got It (1 of 2)

Write $\frac{7}{15}$ as a decimal.

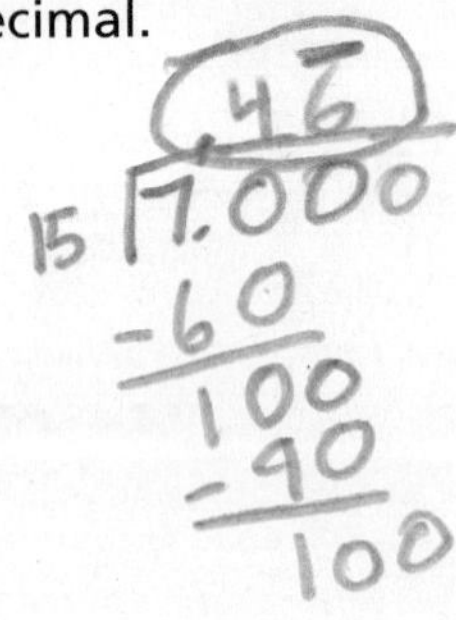

PART 2 Got It (2 of 2)

Look at the decimal expansions below. Make a conjecture about the decimal expansions of $\frac{3}{7}$ and $\frac{6}{7}$. Then prove or disprove your conjecture.

$\frac{1}{7} = 0.\overline{142857}$

$\frac{2}{7} = 0.\overline{285712}$

$\frac{4}{7} = 0.\overline{571428}$

$\frac{5}{7} = 0.\overline{714285}$

Got It?

PART 3 Got It (1 of 2)

In another scene, the special effects artist wants a model submarine to navigate through a cave 6.4 inches wide. The artist wants to make the submarine $6\frac{5}{12}$ inches wide. Will the submarine fit through the cave?

PART 3 Got It (2 of 2)

Calculate $\frac{1}{3}$ of 100. Then calculate 0.33 of 100. What is the difference between the two results? When does the difference matter?

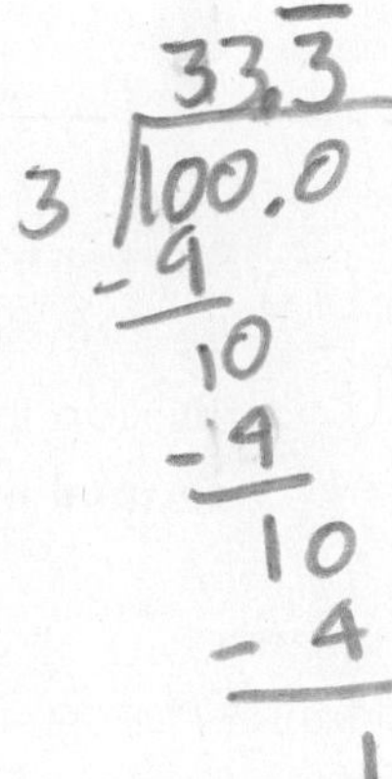

Close and Check

Focus Question

MP6, MP8

When is it helpful to be able to write fractions as decimals? Why is it helpful to show that a decimal repeats?

Do you know HOW?

1. Circle the repeating decimal(s).

12.34345 $\quad$ $9.\overline{012}$

5.25... $\quad$ $23.4380\overline{2}$

2. Write $\frac{1}{13}$ as a decimal.

3. Write $6\frac{5}{12}$ as a decimal.

4. An electrician cuts away a 7.2-inch long section of drywall to make repairs to the electrical system. He has several scraps of drywall he can use to repair the hole. Circle the length(s) of drywall that is large enough to repair the hole.

$7\frac{2}{13}$ $\quad$ $7\frac{3}{14}$ $\quad$ $7\frac{5}{21}$

Do you UNDERSTAND?

5. Writing Your friend compares the values in Exercise 4. She writes the mixed number as an improper fraction. Next she divides the numerator by the denominator to find the decimal value of each number. Describe a shorter method.

6. Reasoning When converting a fraction to a decimal by using long division, how can you know when the decimal is beginning to repeat?

3-2 Terminating Decimals

Digital Resources

CCSS: 7.NS.A.2d: Convert a rational number to a decimal using long division; know that the decimal form of a rational number terminates in 0s or eventually repeats. Also, 7.NS.A.2b.

Launch

MP2, MP6

A certain surly friend of yours likes $1 \div 2$ far better than $1 \div 3$. He says, "At least you can clearly see the answer to $1 \div 2$."

Show and explain with decimals what might make your certain friend surly about $1 \div 3$, but happy about $1 \div 2$.

Reflect How could writing $1 \div 2$ and $1 \div 3$ each as fractions make your friend less surly?

Got It?

PART 1 Got It (1 of 2)

Which are terminating decimals?

I. 0.35

II. 0.00008

III. 16.98...

IV. 0.30030003

PART 1 Got It (2 of 2)

Is 407 a terminating decimal? Explain.

Got It?

PART 2 Got It

A recipe for a six-foot sub calls for $3\frac{7}{8}$ pounds of sliced deli meats. You want to get the exact amount from the deli counter. What decimal number should the digital scale show?

PART 3 Got It (1 of 2)

What is the decimal equivalent of $8\frac{1}{5}$?

PART 3 Got It (2 of 2)

Why isn't $4.67\overline{10000}$ a terminating decimal?

Close and Check

Focus Question

When is it helpful to be able to write fractions as decimals? How is a fraction written as a terminating decimal different from a fraction written as a repeating decimal?

Do you know HOW?

1. Circle the terminating decimal(s).

10.243444   2.010110111...

5.25...   43.98769876

2. Circle the fraction(s) that can be written as a terminating decimal.

$8\frac{7}{12}$ $19\frac{12}{25}$

$4\frac{3}{11}$ $26\frac{2}{15}$

3. The pediatrician weighs a newborn baby on a digital scale. He tells the parents that their baby weighs $6\frac{5}{8}$ pounds. What decimal number did the pediatrician read on the scale?

4. A customer purchases $7\frac{13}{16}$ gallons of gas. What is the decimal equivalent of this mixed number?

Do you UNDERSTAND?

5. Reasoning To compare the values of a decimal and a fraction, should you convert the decimal to a fraction or the fraction to a decimal? Explain.

6. Error Analysis Your friend says every decimal is a repeating decimal because there are an infinite number of 0s at the end of every decimal number. Explain the error in her reasoning.

3-3 Percents Greater Than 100

Digital Resources

CCSS: 7.NS.A.3: Solve real-world and mathematical problems involving the four operations with rational numbers.

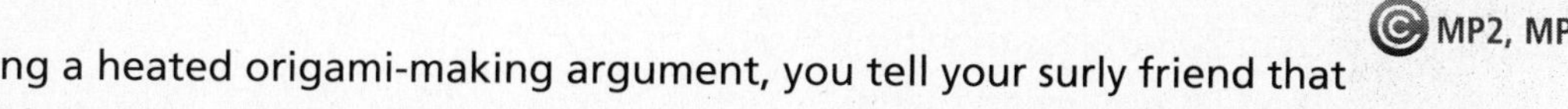

Launch

MP2, MP7

During a heated origami-making argument, you tell your surly friend that you always give 150% effort in folding paper animals. Your surly friend says that he doesn't even know what 150% looks like.

Show a way to represent 150% with pictures or numbers. Explain why your representation works.

Reflect Can you really give more than 100% effort? Provide a possible way in words.

Got It?

PART 1 Got It (1 of 2)

Which is the best estimate for 350% of 20?

% deci + frac are all equal

I. greater than 0 but less than 20
II. greater than 20 but less than 50
III. greater than 50 but less than 100
IV. greater than 100

Discuss with a classmate

What does it mean to estimate 350% of 20?
Which answer choice could you eliminate because it is not reasonable as an estimate for this problem? Explain why it can be eliminated.

PART 1 Got It (2 of 2)

Student A says that 200% of 1 is 2.

Student B says that 200% of 1 is 200.

Which student is correct? Explain.

A because 1 is 100%.

200% of 1
2.0 × 1
2

200% of 1
$\frac{200}{100} \times \frac{1}{1} = \frac{200}{100} = 2$

PART 2 Got It (1 of 2)

During harvest, a cranberry bog is flooded with water to a depth 4,800% of its usual depth of $\frac{1}{4}$ inch. How deep is the water during harvest flooding?

4,800% of 1/4 48.0 × 0.25
12 inches

Got It?

PART 2 Got It (2 of 2)

96 is what percent of 12?

PART 3 Got It (1 of 2)

An artist is making a wall mural from a small sketch. He enlarges the $4\frac{1}{2}$-inch-wide sketch to 900% of the original size to create the final mural. Which statement(s) is/are true?

I. The mural is between 36 and 45 inches wide.

II. The final width of the mural is 4.5 times 900.

III. The final width of the mural is 9 times the width of the sketch.

PART 3 Got It (2 of 2)

Student A says, "A 200% increase of 24 is 48."

Student B says, "200% of 24 is 48."

Who is correct? Explain.

Close and Check

Focus Question

MP1, MP3

What does it mean to have more than 100% of something?

Do you know HOW?

1. Circle the best estimate for 450% of 15.

   A. greater than 0 but less than 30

   B. greater than 30 but less than 60

   C. greater than 60 but less than 100

   D. greater than 100

2. Suppose a small business employs 45 people. Five years later, the same small business employs 380% of the original number of employees. How many employees are there now?

   216 employees

3. Bacterial colonies multiply very quickly. Assume there is a small colony of 560 bacteria that increases 675%. Circle the true statement(s).

   A. The change in the number of bacteria is between 3,000 and 4,000.

   B. The total number of bacteria is 675 times greater than 560.

   C. The total number of bacteria grows to 3,780.

Do you UNDERSTAND?

4. **Compare and Contrast** Compare finding 150% of a number and finding 15% of a number.

   150% means you multiply; 15% means you divide.

5. **Reasoning** The selling price of a sweater is a 175% increase of the purchase price. The markup is $36.75. Explain how to find the purchase price and the selling price.

3-4

Percents Less Than 1

Digital Resources

CCSS: 7.NS.A.3: Solve real-world and mathematical problems involving the four operations with rational numbers.

Launch

MP3, MP6

Explain how these three shaded squares could be used in a representation of 300% or 30%. Use pictures, words, and numbers to model the mathematics.

How the Squares Could Model 300%:

How the Squares Could Model 30%:

Reflect What fractions and decimals would your models model?

Got It?

PART 1 Got It (1 of 2)

Which numbers are equivalent to $\frac{1}{4}\%$?

I. 25% II. $\frac{4}{100}$ III. 0.25 IV. 0.0025

PART 1 Got It (2 of 2)

Why isn't $\frac{1}{3}\%$ equivalent to $33.\overline{3}\%$?

Got It?

PART 2 Got It

What is $\frac{1}{5}$% of 2,400?

PART 3 Got It

About what percent of Colorado's total area is covered by water?

The total area of the state is 104,100 mi^2.

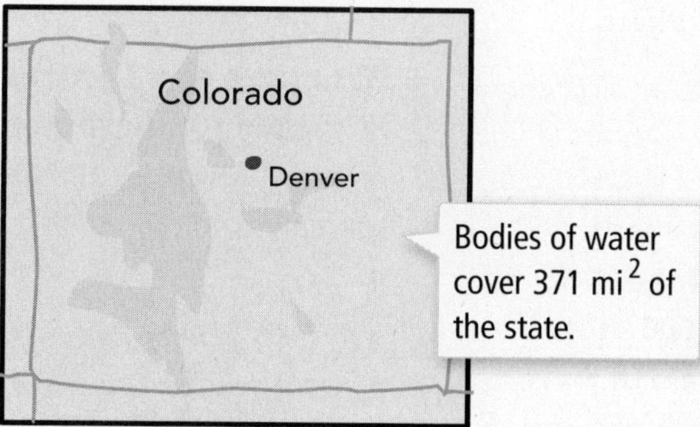

Close and Check

MP1, MP3

Focus Question

What does it mean to have a fractional percent of something?

Do you know HOW?

1. Circle the number(s) that is equivalent to $\frac{1}{5}\%$.

   20% $\frac{2}{100}$

   0.002 0.20

2. Find the solutions.

   What is $\frac{1}{8}\%$ of 800?

   3 is what percent of 1,200?

   19.5 is 0.75% of what?

3. The unemployment rate falls 0.4%. Out of 3,500 unemployed workers, how many people find jobs?

   people

4. Washington, D.C., comprises about 0.0016% of the total area of the U. S. The U.S. covers about 3,790,000 square miles. About how many square miles is Washington, D.C.? Round your answer to the nearest whole number.

   square miles

Do you UNDERSTAND?

5. **Writing** Write a real-world problem that includes a percent less than 1%. Show how to solve your problem.

6. **Compare and Contrast** What is the same and different about a percent less than 100 and a fractional percent?

Fractions, Decimals, and Percents

Digital Resources

CCSS: 7.NS.A.2d: Convert a rational number to a decimal using long division … .. **7.NS.A.3:** Solve real-world and mathematical problems involving the four operations with rational numbers. Also, **7.NS.A.2b.**

Launch

MP2, MP4

The results of an international origami competition show how many animals top folders perfectly folded in fifty minutes.

How could the origami competition organizers use fractions, decimals, or percents to better represent the results? Explain.

Origami Animal Folding Results

Contestant	Perfectly Folded	Folded
Happy Friend	8	12
Surly Friend	6	10
New Friend	4	8
Not a Friend	10	15

Reflect Would you rule out using any form of these representations—fractions, decimals, or percents—to improve the results for any reason? If so, why?

Got It?

PART 1 Got It (1 of 2)

On an 85-question multiple choice exam, a student got 71 questions correct. What percent of the exam did the student get correct? Round to the nearest whole percent.

PART 1 Got It (2 of 2)

On an 85-question multiple choice exam, a student got 71 questions correct. When might representing the results as a fraction, a decimal, and a percent be useful in analyzing this situation?

PART 2 Got It

A koala sleeps for about 75% of the day. Write the ratio of hours a koala is asleep per day to the total number of hours in a day.

Got It?

PART 3 Got It (1 of 2)

Which statement(s) are true?

I. $\frac{1}{4}$, 0.25, and 2.5% are equivalent

II. $\frac{1}{5}$, 0.20, and 20% are equivalent

III. $\frac{2}{5}$, 0.20, and 25% are equivalent

IV. $\frac{5}{8}$, 0.62, and 62.5% are equivalent

Discuss with a classmate

Number lines are useful models for comparing numbers.
Use a number line to justify why the answer you selected shows the values are equivalent.
Use a number line to explain why the other answer choices are incorrect.

PART 3 Got It (2 of 2)

What is 24% of 50? Choose a rational number representation to find the exact answer. Explain why you chose the representation that you used. Use estimation to check your answer.

Close and Check

Focus Question

MP4, MP6

Why are there different representations of rational numbers?

Do you know HOW?

1. There are 78 varieties of cetaceans (whales, dolphins, and porpoises). 11 cetacean species are baleen whales. What percent of cetaceans are baleen whales? Round your answer to the nearest tenth.

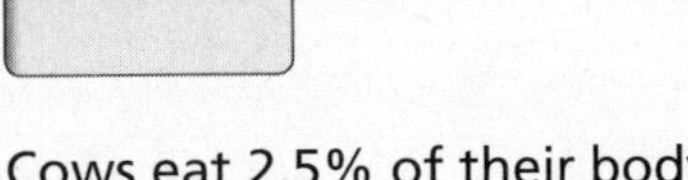

2. Cows eat 2.5% of their body weight in dry food each day. The average cow weighs 1,660 lbs. How many pounds of dry food will the average cow eat each day?

 pounds

3. Complete the table below by filling in equivalent values in different forms.

Fraction	$\frac{1}{4}$			
Decimal		0.04		0.005
Percent			112.5%	

Do you UNDERSTAND?

4. **Writing** Is it easier to change a fraction to a decimal and then to a percent, or is it easier to change a fraction directly to a percent? Explain.

5. **Error Analysis** A score of at least 85% of 220 points is needed to advance to the semi-finals. Can the equation be used to find the number of points needed to advance? Explain.

$$220x = 0.85$$

3-6 Percent Error

Digital Resources

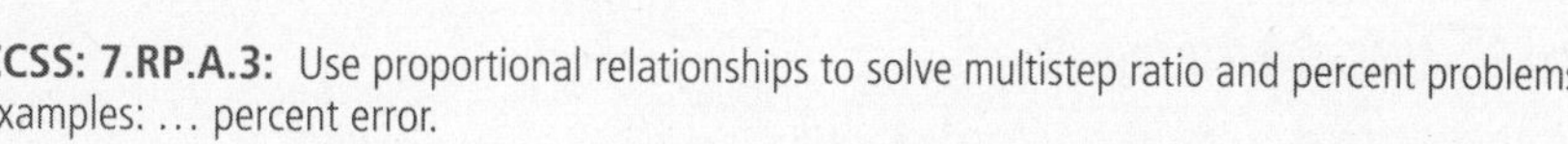

CCSS: 7.RP.A.3: Use proportional relationships to solve multistep ratio and percent problems. Examples: … percent error.

Launch

MP1, MP4

The surly friend and his remaining friends set out to set up an origami shop with a goal of selling 200 animals the first week. After the first week, the surly friend says, "Our sales total is 3 percent from the goal."

Tell how many animals the group sold. Explain whether they made their goal.

Reflect Was the surly friend clear about the sales results? If not, how could he have been clearer?

Got It?

PART 1 Got It (1 of 2)

Find the percent error of the estimated value to the nearest whole percent.

Estimated value: 250
Actual value: 200

PART 1 Got It (2 of 2)

Why does the percent error formula divide by the actual value instead of the estimated value?

PART 2 Got It (1 of 2)

A weatherman predicted 17 inches of snow. The town actually got $1\frac{1}{2}$ feet of snow. By what percent was the weatherman's prediction off?

Got It?

PART 2 Got It (2 of 2)

Why is there an absolute value in the numerator of the percent error formula?

PART 3 Got It (1 of 2)

The dot plot shows the measurements made by a science class. If the rock's actual mass is 5.9 g, what is the greatest percent error among the measurements? Round to the nearest tenth of a percent.

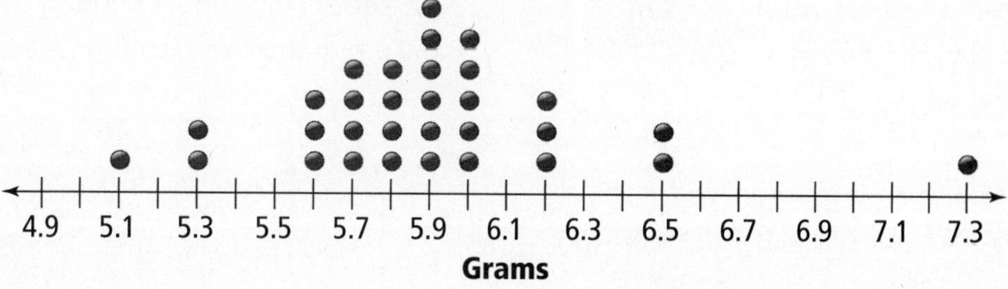

PART 3 Got It (2 of 2)

The dot plot shows the measurements made by a science class. If the rock's actual mass is 5.9 g, what is the least percent error among the measurements? Explain.

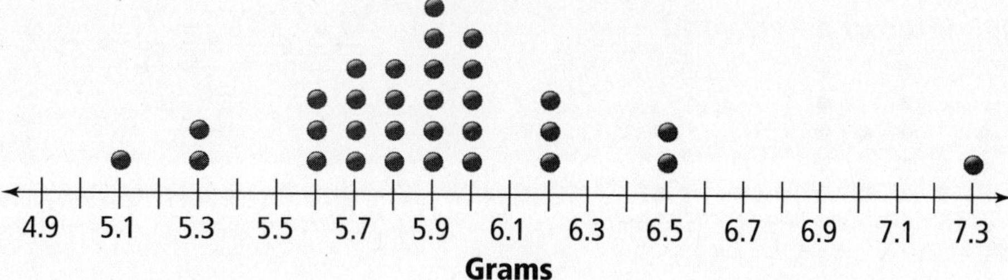

Close and Check

Focus Question

MP4, MP6

How are percents helpful to describe and understand variability in data?

Do you know HOW?

1. Find the percent error of the estimated value to the nearest whole percent.
   Estimated value: 547
   Actual value: 562

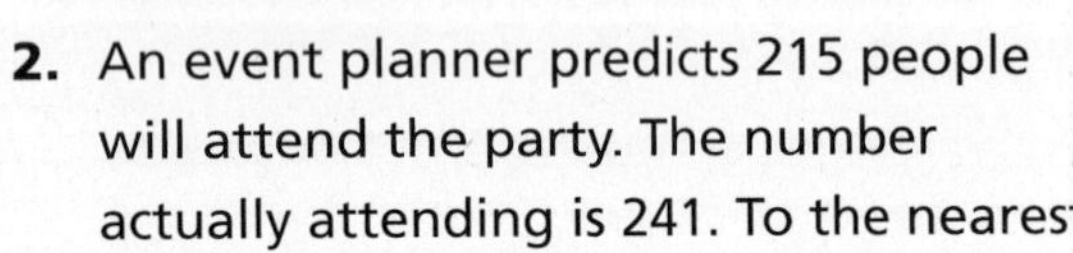

2. An event planner predicts 215 people will attend the party. The number actually attending is 241. To the nearest tenth, find the percent by which the event planner's prediction is off.

3. The actual diameter of a redwood tree is 12.4 feet. To the nearest tenth, find the greatest percent error in the data.

Diameter of a Redwood

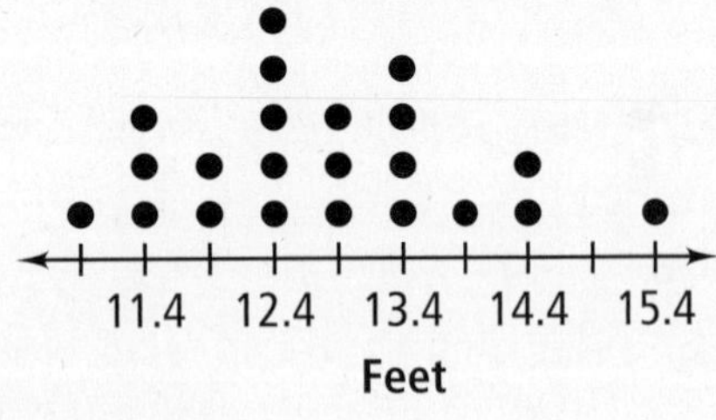

Do you UNDERSTAND?

4. **Reasoning** How does understanding percent error impact making decisions based on a set of data?

5. **Error Analysis** A classmate finds the percent error in Monday's predicted high temperature of 71°F and the actual high temperature of 78°F. Explain her error.

$$\frac{(71 - 78)}{78} = -\frac{7}{78} \approx -9\%$$

Problem Solving

Digital Resources

CCSS: 7.NS.A.3: Solve real-world and mathematical problems involving the four operations with rational numbers.

Launch

MP1, MP3

Your surly friend plans a 400-ft^2 garden to improve his mood. 40% of the garden will be fruit, $\frac{1}{4}$ will be vegetables, 0.1 will be herbs, and the rest flowers.

Choose only one representation—fractions, decimals, or percents—to find the area of each part of the garden. Explain your choice after completing the area calculations.

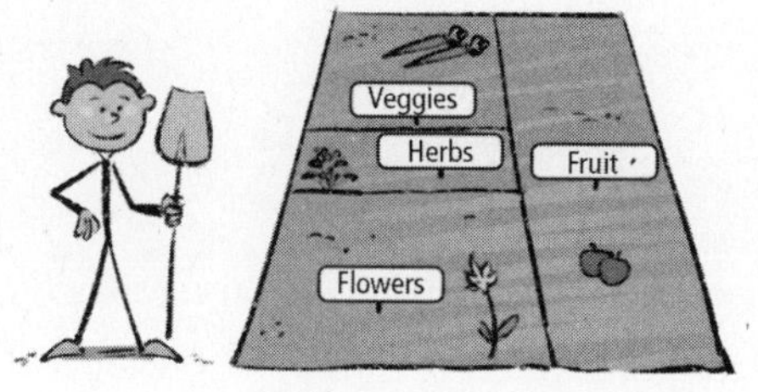

Reflect Do you use fractions, decimals, or percents more often to solve problems? Explain.

Got It?

PART 1 Got It

A student mows a neighbor's lawn for $7.50 an hour. The student does such a good job that the neighbor gives him a 20% raise. Calculate the student's new hourly wage using a percent greater than 100.

PART 2 Got It

A school estimates that the expenses of running a fundraiser will be about 3.25% of the total amount that they collect. The fundraiser collects $16,000 in total, and the amount after expenses is $14,500. Is the estimated expense rate accurate? Explain.

Got It?

PART 3 Got It

Three friends went out to lunch. The bill came to $37.50. Each friend says that she ate 30% of the meal. They want to pay according to how much they ate.

a. How much more or less do they need to pay due to rounding?

b. What is the percent error on what the friends want to pay?

Close and Check

Focus Question

MP1, MP7

How does understanding the relationships among fractions, decimals, and percents help you solve problems?

Do you know HOW?

1. The minimum wage in 2007 was $5.85. The minimum wage rose 24% by 2009. To the nearest cent, find the minimum wage in 2009.

2. On Saturday, a store sells $2,700 in merchandise. The store makes a profit of 15.25% on all sales. The remaining income pays for the store's expenses. How much money goes toward expenses on Saturday?

3. Three roommates split their rent based on the sizes of their bedrooms. Roommate 1's bedroom takes up $\frac{3}{7}$ (43%) of total space. Roommate 2's and Roommate 3's each take up $\frac{2}{7}$ (29%). Find the estimated amount they will pay if total rent is $1900. Then find the percent error on the rent paid.

Estimated amount:

Percent error:

Do you UNDERSTAND?

4. **Writing** Explain how to use estimation to check the reasonableness of your solution to Exercise 2.

5. **Reasoning** If you were one of the roommates from Exercise 3, could you avoid overpaying your rent while still splitting costs according to your room sizes? Explain.

3-R Topic Review

New Vocabulary: accuracy, percent error, repeating decimal, terminating decimal
Review Vocabulary: decimal, fraction, percent, ratio, rational number

Vocabulary Review

Identify two challenging vocabulary terms from this topic. Write one vocabulary term in the center oval, and fill in the surrounding boxes with details that will help you better understand the term.

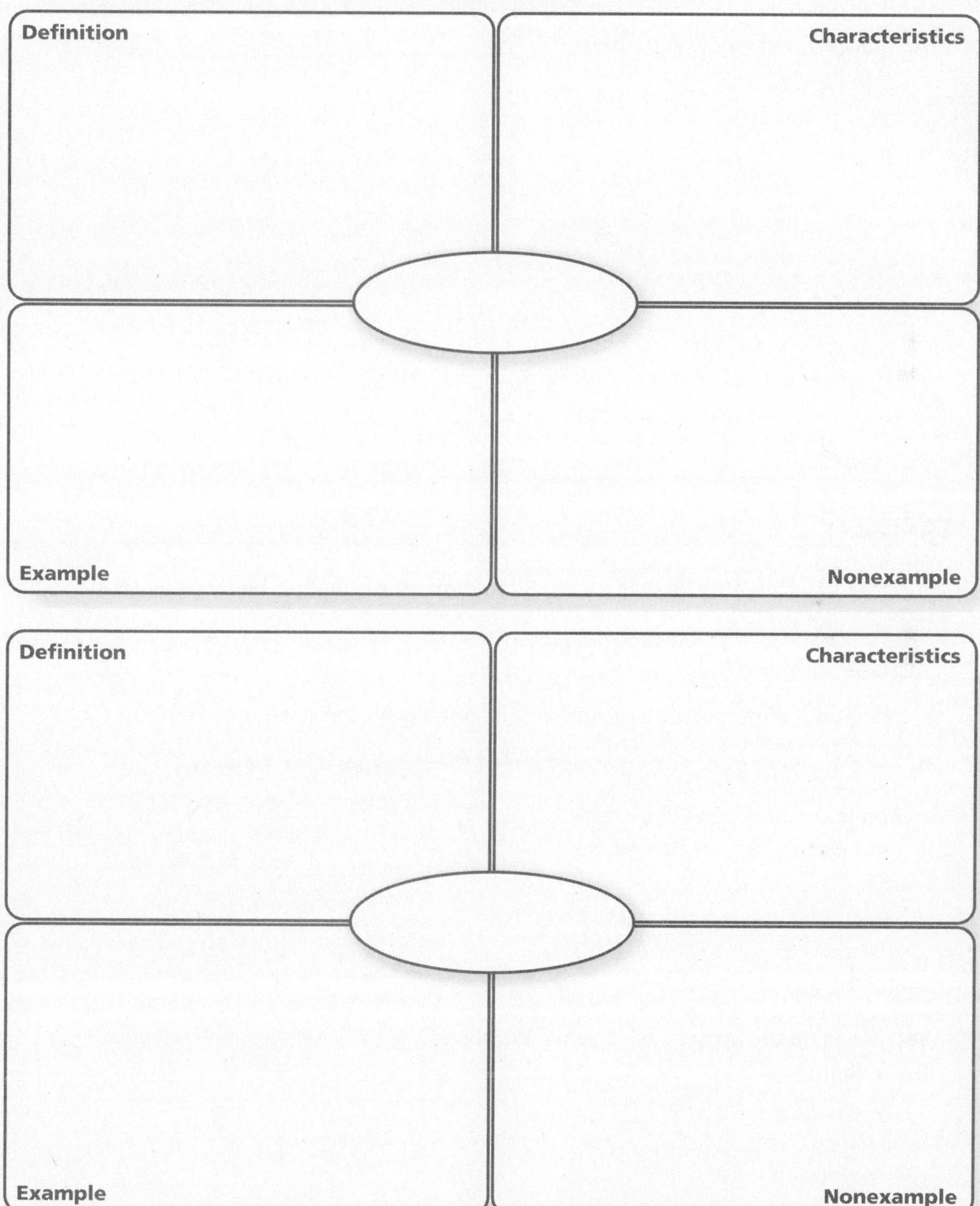

Pull It All Together

TASK 1

A marathon is 26.2 miles. Your friend can run 5 miles. What percent of the race can your friend run?

Your friend could run 5 miles, but increased his running to 164.4% of that distance. How far can your friend run now?

TASK 2

Suppose you have $1,218.29 in a savings account. The equation below represents the account activity.

$1{,}218.29 = p(1.05)^n$

a. What is the interest rate compounded annually on the savings account?

b. At the end of one year, what percent of the principal is the balance?

You have had the account for 3 years. What was the principal originally deposited in the account?

4-1

Expressing Rational Numbers with Decimal Expansions

Digital Resources

CCSS: 8.NS.A.1: … Understand informally that every … numbers show that the decimal expansion repeats eventually, and convert a decimal expansion which repeats eventually into a rational number.

Launch

MP2, MP8

The workers at the local lasagna shack share their tips evenly and entirely at the end of each night. A war of words always erupts when they cannot seem to share the last dollar entirely evenly.

Which nights will the workers argue? Why?

Day	Last Dollar	Number of Workers	Even Split
M	\$1	2	50¢ each
T	\$1	4	25¢ each
W	\$1	3	$0.\overline{3}$ (arguing, $0.\overline{3}$ is ∞)
TH	\$1	5	20¢ each
F	\$1	6	$0.1\overline{6}$ (arguing, $0.1\overline{6}$ is ∞)

Reflect Suppose you could divide the last dollar to as many decimal places as needed. Would that solve all the problems of dividing the money evenly?

Got It?

PART 1 Got It

Wheels on some in-line skates can be removed using a $\frac{5}{32}$-in. Allen wrench. What is $\frac{5}{32}$ written as a decimal?

PART 2 Got It

Elena Kagan's confirmation to the U.S. Supreme Court was historic. For the first time, 3 of the 9 justices on the court were female. What is $\frac{3}{9}$ written as a decimal?

Got It?

PART 3 Got It

There are two parking lots near a concert hall. The covered parking lot is $\frac{5}{6}$ mi away. The open-air parking lot is 0.8 mi away. Which parking lot is closer to the concert hall? Explain.

Close and Check

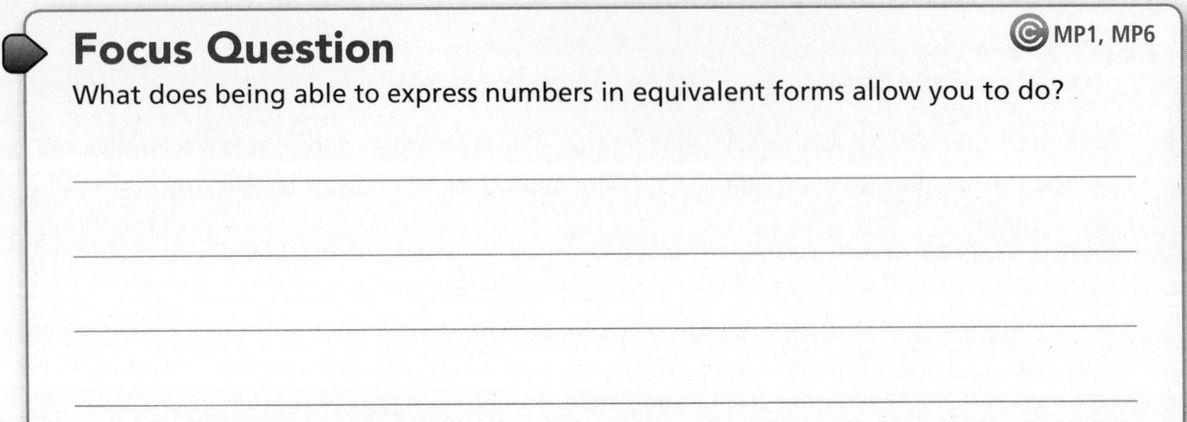

Focus Question

MP1, MP6

What does being able to express numbers in equivalent forms allow you to do?

Do you know HOW?

1. What is $\frac{1}{8}$ written as a decimal?

2. Use = or ≠ to correctly complete each statement.

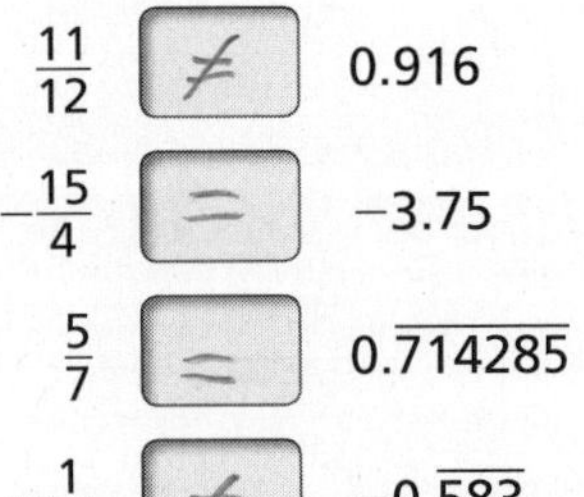

$\frac{11}{12}$ ☐ 0.916

$-\frac{15}{4}$ ☐ -3.75

$\frac{5}{7}$ ☐ $0.\overline{714285}$

$-\frac{1}{12}$ ☐ $-0.5\overline{83}$

3. The North Vista hiking trail is $\frac{11}{16}$ mi. The Scenic Overlook trail is 0.688 mi. Use <, >, or = to correctly complete the statement.

$\frac{11}{16}$ ☐ 0.688

Do you UNDERSTAND?

4. Error Analysis A classmate says that $0.\overline{285714}$ is not a rational number because it does not terminate. Explain her error.

5. Reasoning Two chefs are trying to break the world's record for the longest strand of spaghetti. Chef A measures his spaghetti strand to be $503\frac{2}{3}$ ft. Chef B measures his spaghetti strand to be $503.\overline{66}$ ft. Since $503.\overline{66}$ rounds to 503.7, the judges declare Chef B the winner. Explain why Chef A should protest the judges' decision.

4-2 Exploring Irrational Numbers

Digital Resources

CCSS: 8.NS.A.1: Know that numbers that are not rational are called irrational. Understand informally that every number has a decimal expansion; for rational numbers show that the decimal expansion repeats eventually … .

Launch

MP1, MP6

Complete the table and then draw each square. Provide exact lengths. Describe any problems you have.

	Side Length	Area
Square 1		1 $unit^2$
Square 2		2 $units^2$
Square 3		4 $units^2$

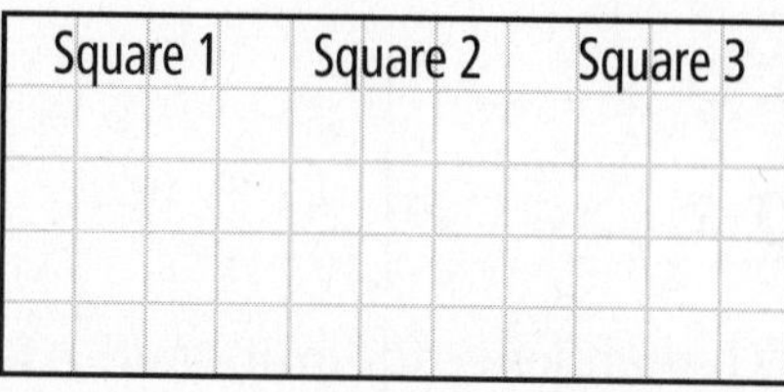

Reflect Do you think you could find an exact side length for all of the squares if you kept trying? Explain.

Got It?

PART 1 Got It

Which numbers are irrational?

I. $\sqrt{25}$ II. $\sqrt{50}$ III. $\sqrt{125}$

PART 2 Got It

Which number is *not* irrational? Assume each pattern continues.

I. 3.202002000200002...

II. 3.213213213213...

III. 3.121221222...

PART 3 Got It

What are all the possible names for $1\frac{2}{9}$?

Close and Check

Focus Question

MP3, MP6

What is the difference between an irrational number and a rational number? Can a number be both irrational and rational?

Do you know HOW?

1. Circle the irrational numbers.

$\sqrt{111}$ $\sqrt{400}$ $\sqrt{160}$

$\sqrt{144}$ $\sqrt{220}$ $\sqrt{200}$

2. Circle the rational numbers. Assume each pattern continues.

4.014014 6.232342345

0.717717 1.594593592

12.12211222 9.96939693

3. Indicate all the possible names for each number.

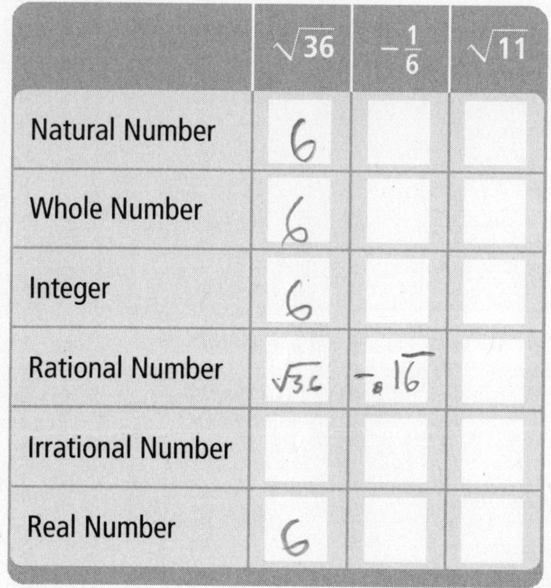

	$\sqrt{36}$	$-\frac{1}{6}$	$\sqrt{11}$
Natural Number			
Whole Number			
Integer			
Rational Number			
Irrational Number			
Real Number			

Do you UNDERSTAND?

4. Reasoning Can an irrational number ever be a natural number? A whole number? Explain.

5. Compare and Contrast What is the difference between locating $\frac{3}{5}$ on a number line and locating $\sqrt{5}$ on a number line?

This page intentionally left blank.

4-3

Approximating Irrational Numbers

Digital Resources

CCSS: 8.NS.A.2: Use rational approximations of irrational numbers to compare the size of irrational numbers, locate them approximately on a number line diagram, and estimate the value of expressions.

Launch

MP1, MP2

Due to the sauciness of their sauce, the local lasagna shack decides to expand its old square napkin to a new square napkin.

Find the approximate side length of the new square napkin. Explain what you did.

Old Napkin
100 in.^2

New Napkin
150 in.^2

Reflect Why would it be useful to write the side length of the new square napkin as an approximate length instead of an exact length?

Got It?

PART 1 Got It (1 of 2)

On a number line, between which two consecutive whole numbers would $\sqrt{70}$ be located?

PART 1 Got It (2 of 2)

The square root of an integer *n* is between 9 and 10. What are all the possible values for *n*? Explain.

PART 2 Got It (1 of 2)

What is $\sqrt{50}$ to the nearest tenth?

Got It?

PART 2 Got It (2 of 2)

Is it possible to find the exact decimal value for $\sqrt{50}$? Explain.

PART 3 Got It (1 of 2)

A square has an area of 112 cm^2. What is the approximate perimeter of the square?

PART 3 Got It (2 of 2)

You estimate $\sqrt{112}$ to the nearest tenth. Is the estimated value *rational* or *irrational*? Explain.

Discuss with a classmate
Read your explanation to this problem out loud.
Check for the following:
Is the explanation clear?
Are the key words, such as rational number, used correctly in the explanation?
If not, discuss how to improve the explanation.

Close and Check

Focus Question

MP2, MP5

How do you estimate an irrational number? Why might you need to be able to estimate an irrational number?

Do you know HOW?

1. On a number line, between which two whole numbers would $\sqrt{136}$ be located?

   11 and 12

2. The square root of an integer n is between 6 and 7. Write an inequality that expresses all the possible values for n.

3. Which value is farther to the right on a number line?

   2.5^2 $\sqrt{81}$

   $\sqrt{81}$

4. A square sandbox has an area of 42 ft^2. What is the approximate perimeter of the sandbox to the nearest hundredth?

Do you UNDERSTAND?

5. **Reasoning** Two classmates estimate the location of $\sqrt{60}$ on a number line. One student locates the point at 7.7. The other student says the point is located at 7.75. Can both students be correct? Explain.

6. **Writing** Pi (π) is an irrational number used to find the circumference and area of circles. Are the circumference and area of a circle actual or estimated measures? Explain.

4-4

Comparing and Ordering Rational and Irrational Numbers

CCSS: 8.NS.A.2: Use rational approximations of irrational numbers to compare the size of irrational numbers, locate them approximately on a number line diagram, and estimate the value of expressions.

Digital Resources

Launch

MP4, MP7

For people who prefer pizza, the local lasagna shack also offers thin crust pizzas in three different shapes. Each costs $20.

Which deal is the best and which deal is the worst? Explain.

Reflect Do you think all the pizza areas are rational? Explain.

Got It?

PART 1 Got It (1 of 2)

What symbol correctly completes the statement?

$\frac{4}{3}$ ☐ $\sqrt{2}$

PART 1 Got It (2 of 2)

Your friend claims that for any positive real number a, $a > \sqrt{a}$. Is your friend correct? Explain. If your friend is incorrect, give a counterexample in your explanation.

Discuss with a classmate
Compare your explanations for this problem.
What does counterexample mean?
What does counterexample mean for a math problem?

Got It?

PART 2 Got It

Order the values from least to greatest.

π, $\sqrt{11}$, 3.4, 3.1

PART 3 Got It

Order the values from least to greatest.

$-\sqrt{16}$, $-\frac{16}{6}$, $\sqrt{8}$, 2.6, $-\sqrt{10}$

Close and Check

Focus Question

MP2, MP3

How can you compare rational and irrational numbers? Why might you want to?

Do you know HOW?

1. Use $<$, $>$, or $=$ to complete each statement.

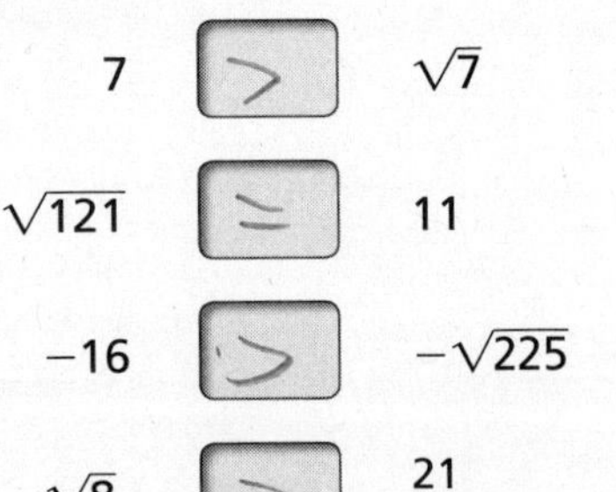

7 ☐ $\sqrt{7}$

$\sqrt{121}$ ☐ 11

-16 ☐ $-\sqrt{225}$

$\sqrt{8}$ ☐ $\frac{21}{8}$

2. Order the values from least to greatest.

$\frac{25}{7}$ $\sqrt{3}$ 5.85 4^2 π

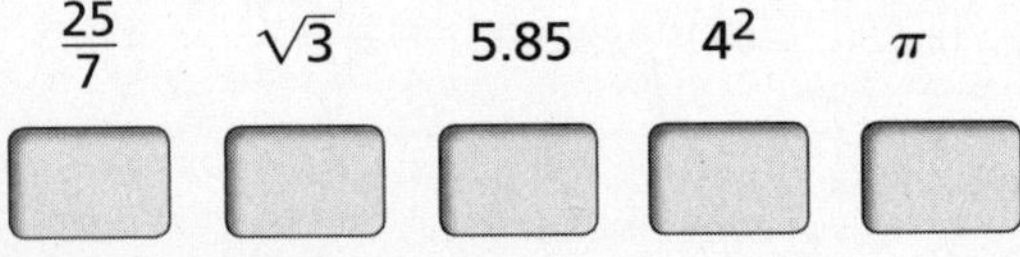

3. Match each point on the number line to the nearest value.

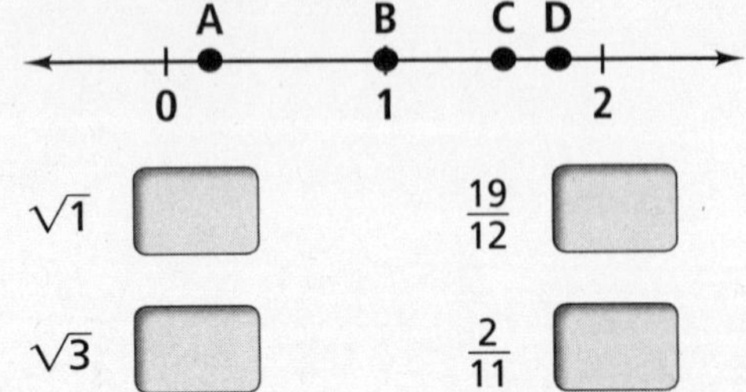

$\sqrt{1}$ ☐ $\frac{19}{12}$ ☐

$\sqrt{3}$ ☐ $\frac{2}{11}$ ☐

Do you UNDERSTAND?

4. **Reasoning** The owners want to remake the pizza in Deal #3 of the Launch. Can they make a square pizza with exactly the same area? Explain.

5. **Writing** What strategies can you use to order the numbers in Exercise 2 without changing them all to decimals?

4-5

Problem Solving

Digital Resources

CCSS: 8.NS.A.1: Know that numbers that are not rational are called irrational ... and convert a decimal expansion which repeats eventually into a rational number. 8.NS.A.2: Use rational approximations of irrational numbers to ... estimate the value of expressions.

Launch

MP5, MP6

Your friend said the square root of 14 is somewhere in between 3 and 4 as shown.

Explain whether you agree. Then show where would be a more precise spot to place the square root of 14 and tell why your estimate is better.

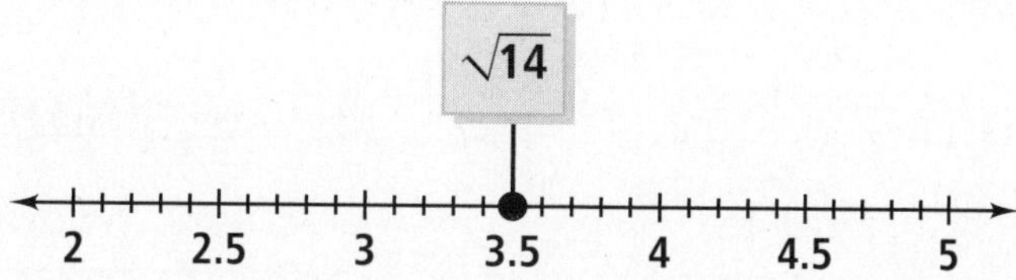

Reflect When is precision important and when is it not so important? Provide an example for each.

Got It?

PART 1 Got It

If $x = 12$, what is the smallest natural number y that makes $\sqrt{x^2 + y^2}$ rational?

PART 2 Got It

You have a rope that is marking off a square plot of land with an area of 6 ft^2. Is the rope long enough to mark off a circular area with a diameter of 3 ft? Explain.

Got It?

PART 3 Got It (1 of 2)

Write $0.\overline{24}$ as a fraction in simplest form.

PART 3 Got It (2 of 2)

Write $0.5\overline{3}$ as a fraction in simplest form.

Close and Check

Focus Question

MP2, MP8

How is solving a problem that includes rational numbers similar to solving a problem that includes irrational numbers? How is it different?

Do you know HOW?

1. If $x = 6$, what is the smallest natural number y that makes $\sqrt{x^2 + y^2}$ rational?

$y =$ ______

2. A carnival ride must be enclosed within a fence. The ride requires 676 ft^2 of space to operate. What is the minimum number of feet of fencing required to enclose the ride?

______ ft

3. A square billboard is shown below. What is the approximate length and width of the billboard to the nearest hundredth?

$A = 5{,}200 \text{ ft}^2$

______

Do you UNDERSTAND?

4. Reasoning A square pool with side lengths of 16 ft sells for $\frac{2}{3}$ the price of a circular pool with a diameter of 18 ft. If the shape does not matter, which is the better deal? Explain.

5. Error Analysis Your friend says that 0.2 and $0.\overline{2}$ can both be written as the fraction $\frac{1}{5}$. Explain his mistake.

4-R Topic Review

New Vocabulary: irrational numbers, perfect square, real numbers, repeating decimal, square root, terminating decimal
Review Vocabulary: integer, natural numbers, rational numbers, whole numbers

Vocabulary Review

Identify two challenging vocabulary terms from this topic. Write one vocabulary term in the center oval, and fill in the surrounding boxes with details that will help you better understand the term.

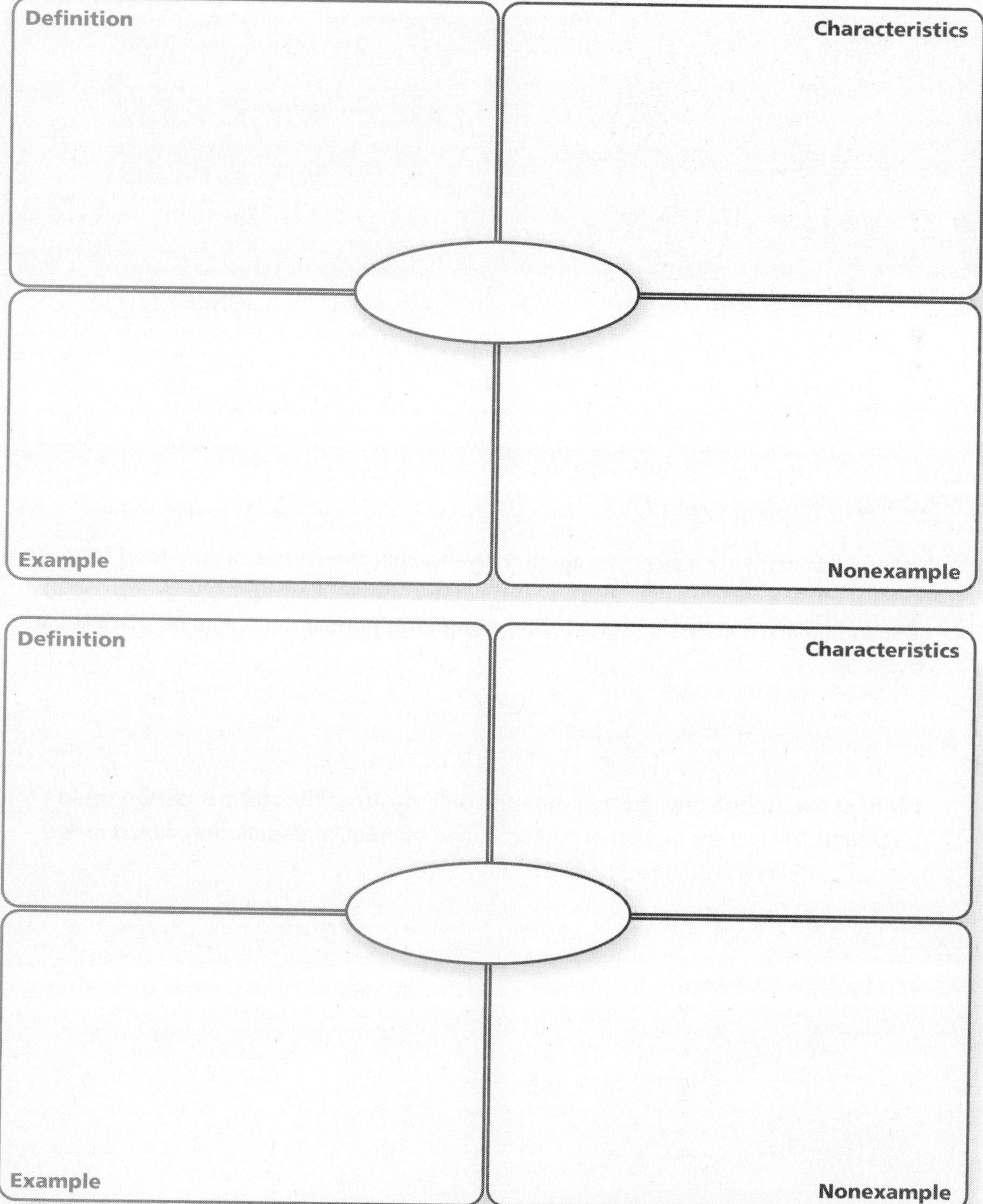

Pull It All Together

TASK 1

You want to fence in a square region with twice the area of the square garden shown. To the nearest foot, how much fencing will you need?

7 ft

7 ft

TASK 2

You and some of your classmates agree to evenly split the cost of buying food for a party. The cost per person comes to $\$1.\overline{63}$. What is the least amount the group could be spending on food? What is the fewest number of people that could be sharing the cost?

Is your answer to the previous question the only way that the cost per person could come to $\$1.\overline{63}$? Is there any other total cost and number of people that would make the cost per person equal to $\$1.\overline{63}$? Explain.

5-1

Perfect Squares, Square Roots, and Equations of the Form $x^2 = p$

Digital Resources

CCSS: 8.EE.A.2: Use square root and cube root symbols to represent solutions to equations of the form $x^2 = p$ and $x^3 = p$, where p is a positive rational number. Evaluate square roots of small perfect squares and cube roots of small perfect cubes.

Launch

MP3, MP6

Your friend claims that x^2 is the same as $2x$. Tell how he could have come to that conclusion. Explain whether you agree.

Reflect When have you used expressions with exponents like x^2 in mathematics before? Explain.

Got It?

PART 1 Got It

Solve $y^2 = 625$.

PART 2 Got It

Solve $y^2 = \frac{4}{9}$.

Got It?

PART 3 Got It

A square painting has an area of 460 cm^2. What is the length of one side of the painting to the nearest tenth of a centimeter?

Close and Check

Focus Question

How can you apply what you know about squares and square roots to write and solve equations of the form $x^2 = p$? How can you use equations in that form?

Do you know HOW?

1. Solve each equation.

A. $x^2 = 36$

B. $x^2 = 64$

C. $x^2 = 400$

D. $x^2 = 121$

2. Solve $y^2 = \frac{144}{169}$.

3. A square flower garden has an area of 136 ft^2. Find the length of one side of the garden to the nearest tenth of a foot.

ft

4. A square playground has an area of 1,500 ft^2. Find the length of one side of the playground to the nearest tenth of a foot.

ft

Do you UNDERSTAND?

5. Vocabulary What is the relationship between perfect squares and square roots? Give an example.

6. Error Analysis The square-shaped downtown region of a town has an area of 144 km^2. Your friend says the length of one side can be represented by $\sqrt{144} = \pm 12$. Explain the error she made in her solution.

5-2

Perfect Cubes, Cube Roots, and Equations of the Form $x^3 = p$

Digital Resources

CCSS: 8.EE.A.2: Use square root and cube root symbols to represent solutions to equations of the form $x^2 = p$ and $x^3 = p$, where p is a positive rational number. Evaluate square roots of small perfect squares and cube roots of small perfect cubes.

Launch

MP1, MP6

Draw a line from each measurement to the figure it could represent. Explain how you know you are correct.

64 in.^{2}

64 in.^{3}

Reflect Could one of the measurements somehow represent something about both figures? Could the other?

Got It?

PART 1 Got It

Solve $y^3 = -64$.

PART 2 Got It

Solve $y^3 = \frac{1}{1000}$.

Got It?

PART 3 Got It

A mailing carton in the shape of a cube has a volume of 684 cubic inches. What is the length of one side of the carton to the nearest tenth of an inch?

Close and Check

Focus Question

MP1, MP7

How is solving an equation that includes cubes similar to solving an equation that includes squares? How is it different?

Do you know HOW?

1. Solve each equation.

A. $x^3 = 343$ 

B. $x^3 = -1{,}000$ 

C. $x^3 = -729$ 

D. $x^3 = 216$ 

2. Solve $y^3 = \frac{27}{512}$.

3. A storage unit in the shape of a cube has a volume of 3,000 cubic feet. Find the length of one side of the storage unit to the nearest tenth of a foot.

ft

4. An abstract sculpture in the shape of a cube has a volume of 925 ft^3. Find the approximate length of one side of the sculpture to the nearest tenth of a foot.

 ft

Do you UNDERSTAND?

5. Error Analysis A salesperson says the volume of a cube-shaped birdcage is 64 ft^3. What error does the salesperson make when solving the equation? Write the correct solution and explain what it means.

$$x^3 = 64$$
$$\sqrt[3]{x^3} = \sqrt[3]{64}$$
$$x = \pm 4$$

6. Reasoning Can the cube root of a positive number ever be negative? Explain.

5-3 Exponents and Multiplication

Digital Resources

CCSS: 8.EE.A.1: Know and apply the properties of integer exponents to generate equivalent numerical expressions. *For example,* $3^2 \times 3^{-5} = 3^{-3} = \frac{1}{3^3} = \frac{1}{27}$.

Launch

MP3, MP7

The city's second-best scientist's first rocket fails to reach orbit. He promises his second rocket will fly twice as fast as his first and his third rocket will fly twice as fast as the second.

How fast will Rockets 2 and 3 fly? Show how you know.

Rocket 1

2^{14} mph

Rocket 2

Rocket 3

Reflect What do you know about the factors in the expression 2^{14}? Explain.

Got It?

PART 1 Got It (1 of 2)

Simplify the expression.

$3y^4 \cdot 5y^7$

PART 1 Got It (2 of 2)

Does $x^8 \cdot x^2$ have the same value as $x^5 \cdot x^5$? Justify your answer.

Discuss with a classmate

Compare your answers to this problem.
What steps did you take to justify your answers?
Test your answers using replacements for the variable x and see if your explanations are still valid. If they are not, revise them as needed.

Got It?

PART 2 Got It

Simplify the expression.

$(g^9)^6$

PART 3 Got It

Simplify the expression.

$(2s^5t^9)^4$

Close and Check

Focus Question

MP1, MP2

How can you apply what you know about multiplying numerical expressions to multiplying algebraic expressions containing exponents?

Do you know HOW?

1. Simplify the expression.
$4x^6 \cdot 12x^9$

2. Simplify the expression.
$(f^8)^3$

3. Simplify the expression.
$(4st)^4$

4. Simplify the expression.
$(7q^7r^3)^3$

5. Circle the expression(s) that is equivalent to $216a^9b^{15}c^{27}$.

A. $(72a^6b^{12}c^{24})^3$

B. $(72a^3b^5c^9)^3$

C. $(6a^6b^{12}c^{24})^3$

D. $(6a^3b^5c^9)^3$

Do you UNDERSTAND?

6. Writing Use arithmetic to prove it is incorrect to add the exponents of unlike bases. Use the equation $a^2b^2 \neq (ab)^4$.

7. Error Analysis A classmate says $3s^4 \cdot 5s^2 = (15s)^6$. Explain why your classmate is incorrect. Rewrite the equation to make a true statement.

5-4 Exponents and Division

Digital Resources

CCSS: 8.EE.A.1: Know and apply the properties of integer exponents to generate equivalent numerical expressions. *For example,* $3^2 \times 3^{-5} = 3^{-3} = \frac{1}{3^3} = \frac{1}{27}$.

Launch

MP1, MP2, MP7

The city's second-best scientist likes to look overly complex. That's why he's second best. He presents the cost of a rocket bolt on Rocket 1 as shown.

How much does a bolt really cost? Show how you know.

$$\frac{5 \cdot 6 \cdot 2 \cdot 17 \cdot 31 \cdot 4 \cdot 4}{31 \cdot 4 \cdot 2 \cdot 17 \cdot 6 \cdot 5}$$ **dollars each**

Reflect What was the key to solving this problem? Explain.

Got It?

PART 1 Got It (1 of 2)

Simplify the expression $\frac{g^{35}}{g^{23}}$.

PART 1 Got It (2 of 2)

Does $\frac{a^{12}}{a^{8}}$ have the same value as $\frac{a^{6}}{a^{2}}$? Justify your answer.

PART 2 Got It

Simplify the expression $\left(\frac{a^2}{4b^3}\right)^4$.

Close and Check

Focus Question

How can you apply what you know about dividing numerical expressions to dividing algebraic expressions containing exponents?

Do you know HOW?

1. Simplify the expression.

$\frac{x^{27}}{x^{13}}$

2. Simplify the expression.

$\frac{r^{55}}{r^{32}}$

3. Simplify the expression.

$\left(\frac{2r^9}{3m}\right)^3$

4. Simplify the expression.

$\left(\frac{2d^3g^{12}}{4s^{12}w^6}\right)^5$

Do you UNDERSTAND?

5. Writing Can the exponent in the denominator be subtracted from the exponent in the numerator when the bases are different? Explain.

6. Error Analysis When asked to simplify the expression, your classmate writes the following:

$$\left(\frac{c^3}{3d^5}\right)^2 = \frac{2c^5}{6d^7}$$

What errors did your classmate make? What should she have written?

This page intentionally left blank.

5-5 Zero and Negative Exponents

Digital Resources

CCSS: 8.EE.A.1: Know and apply the properties of integer exponents to generate equivalent numerical expressions. *For example,* $3^2 \times 3^{-5} = 3^{-3} = \frac{1}{3^3} = \frac{1}{27}$.

Launch

MP7, MP8

Complete the table. Describe three patterns you see in the table.

2^x	10^x
$2^5 = 32$	$10^5 = 100{,}000$
$2^4 = 16$	$10^4 = 10{,}000$
$2^3 = 8$	$10^3 = 1{,}000$
$2^2 = 4$	$10^2 = 100$
$2^1 =$	$10^1 =$
$2^0 =$	$10^0 =$
$2^{-1} =$	$10^{-1} =$

Reflect Did you figure out the pattern in the left or right column first? Explain.

Got It?

PART 1 Got It

Simplify the expression $(-3.6)^0$.

PART 2 Got It (1 of 2)

Simplify the expression $\frac{m^2n^4}{m^5n^3}$.

Got It?

PART 2 Got It (2 of 2)

Is -3^{-2} *positive* or *negative*? Justify your answer.

PART 3 Got It

Is 4^{-3} greater than 1, equal to 1, or less than 1?

Close and Check

Focus Question

MP3, MP7

When do you need an exponent that is equal to zero? When do you need an exponent that is negative? What makes these exponents useful?

Do you know HOW?

1. Simplify the expression.

$\frac{n^{15}}{n^{15}}$

2. Simplify the expression.

$\frac{12k^{15}}{3k^{18}}$

3. Tell whether each expression is > 1, < 1, or $= 1$.

5^{-3}

100^{0}

25^{-2}

7^{2}

Do you UNDERSTAND?

4. **Reasoning** In the expression $\frac{a^3}{a^3}$, why can the variable *not* be equal to 0? Use substitution to justify your argument arithmetically.

5. **Error Analysis** Your classmate simplified the expression below. Explain his error and write the correct simplified expression.

$$\frac{6w^{12}}{3w^{12}} = 2w^0 = 2 \cdot 0 = 0$$

5-6 Comparing Expressions with Exponents

CCSS: 8.EE.A.1: Know and apply the properties of integer exponents to generate equivalent numerical expressions. *For example,* $3^2 \times 3^{-5} = 3^{-3} = \frac{1}{3^3} = \frac{1}{27}$.

Digital Resources

Launch

MP3, MP6

Use the tiles to create an expression with the least value and an expression with the greatest value. For each expression, you must use each number tile and the negative sign tile in only one location.

Tell how you decided the tile locations.

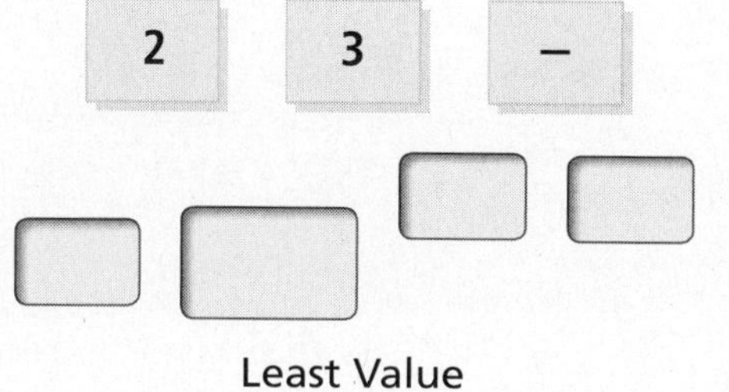

Least Value

Greatest Value

Reflect What did you decide first in solving the problem? Explain.

Got It?

PART 1 Got It

Which expressions are equivalent to 5^8?

I. $5^1 \cdot 5^8$

II. $5^2 \cdot 5^6$

III. $\frac{5^{16}}{5^2}$

IV. $(5^2)^4$

PART 2 Got It

Use <, >, or = to complete the statement.

9^{12} ☐ $\frac{9^{36}}{9^3}$

Got It?

PART 3 Got It

Use $<$, $>$, or $=$ to complete the statement.

27^5 ☐ $\frac{9^8}{3^4}$

Close and Check

Focus Question

MP4, MP7

What does being able to write expressions with exponents in equivalent forms allow you to do?

Do you know HOW?

1. Which expression(s) is equivalent to 6^{12}?

   I. $2^{10} \cdot 3^2$

   II. $6^0 \cdot 6^{12}$

   III. $(6^{10})^2$

   IV. $(6^2)^6$

2. Use $>$, $<$, or $=$ to complete each statement.

   8^0 ☐ $\frac{8^3}{1^3}$

   12^6 ☐ $(12^2)^3$

   25^8 ☐ 125^5

   27^{12} ☐ $(9^6)^3$

   $(8^6)^6$ ☐ $(4^4 \cdot 2^2)^6$

Do you UNDERSTAND?

3. **Compare and Contrast** What is the difference between comparing exponential numbers with like bases and comparing those with unlike bases?

4. **Error Analysis** A classmate writes equivalent expressions. Her work is shown below. Is she correct? Explain.

   $(4^2 \cdot 3^2)^6 = (12^4)^6 = 12^{24}$

5-7

Additional Problem Solving

Digital Resources

CCSS: 8.EE.A.1: Know and apply the properties of integer exponents to generate equivalent numerical expressions. *For example,* $3^2 \times 3^{-5} = 3^{-3} = \frac{1}{3^3} = \frac{1}{27}$.

Launch

MP7, MP8

Look for a pattern in the table.

Based on the pattern, what value of x makes the statement $4^{15} = 2^x$ true?

Powers of 4	Powers of 2
$4^2 = 16$	$2^4 = 16$
$4^3 = 64$	$2^6 = 64$
$4^4 = 256$	$2^8 = 256$
$4^5 = 1024$	$2^{10} = 1024$

Reflect What property of exponents did you apply to help you solve this problem?

Did you use an equation to find the value of x? If so, what equation did you use?

Got It?

PART 1 Got It

For what value(s) of m is the expression $3m^5$ reasonable in representing the area of a rectangle?

PART 2 Got It

For what values of a, if any, does $-3a^2 = -243$?
Explain your reasoning.

Close and Check

Focus Question

What kind of problems can you solve using expressions and equations containing exponents?

Do you know HOW?

1. Circle the value(s) of s for which the expression $-9s^3$ is reasonable for representing the volume of a cube.

   A. $s = 0$

   B. s can be any negative number.

   C. s can be any positive number.

2. Circle the value(s) of y for which the expression $35y^2$ is reasonable for representing the number of square yards your friend mows.

   A. $y = 0$

   B. y can be any negative number.

   C. y can be any positive number.

3. For what values of d, if any, will $2d^4 = 1{,}250$?

Do you UNDERSTAND?

4. **Reasoning** How would the solution to Exercise 3 change if the equation was $2d^4 = -1{,}250$? How do you know?

5. **Error Analysis** Your friend writes an expression to represent the score of a game. Is his expression useful? Explain.

$$\frac{5p^6}{(p^2)^3}$$

This page intentionally left blank.

5-R Topic Review

New Vocabulary: cube root, Negative Exponent Property, perfect cube, Zero Exponent Property
Review Vocabulary: base, exponent, inverse operations, perfect square, power, square root

Vocabulary Review

Identify two challenging vocabulary terms from this topic. Write one vocabulary term in the center oval, and fill in the surrounding boxes with details that will help you better understand the term.

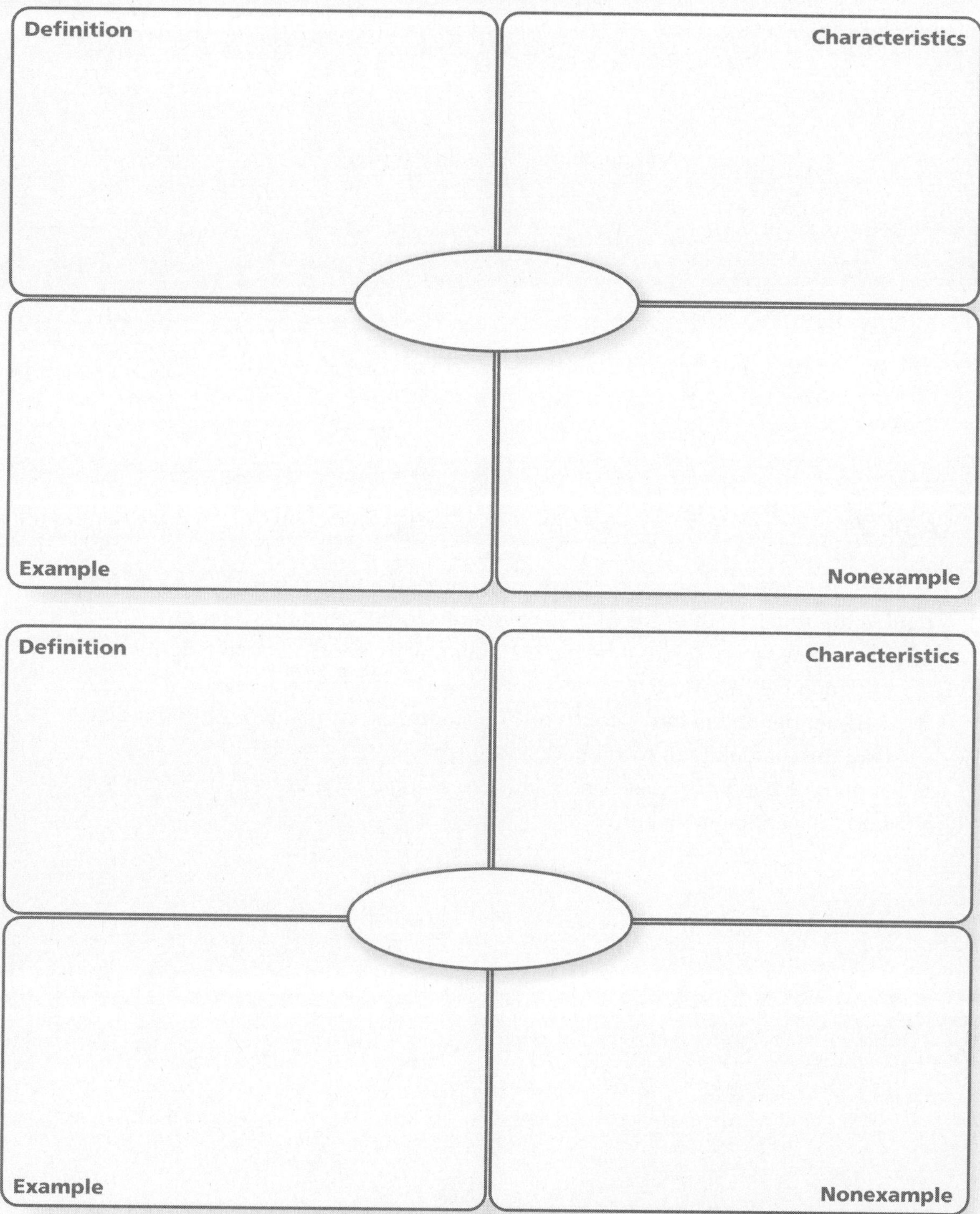

Pull It All Together

TASK 1

In a computer game, players collect objects. Objects come in clusters, mega-clusters, and super-mega-clusters. A cluster is 3^2 objects. A mega-cluster is 3^7 clusters. A super-mega-cluster is 3^{11} clusters.

a. How many objects are in a mega-cluster?

b. How many objects are in a super-mega-cluster?

c. How many mega-clusters are in a super-mega-cluster?

TASK 2

To find the number of seconds it takes a certain pendulum to swing back and forth, double the square root of the number of meters in the pendulum's length.

a. How many seconds does it take a pendulum with length 25 meters to swing back and forth?

b. Another pendulum has a length of 15.85 meters. How many seconds does it take this pendulum to swing back and forth?

c. Suppose a pendulum takes one minute to swing back and forth. How can you find the pendulum's length?

6-1 Exploring Scientific Notation

Digital Resources

CCSS: 8.EE.A.3: Use numbers expressed in the form of a single digit times an integer power of 10 to estimate very large or very small quantities .... 8.EE.A.4: Perform operations with numbers expressed in scientific notation ....

Launch

MP2, MP6

Order the tiles from least to greatest numeric value. Explain how you know your order is correct.

30,000	$3 \cdot 10^3$	30	$3 \cdot 10^2$
300	$3 \cdot 10^1$	3,000	$3 \cdot 10^4$

Reflect Is there a pattern between the numbers and the expressions? If so, describe it.

Got It?

PART 1 Got It

Order the following numbers from least to greatest.

I. 2.34×10^2 II. 2.34×10^{-2} III. 2.34

II, III, I

PART 2 Got It

Which of the following numbers are not expressed in scientific notation?

I. 1.7×10^7 II. 27.3×10^3 III. 8.04×10^{-2}

II

Got It?

PART 3 Got It

Suppose your calculator display shows 7.7E–11. Express this result in scientific notation.

Close and Check

Focus Question

MP3, MP8

Why might you use powers of 10 to write numbers?

Do you know HOW?

1. Order the numbers from least to greatest.

Least

7.29×10^0	7.29×10^{-5}
7.29×10^{-5}	7.29×10^{-3}
7.29×10^3	7.29×10^0
7.29×10^{-3}	

Greatest

2. Circle the numbers that are expressed in scientific notation.

34.5×10^7 5.02×10^3 (circled)

2×10^9 (circled) 0.4×10^1

3. Write 745,000 in scientific notation.

7.45×10^5

Do you UNDERSTAND?

4. Reasoning Explain the strategy you used to order the numbers in Exercise 1.

5. Vocabulary How is scientific notation useful in mathematics?

6-2

Using Scientific Notation to Describe Quantities

CCSS: 8.EE.A.3: Use numbers expressed in the form of a single digit times an integer power of 10 to estimate very large or very small quantities, and to express how many times as much one is than the other … .

Digital Resources

Launch

MP3, MP6, MP7

Your friend writes 5×2^6 as a shortcut for writing 1×10^6. Explain your friend's shortcut thinking. Is your friend's thinking more science or fiction?

Reflect Why is it helpful to write numbers in scientific notation using powers of 10? Why is this better than using powers of 2? Explain.

Got It?

PART 1 Got It

Light travels at a constant speed of 186,000 mi/s. Express the speed of light in scientific notation.

Discuss with a classmate

Take turns reading your response to this problem.
How did your prior experiences help you determine a large measurement that could be written in scientific notation? Did you both choose the same type of measurement? Can you think of another measurement different from either of the ones you wrote about?

PART 2 Got It (1 of 2)

The moon is about 2.4×10^5 miles from Earth. Express this distance in standard form.

PART 2 Got It (2 of 2)

Describe at least one large measurement (unrelated to astronomy) that you might want to write in scientific notation rather than in standard form.

Got It?

PART 3 Got It

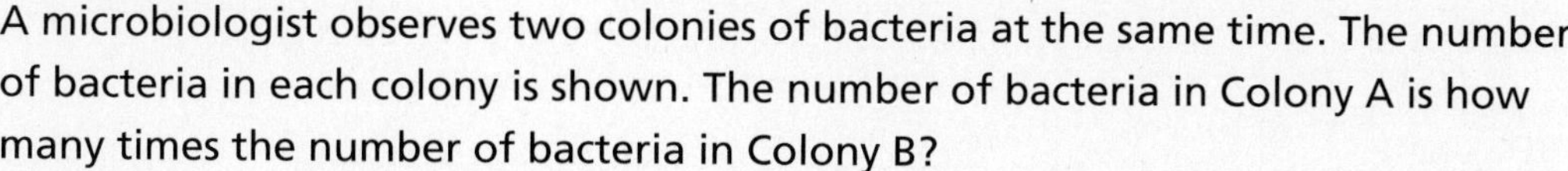

A microbiologist observes two colonies of bacteria at the same time. The number of bacteria in each colony is shown. The number of bacteria in Colony A is how many times the number of bacteria in Colony B?

Colony A	Colony B
4×10^6	2×10^5

Close and Check

Focus Question

MP6, MP8

How can positive powers of 10 make large and small numbers easier to write and compare?

Do you know HOW?

1. The X-15 aircraft holds the world speed record at 23,865,600 ft/hr. Express the world record speed in scientific notation.

2. The population on Earth increased by about 7.62×10^8 people during the first decade of the 21st century. Express the population growth in standard form.

 people

3. One giant ant colony is reported to have about 3.06×10^8 worker ants and 1.02×10^6 queen ants. The number of worker ants is how many times the number of queen ants?

Do you UNDERSTAND?

4. **Writing** Your best friend has never learned about scientific notation. Explain how to use scientific notation to rewrite very large numbers.

5. **Error Analysis** A friend says the average distance to the moon is 382,500 km. Is the number he wrote accurate? Explain.

3.825×10^6

Using Scientific Notation to Describe Very Small Quantities

Digital Resources

CCSS: 8.EE.A.3: Use numbers expressed in the form of a single digit times an integer power of 10 to estimate very large or very small quantities, and to express how many times as much one is than the other … .

Launch

MP2, MP4

Your friend says a zeptometer is 1×10^{-21} based on its standard form. Explain your friend's zepto-reasoning. Is your friend's thinking more science or fiction?

Unit	Scientific Notation (m)	Standard Form (m)
Meter	1×10^{0}	1
Decimeter	1×10^{-1}	0.1
Centimeter	1×10^{-2}	0.01
Millimeter	1×10^{-3}	0.001
Zeptometer		0.000000000000000000001

Reflect Does it make more sense to use scientific notation or standard form to represent 1 zeptometer?

Got It?

PART 1 Got It (1 of 2)

An X-ray can have a wavelength of 0.00000001 m. Express this wavelength in scientific notation.

PART 1 Got It (2 of 2)

Wavelengths of visible light range from 0.0000004 m to 0.0000007 m. A nanometer is one-billionth of a meter. Which unit, meters or nanometers, might be more appropriate for measuring the wavelength of light? Explain your reasoning.

Got It?

PART 2 Got It

Express the diameter of the red blood cell shown in standard form.

PART 3 Got It

The length of cell A is 3×10^{-4} m and the length of cell B is 3×10^{-5} m. How many times as long is cell A than cell B?

Close and Check

Focus Question

MP6, MP8

How can negative powers of 10 make small numbers easier to write and compare?

Do you know HOW?

1. The diameter of an average snowflake is about 10 micrometers. That is approximately 0.0003937 in. Express the diameter of a snowflake in scientific notation.

   3.937×10^{-4}

2. The diameters of atoms can vary. One particular atom has a diameter of 5.0×10^{-8} cm. Express the diameter of the atom in standard form.

   0.00000005

3. The measurement 8.16 micrometers equals 8.16×10^{-6} meter. The measurement 2.04 centimeters equals 2.04×10^{-2} meter. How many times greater is the centimeter measurement than the micrometer measurement?

Do you UNDERSTAND?

4. **Writing** Do you agree or disagree with the statement below? Explain.

   Scientific notation is a method used to rewrite very large or very small numbers as a number n greater than 0 times an integer power of 10.

5. **Error Analysis** An earthworm travels 0.0000425 miles per second. A friend writes the rate as 4.25×10^{5} mps. Explain her error. Write the correct rate in scientific notation.

6-4

Operating with Numbers Expressed in Scientific Notation

Digital Resources

CCSS: 8.EE.A.3: Use numbers expressed in the form of a single digit times an integer power of 10 . . . . **8.EE.A.4:** Perform operations with numbers expressed in scientific notation, including problems where both decimal and scientific notation are used.

Launch

MP1, MP6

The scientific notation cards shown represent place values. Arrange at least six of the cards in place-value order to represent a three-digit number.

Then write your number in standard form and explain why the cards you chose represent your number.

1×10^2 1×10^2 1×10^0 1×10^1 1×10^1

1×10^1 1×10^0 1×10^2 1×10^2 1×10^2

Reflect How is using the cards the same as using place value blocks? How is it different?

Got It?

PART 1 Got It (1 of 2)

Simplify $(5.9 \times 10^5) + (4.3 \times 10^5) - (2.2 \times 10^5)$.

PART 1 Got It (2 of 2)

Is it possible to add or subtract two numbers in scientific notation when they do not have the same power of 10? Explain.

Got It?

PART 2 Got It

About 1.0×10^8 bacteria live in a human body. If there are 2,000 spectators at a football game, how many bacteria are living in the spectators?

PART 3 Got It

The biggest stars are known as red supergiants. One example, Betelgeuse, is about 300 million miles wide. One AU is about 93,000,000 miles. What is the width of Betelgeuse in AU?

Close and Check

Focus Question

MP2, MP7

You previously learned how to multiply and divide expressions with exponents. How can you apply what you know to operations with numbers in scientific notation?

Do you know HOW?

1. Simplify.
$(6.9 \times 10^{12}) - (2.6 \times 10^{12}) + (3.4 \times 10^{12})$

2. One gram of dust can contain 2.5×10^5 dust mite droppings. The average six-room home collects about 1.5×10^3 grams of dust each month. In scientific notation, how many dust mite droppings can be found in an average home each month?

droppings

3. The smallest ant is about 4.9×10^{-4} m in length. The distance around the earth at the equator is about 4×10^7 m. In scientific notation to the nearest tenth, how many of these small ants would it take to circle the earth at the equator?

ants

Do you UNDERSTAND?

4. **Compare and Contrast** How are the processes for multiplying and dividing numbers written in scientific notation alike and different?

5. **Error Analysis** Your friend says this problem has no solution because 8.3 cannot be subtracted from 2.5. Do you agree? Explain.

Statistically, 2.5×10^7 plastic beverage bottles are used each day. If 8.3×10^6 bottles are recycled, how many end up in landfills?

6-5 Problem Solving

Digital Resources

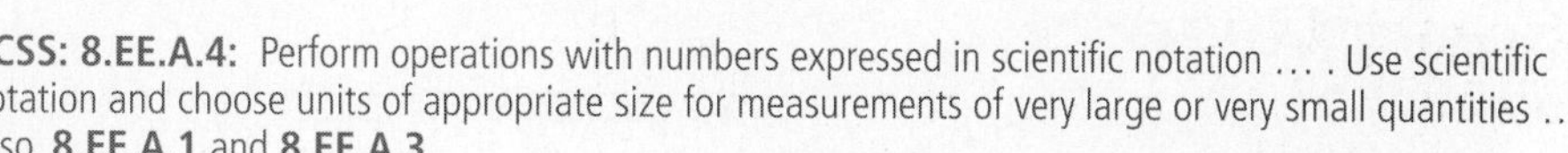

CCSS: 8.EE.A.4: Perform operations with numbers expressed in scientific notation .... Use scientific notation and choose units of appropriate size for measurements of very large or very small quantities .... Also, **8.EE.A.1** and **8.EE.A.3.**

Launch

MP4, MP7

Approximate population data for adults and children in the most and least populous U.S. states in one year, according to the U.S. Census Bureau, are shown.

What is the total population for each state in scientific notation? Justify your answers.

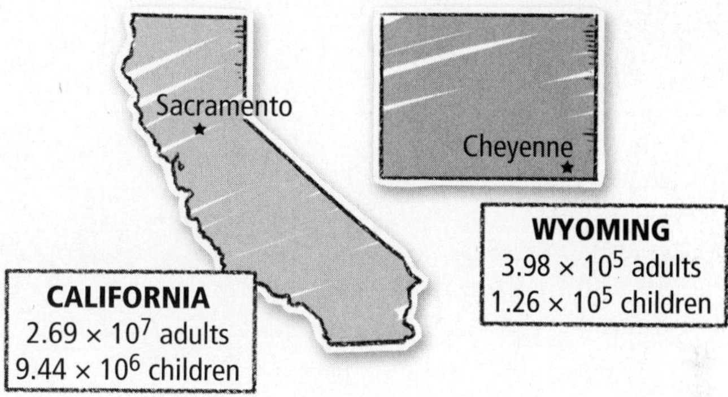

Reflect How can you tell that California has more people than Wyoming just by comparing the adult and children populations?

Got It?

PART 1 Got It

Which of the following is the most appropriate way to represent the distance from our solar system to our nearest star, Proxima Centauri?

I. 1.3×10^{17} feet **II.** 4.22 light-years **III.** 3.97×10^{16} m

PART 2 Got It

What is the value of n?

$1.5 \times 10^{21} = (3 \times 10^{14})(5 \times 10^{n})$

Close and Check

Focus Question

MP1, MP7

How can you use scientific notation to help you solve problems?

Do you know HOW?

1. It takes light 8.5 minutes to travel from the sun to the earth. Light travels at 9.82×10^8 feet per second. How far does light travel from the sun to the earth? Express this distance in scientific notation using the most appropriate unit from the given list.

   5280 ft = 1760 yd
   1760 yd = 1 mi

2. The area of the world's largest country is about 6.6×10^6 mi^2. The area of the world's smallest country is about 1.7×10^{-1} mi^2. About how many times larger is the area of the largest country than the area of the smallest country? Express your answer in scientific notation.

3. Find the value of n.
   $1.887 \times 10^{12} = (5.1 \times 10^8)(3.7 \times 10^n)$

4. Find the value of n.
   $(4.5 \times 10^9) \div (9 \times 10^n) = 5 \times 10^2$

Do you UNDERSTAND?

5. **Reasoning** Explain why you chose the unit of measure that you did in Exercise 1. Explain why you did not choose the others.

6. **Compare and Contrast** How can understanding operations on exponential numbers help you solve problems involving scientific notation?

This page intentionally left blank.

Topic Review

New Vocabulary: scientific notattion
Review Vocabulary: base, exponent, power, standard form

Vocabulary Review

Identify two challenging vocabulary terms from this topic. Write one vocabulary term in the center oval, and fill in the surrounding boxes with details that will help you better understand the term.

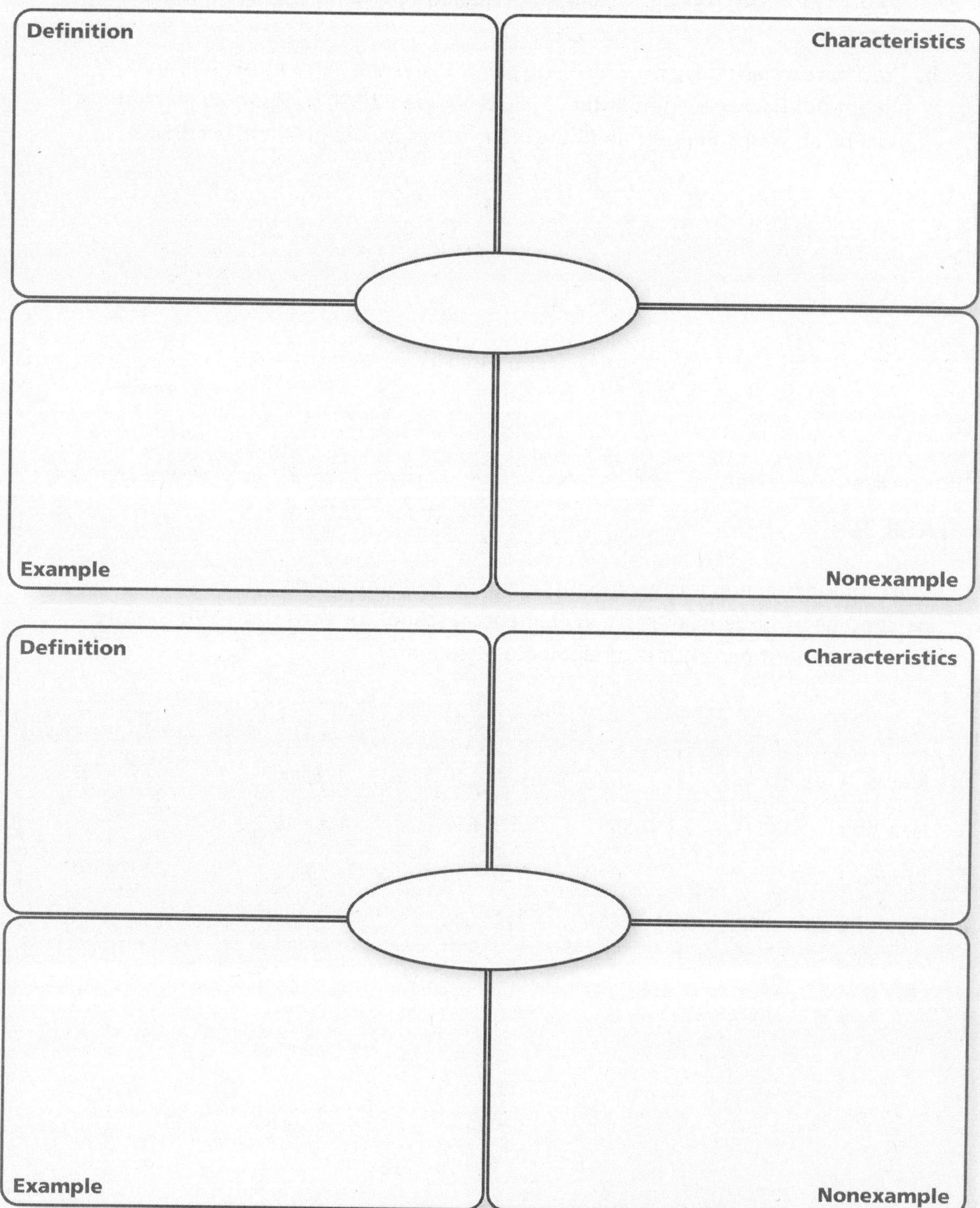

Pull It All Together

TASK 1

You want to download music on your computer. You decide that a song file should be 3.9×10^{-3} GB or less to preserve memory space. Your computer has 9 GB of memory space available for song files.

a. You want to download 2,500 songs of your preferred maximum size (3.9×10^{-3} GB). Do you have enough memory space on your computer? Explain.

b. You have a flash drive on which you can transfer the extra music files that might not fit on your computer. If you download 2,500 songs, how many songs will be on your computer and how many songs will be on the flash drive?

TASK 2

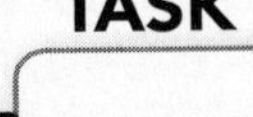

The table shows numbers of students in school in 4 states. Determine the percentage of students that are in elementary school for each state. Which state had the greatest percentage of elementary students?

	Elementary	High School	College	Total Students
Kansas		1.65×10^5	176,000	6.67×10^5
New York	2,210,000	1.1×10^6	1.3×10^6	
Oregon		1.91×10^5	2.05×10^5	7.81×10^5
South Carolina	4.74×10^5	230,000	2.17×10^5	

7-1 Equivalent Ratios

Digital Resources

CCSS: 7.RP.A.1: Compute unit rates associated with ratios of fractions, including ratios of lengths, areas and other quantities measured in like or different units.

Launch

MP2, MP6

Your friend can't help but compare. During a game of stickball in the street, you notice him making all sorts of number comparisons. He asks for help making number comparisons on one building.

Name at least five number comparisons you can make by looking at the building.

Reflect Do you make number comparisons? Provide an example of a number comparison you've made and why you made it.

Got It?

PART 1 Got It

Write the ratio of the number of pins left standing to the number of pins knocked down in three different ways.

7:3 $\frac{7}{3}$ 7 to 3

PART 2 Got It

Find a ratio equivalent to $\frac{12}{15}$ with lesser terms.

4:5

Got It?

PART 3 Got It (1 of 2)

A kitten weighs 12 oz. A puppy weighs 3 lb. Write the ratio of the kitten's weight to the puppy's weight as a fraction in simplest form.

$\frac{1}{4}$

PART 3 Got It (2 of 2)

Use the ratio of the kitten's weight to the puppy's weight. Describe the puppy's weight in terms of the kitten's weight.

The puppy's weight is 4 times that of the kitten's.

Close and Check

Focus Question

MP4, MP6

What does it mean if two different ratios describe the same situation? How can being able to describe the situation in multiple ways help you to solve problems?

Do you know HOW?

1. Write the ratio of the number of bees to the number of flowers in three different ways.

2. Find a ratio equivalent to $\frac{63}{77}$ with lower terms.

3. A baby boy weighs 7 lb 8 oz. A five-year-old boy weighs 48 lb. Write the ratio of the baby's weight to the boy's weight as a fraction in simplest form.

Do you UNDERSTAND?

4. **Vocabulary** How can the terms of a ratio be used to write an equivalent ratio?

5. **Reasoning** Two students each write a ratio comparing the two shapes in the group. Can both students be correct? Explain.

$\frac{6}{4}$ $\frac{2}{3}$

7-2 Unit Rates

Digital Resources

CCSS: 7.RP.A.1: Compute unit rates associated with ratios of fractions, including ratios of lengths, areas and other quantities measured in like or different units.

Launch

MP4, MP7

Three teams train turtles for the Third Annual Turtle Trot, a 30-foot race. If the turtles trot at their training pace, which turtle will win the race? By how many minutes? Explain your reasoning.

Team 1 Turtle	Team 2 Turtle	Team 3 Turtle
18 feet in 6 minutes	12 feet in 4 minutes	10 feet in 2 minutes

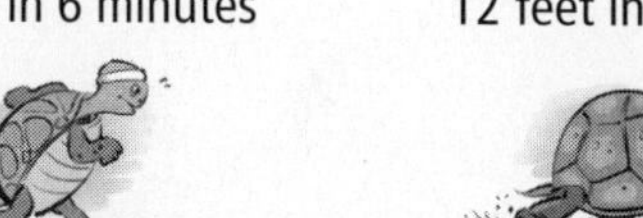

10 min 10 min 6 min

Team 3 b/c it will take him 6 mins. He'd win by 4 mins.

Reflect Could you have solved the problem without unit rates? Explain.

Got It?

PART 1 Got It

Find the unit rate for 219 heartbeats in 3 minutes.

73 bpm

PART 2 Got It

You also need to buy dye for the tie-dying activity. You can buy the dye in various sizes. Which is the best buy?

- 2 fl oz for $3.96 ✗
- 4 fl oz for $8.36 ✗
- 8 fl oz for $14.24 ✓ ← this one
- 16 fl oz for $28.96 ✗

PART 3 Got It

A satellite travels about 2,272 mi in 8 min. About how many miles does the satellite travel in 3 min?

Discuss with a classmate

Compare your answers to this problem.
Discuss what it means for an answer to be reasonable.
How can you apply what you know about checking an answer for reasonableness to the answers to this problem?

Close and Check

Focus Question

MP1, MP7

How can you identify a rate? How can unit rates help you to solve problems?

Do you know HOW?

1. The Earth rotates 1.25 degrees in 5 minutes. How many degrees does it rotate in 1 minute?

   0.25 degrees

2. A driver fills his tank with 15 gallons of gas for $45.60 at a gas station. The next time he stops he fills up with 12 gallons for $39.00. Find the unit price for gas at each station and circle which has the better deal.

   1st Station: 3.04

   2nd Station: 3.25

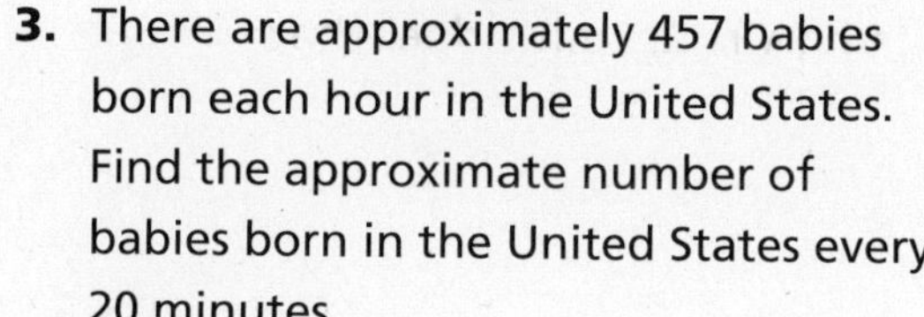

3. There are approximately 457 babies born each hour in the United States. Find the approximate number of babies born in the United States every 20 minutes.

   152 babies

Do you UNDERSTAND?

4. **Writing** A company earns a profit of $50 for every 10 items sold. Explain how the company can find the amount of profit for 50 items sold.

5. **Error Analysis** A classmate writes a rate for Exercise 1 to express the degrees rotated in 2 minutes. Explain her error and give the correct rate.

$$\frac{1.25 \div 2}{5 \div 2} = \frac{0.625}{2.5}$$

This page intentionally left blank.

7-3 Ratios With Fractions

Digital Resources

CCSS: 7.RP.A.1: Compute unit rates associated with ratios of fractions, including ratios of lengths, areas and other quantities measured in like or different units.

Launch

MP2, MP8

How many pears must you place on Plate 3 so that the ratios of apples to pears are equivalent for all three plates?

Write the ratio of apples to pears for each plate. Explain your reasoning.

Plate 1	Plate 2	Plate 3
☐ : ☐ apples to pears	☐ : ☐ apples to pears	☐ : ☐ apples to pears

Reflect Can you compare quantities that aren't in whole number units? Explain.

Got It?

PART 1 Got It

An athlete runs on a treadmill for $\frac{3}{4}$ h. The athlete then lifts weights for 2 h. Write the ratio of the running time to the weight-lifting time as a fraction in simplest form.

PART 2 Got It

Write the ratio $\dfrac{\frac{3}{4}\text{gal}}{\frac{9}{10}\text{gal}}$ in simplest form.

Got It?

PART 3 Got It

A model boat is $6\frac{1}{4}$ in. wide. The actual boat is $12\frac{1}{2}$ ft wide. What is the ratio of the width of the model boat to the width of the actual boat, in simplest form?

Close and Check

Focus Question

MP1, MP6

Previously you have written ratios as fractions. How can you write a ratio if at least one term is a fraction? How is this different from writing a ratio where both the terms are whole numbers?

Do you know HOW?

1. A bakery has $\frac{3}{4}$ dozen whole-grain muffins and 6 dozen mixed-berry muffins. Write the ratio of whole-grain muffins to mixed-berry muffins as a fraction in simplest form.

2. Write the ratio $\frac{\frac{6}{7}}{\frac{8}{9}}$ in simplest form.

3. A scale model of a van is $4\frac{1}{5}$ feet long. The actual van is $22\frac{2}{5}$ feet long. What is the ratio of the length of the model to the actual length of the van in simplest form?

Do you UNDERSTAND?

4. **Reasoning** Can any ratio be written as a unit rate? Explain.

5. **Error Analysis** A store sells 8 unscented candles for $2 or 9 scented candles for $3. A classmate writes the unit rates $\frac{4}{1}$ and $\frac{3}{1}$. She says one scented candle costs $3, and one unscented candle costs $4. Do you agree? Explain.

7-4 Unit Rates with Fractions

Digital Resources

CCSS: 7.RP.A.1: Compute unit rates associated with ratios of fractions, including ratios of lengths, areas and other quantities measured in like or different units.

Launch

MP3, MP4

Two clowns get a call as they race to the circus. Clown 2 pleads, "We're going 10 miles per half-hour. We can't go any faster." The caller replies, "You'd better double your speed or you'll never make it."

Show two different ways to write a speed that is twice as fast. Explain your reasoning.

Reflect Is reporting speed in miles per half hour useful? Is there a better way? Explain.

Got It?

PART 1 Got It (1 of 2)

Your dog eats $\frac{7}{8}$ lb of food in 4 meals. How much food does your dog eat per meal?

PART 1 Got It (2 of 2)

If your dog eats $\frac{7}{8}$ lb of food in 4 meals, how many meals will it take your dog to eat 1 lb of food?

Discuss with a classmate

Read the problem aloud. Discuss the units of measure in the problem and what they mean.

Then, use a graphic organizer, such as Know-Need-Plan, to manage all the units of measure in the problem.

Got It?

PART 2 Got It

You are planning to build a boat. You have a sample board of the wood that you want to use. The board has an area of $\frac{1}{3}$ ft^2 and weighs $\frac{1}{5}$ lb. What is the weight of the wood in pounds per square foot?

PART 3 Got It

You ran $3\frac{1}{2}$ mi in $\frac{3}{4}$ h. Your friend ran $1\frac{2}{5}$ mi in $\frac{1}{3}$ h. Which of you ran faster? Explain.

Close and Check

Focus Question

MP1, MP2

How can you write a unit rate if at least one term is a fraction? How is this different from writing a unit rate where both terms are whole numbers?

Do you know HOW?

1. A craft project requires $\frac{5}{6}$ yard of ribbon to make 4 refrigerator magnets. How many inches of ribbon are needed for each magnet?

   ☐ inches

2. If it takes $\frac{5}{6}$ yard of ribbon to make 4 magnets, how many complete magnets can be made with $\frac{2}{3}$ yard of ribbon?

   ☐ magnets

3. Machine A packs $4\frac{1}{4}$ cartons in $\frac{1}{5}$ hour. Machine B packs $4\frac{3}{5}$ cartons in $\frac{1}{4}$ hour. Which machine packs faster? How many cartons per hour can the faster machine pack?

   Machine: ☐

   Unit Rate: ☐

Do you UNDERSTAND?

4. **Writing** How do you convert a rate to a unit rate?

5. **Error Analysis** An elevator has a floor area of 38 ft^2 and holds a load of 3,500 lb. The engineer writes this equation to find the number of pounds per square foot.

$$\frac{\frac{3500}{1}}{\frac{38}{1}} = \frac{\frac{3500}{1} \cdot \frac{38}{1}}{1} = \frac{133{,}000}{1} \text{ lb/ft}^2$$

   Explain his error and write the correct pounds per square foot.

Problem Solving

Digital Resources

CCSS: 7.RP.A.1: Compute unit rates associated with ratios of fractions, including ratios of lengths, areas and other quantities measured in like or different units.

Launch

MP1, MP4, MP7

Two nosy neighbors constantly try to outdo each other. Neighbor 1 mows her lawn in $1\frac{3}{4}$ hours. Neighbor 2 insists she's faster and she took $2\frac{1}{4}$ hours.

Who's correct? Show how you know.

Reflect How were unit rates useful in this problem? Explain.

Got It?

PART 1 Got It

The image on a digital camera's screen is $1\frac{1}{2}$ in. by 1 in. When the image is printed, it is $\frac{1}{2}$ ft by $\frac{1}{3}$ ft. What is the ratio of the area of the image on the camera's screen to the area of the print?

PART 2 Got It

You are parked $\frac{7}{8}$ mi from the football stadium. You walk at a constant speed of $3\frac{1}{4}$ mi/h. The game starts in 14 min. Will you make it to the stadium before the game starts? Explain.

Got It?

PART 3 Got It

The spice recipe calls for $\frac{1}{2}$ tsp of crushed red pepper flakes for every $1\frac{1}{4}$ tsp of black pepper. You use 3 tsp of crushed red pepper. How many teaspoons of black pepper do you need?

Close and Check

Focus Question

MP1, MP6

In this topic you have learned how to compare quantities other than whole numbers. Are some comparisons more helpful for solving problems than others?

Do you know HOW?

1. Your neighbor is replacing her old TV. The old TV screen is $14\frac{2}{5}$ in. tall by $21\frac{1}{2}$ in. wide. The new TV screen is $28\frac{4}{5}$ in. tall and 43 in. wide. What is the ratio of the area of the old TV screen to the area of the new TV screen?

2. A mountain bike race is two laps around a $25\frac{1}{2}$ mi course. Rider A completes the first lap in $1\frac{1}{4}$ hours and the second lap in $1\frac{1}{2}$ hours. Rider B completes both laps at a constant speed of 20 miles per hour. Which rider had the faster combined time for both laps?

3. A recipe for lemonade calls for a ratio of 1 part fresh lemon juice to 8 parts cold water. You have $\frac{2}{3}$ cup of lemon juice. How much water should you add?

Do you UNDERSTAND?

4. **Vocabulary** In one weekend, you earn \$27 and your friend earns \$35. Would a ratio or a unit rate be more helpful to compare the two amounts? Explain.

5. **Reasoning** An entertainment center for the new TV in Exercise 1 has an area of 1,548 ft^2. Explain how to find the ratio of the area of the entertainment center to the area of the TV. What is the unit ratio?

7-R Topic Review

New Vocabulary: equivalent ratios, rate, ratio, terms of a ratio, unit price, unit rate
Review Vocabulary: greatest common factor, least common multiple, simplest form

Vocabulary Review

Identify two challenging vocabulary terms from this topic. Write one vocabulary term in the center oval, and fill in the surrounding boxes with details that will help you better understand the term.

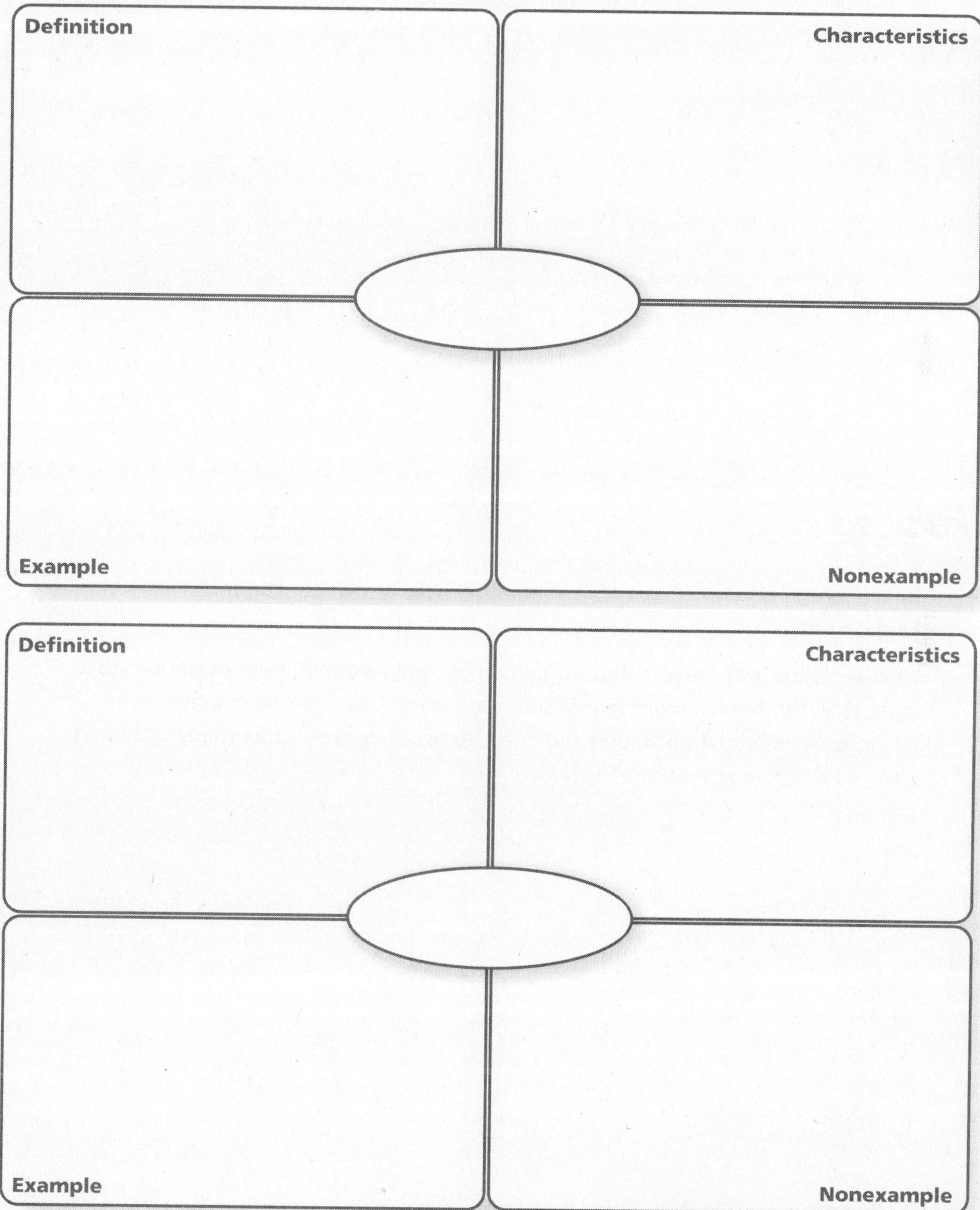

Pull It All Together

TASK 1

Your neighbor's car uses $2\frac{1}{4}$ gallons of gasoline to travel 45 miles. Your neighbor is planning a trip of 243 miles. How many gallons of gasoline will your neighbor need for the trip if the car continues to use gasoline at the same rate?

TASK 2

Your neighbor needs $12\frac{3}{20}$ gal of gasoline for a trip of 243 mi. The car's tank holds $13\frac{1}{2}$ gal of gas.

a. Write the ratio of the number of gallons needed to the number of gallons the gas tank can hold as a fraction in simplest form.

b. If your neighbor needs to make this trip 10 times in a row, how many full tanks of gas will your neighbor need?

8-1

Proportional Relationships and Tables

CCSS: 7.RP.A.2: Recognize and represent proportional relationships .... 7.RP.A.2a: Decide whether two quantities are in a proportional relationship, e.g., by testing for equivalent ratios in a table or graphing on a coordinate plane and observing whether the graph is a straight line through the origin.

Digital Resources

Launch

MP1, MP7

A company manufactures custom car paints. A manager receives orders for 25, 35, and 105 gallons of their Powerful Purple paint shade. The paint manager panics and says, "None of the orders match our mixing chart. How can we make these orders?"

Provide a solution for the panicked paint man.

Powerful Purple Mixing Guide

Gallons of Red Paint	Gallons of Blue Paint
2	3
4	6
20	30
40	60

Reflect How do you know if two ratios are equivalent?

Got It?

PART 1 Got It

The diagram shows a series of squares drawn on graph paper. The side length and area of each square are labeled.

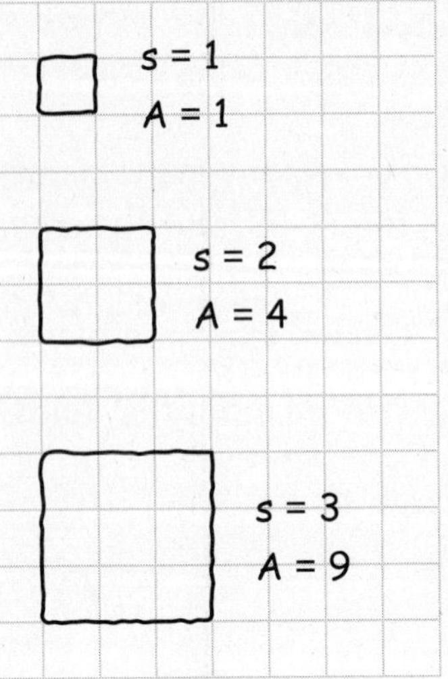

Use the diagram to complete the table. Draw the next few squares as needed. Write all the ratios in simplest form.

Is the relationship between the side length and area of a square proportional? How do you know?

Side length	1	2	3		5	
Area	1			16		36
Ratio $\frac{\text{area}}{\text{side length}}$		$\frac{4}{2} = \frac{2}{1}$				

PART 2 Got It

Does the table show a proportional relationship between *x* and *y*? Explain.

x	y
5	1
3	15
2	$\frac{2}{5}$
$\frac{8}{5}$	8

Got It?

PART 3 Got It

Does the table show a proportional relationship between the number of heartbeats and time? Explain.

Resting Heart Rate

Time(s)	Heartbeats
4	6
6	9
10	15
12	18

Close and Check

Focus Question

MP2, MP7

What does it mean for two quantities to have a proportional relationship? How can you tell if a table shows a proportional relationship between two quantities?

Do you know HOW?

1. The table shows a proportional relationship between the number of teachers and the number of students. Complete the table.

Teachers	3	5		10
Students		75	120	
Ratio students/ teachers				

2. Tell whether the relationship between *x* and *y* shown in the table is *proportional* or *not proportional*.

x	1	2	3	4
y	0	6	12	18

3. Circle the ratios that are proportional to $\frac{27}{9}$.

$\frac{9}{3}$ $\frac{36}{4}$ $\frac{3}{1}$

$\frac{6}{2}$ $\frac{54}{18}$ $\frac{1}{9}$

Do you UNDERSTAND?

4. **Writing** Explain how you determined the proportional ratios in Exercise 3.

5. **Writing** Give a real-world example of when you might use proportional relationships. Explain why it is proportional.

8-2

Proportional Relationships and Graphs

Digital Resources

CCSS: 7.RP.A.2a: Decide whether two quantities are in a proportional relationship, e.g., … graphing on a coordinate plane and observing whether the graph is a straight line through the origin. Also, **7.RP.A.2d.**

Launch

MP2, MP4

The manager of the car paint company prepares orders for its Granny Apple Green paint.

Tell how the graph can help you find the amounts of blue and yellow paint needed to make 8 gallons, 24 gallons, and 56 gallons of Granny Apple Green paint.

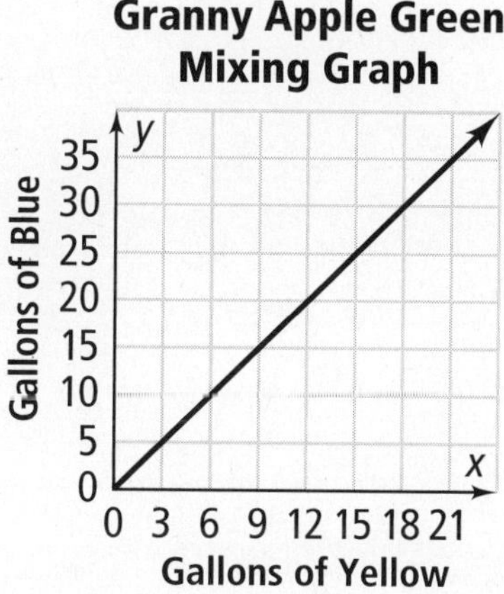

Reflect Do you think a graph or a table makes it easier for the company to find the correct mix of blue and yellow paint to make Granny Apple Green?

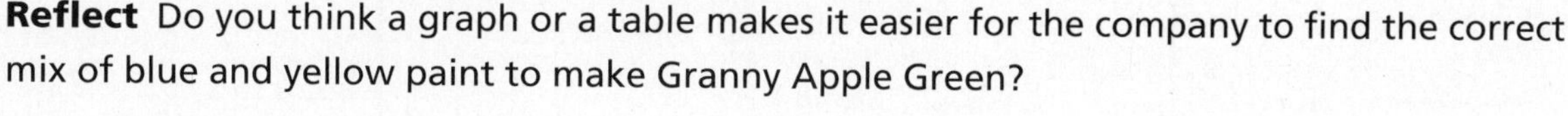

Got It?

PART 1 Got It (1 of 2)

Does the graph show a proportional relationship between x and y? Explain.

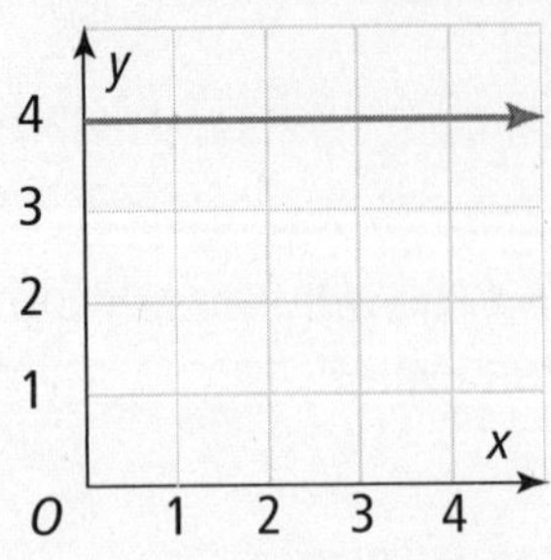

PART 1 Got It (2 of 2)

Does the graph show a proportional relationship between x and y? Explain.

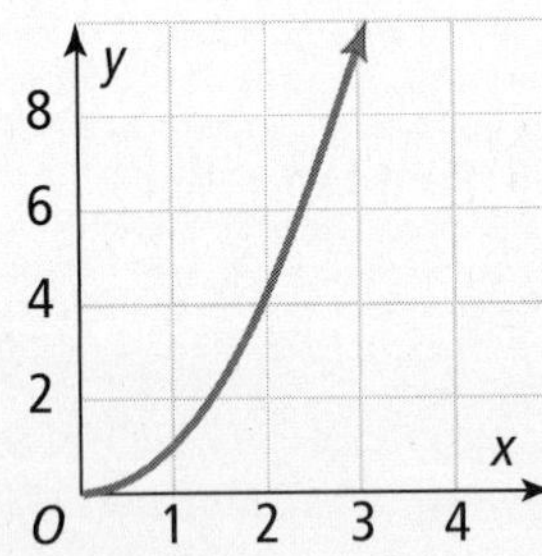

Got It?

PART 2 Got It

Does the equation $y = 4x + 1$ show a proportional relationship between x and y? Explain.

PART 3 Got It

The graph shows a proportional relationship between the amounts of nuts and dried fruit in a trail mix. You want to know how many pounds of dried fruit there are per pound of nuts. What point represents this unit rate?

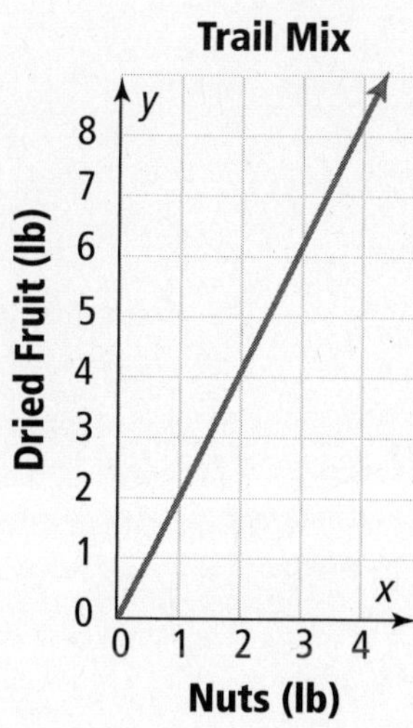

Close and Check

Focus Question

MP2, MP7

How can you tell if a graph shows a proportional relationship between two quantities?

____

____

____

____

Do you know HOW?

1. The relationship between time x and distance y can be represented by the equation $y = 2x$. Complete the table and graph.

$y = 2x$

x	y
0	
1	
2	
3	
4	
5	

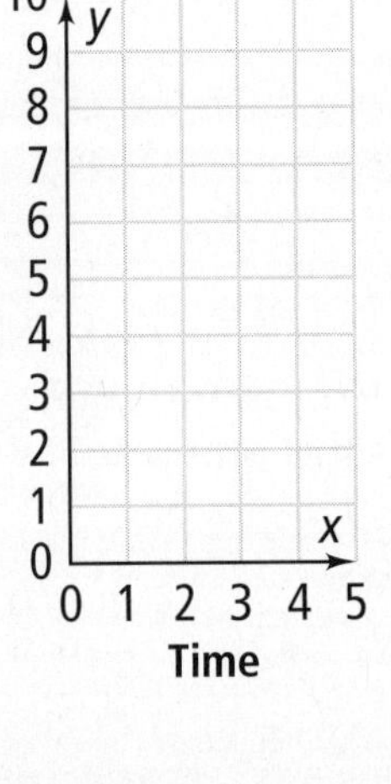

2. What is the distance when time is equal to 15?

[ ] units

3. What is the unit rate of the graph?

[ ]

Do you UNDERSTAND?

4. **Writing** Does the graph in Exercise 1 represent a proportional relationship? Explain how you know.

____

____

____

5. **Reasoning** Do all linear graphs represent proportional relationships? Explain.

____

____

____

6. **Error Analysis** A classmate says that not all proportional relationships are linear. Do you agree? Explain.

____

____

____

____

8-3 Constant of Proportionality

Digital Resources

CCSS: **7.RP.A.2:** Recognize and represent proportional relationships between quantities. **7.RP.A.2b:** Identify the constant of proportionality (unit rate) in tables, graphs, equations, diagrams, and verbal descriptions of proportional relationships. Also, **7.NS.A.2d.**

Launch

MP3, MP6

The car paint company provides a perplexing pay graph for new managers.

What does the graph show? Which point—*A, B,* or *C*—might be the most useful? Explain.

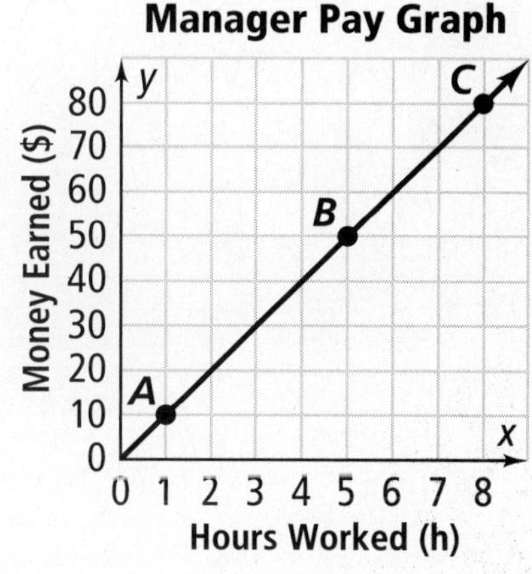

What the Graph Shows:

Which Point Might Be Most Useful:

Reflect Which point may be the least useful? Explain.

Got It?

PART 1 Got It

Each shoebox is the same height. The height of the display depends on the number of shoeboxes in one column of shoeboxes. What is the constant of proportionality for this situation?

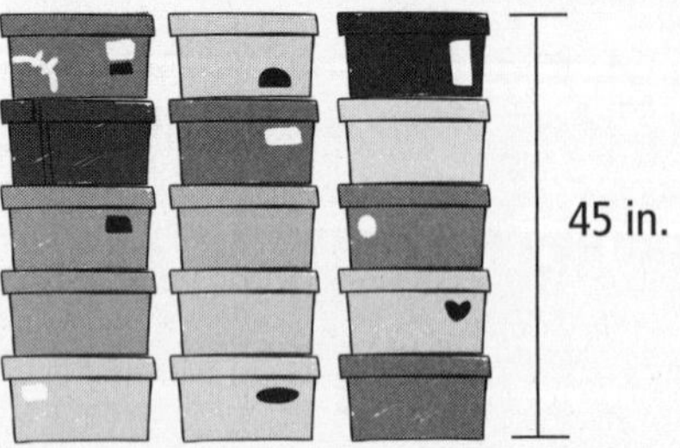

PART 2 Got It

You run on a treadmill daily at a constant speed. On Monday, you ran 2.25 mi in 22.5 min. On Tuesday, you ran 2.35 mi in 25 min. Are the constants of proportionality the same for the two days? How do you know?

Got It?

PART 3 Got It

The table shows the time it takes to pump gasoline based on the number of gallons pumped. What is the constant of proportionality for this situation?

Pump Rate

Gasoline (gal)	Time (s)
17	136
12	96
10.5	84
9.25	74

PART 4 Got It

The graph shows the distance a cyclist traveled based on time. What is the constant of proportionality for this situation?

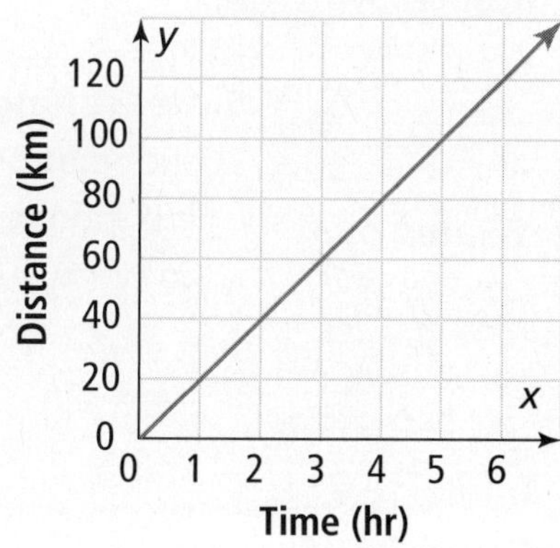

Close and Check

Focus Question

MP1, MP4

What is a constant of proportionality? What does the constant of proportionality tell you?

Do you know HOW?

1. Each bus carries 24 passengers. The number of buses needed for a field trip depends on the number of students going on the trip. What is the constant of proportionality for this situation?

   ______ per ______

2. Your class collects cans for a local food bank. On Monday, 7 students collect 63 cans. Using the constant of proportionality, find the number of students who collect 90 cans on Tuesday.

   ______ students

3. The table shows the number of concert tickets sold based on the number of hours the tickets are available. What is the constant of proportionality for this situation?

Ticket Sales

Time (hr)	Tickets
3	240
5	400
9	720
15	1200

Do you UNDERSTAND?

4. **Writing** Which variable in Exercise 3 represents the independent variable and which represents the dependent variable? Explain.

5. **Reasoning** How can you use the relationship between the independent and dependent variables to write a unit rate?

8-4 Proportional Relationships and Equations

Digital Resources

CCSS: 7.RP.A.2: Recognize and represent proportional relationships between quantities. **7.RP.A.2b:** Identify the constant of proportionality (unit rate) in … equations … of proportional relationships. **7.RP.A.2c:** Represent proportional relationships by equations … .

Launch

MP6, MP7

The paint company manager grows tired of answering a particular pay question from employees. He mulls over two equations to help the employees.

What question could employees keep asking? Which equation would help them? Explain.

Reflect If you could have had one more piece of information before starting to answer the problem, what would it be and why?

Got It?

PART 1 Got It

The equation $P = 4s$ represents the perimeter P of a square with side length s. What is the constant of proportionality? What is the perimeter of a square with side length 1.6 m?

PART 2 Got It

You paid $2.50 for 5 apples. Write an equation to represent the total cost y of buying x apples.

PART 3 Got It

You have returned from your trip with euros left over. Use the table to write an equation you can use to find about how many U.S. dollars y you will receive in exchange for x euros.

Currency Exchange

U.S. Dollars($)	Euros(€)
50	37.50
100	75
120	90
175	131.25

Discuss with a classmate

What does currency exchange mean? Have you ever traveled to a place where the currency was not the U.S. dollar?

Got It?

PART 4 Got It (1 of 2)

The ratio of defensive players to the total number of players in a different soccer league is about 9 to 30. If the league has 890 players, about how many defensive players are in the league?

PART 4 Got It (2 of 2)

Explain how you can solve the proportion $\frac{19}{x} = \frac{152}{4}$ for x.

Close and Check

Focus Question

MP2, MP6

How can you tell if an equation shows a proportional relationship between two quantities? How can you identify the constant of proportionality in an equation that represents a proportional relationship?

Do you know HOW?

1. The equation $q = 12c$ represents the quantity q of t-shirts in any number of cartons c.
   a. What is the constant of proportionality?
   b. How many shirts are in 8 cartons?
   shirts

2. A car manufacturer completes 81 cars every 180 seconds. Write an equation to represent the total number of cars y for x seconds of production.

3. Use the table to write an equation to find how much money y is received for x ounces of silver on the open market.

Silver Exchange Rate			
Silver (oz)	5	9	12
Price ($)	151.35	272.43	363.24

Do you UNDERSTAND?

4. **Writing** Can setting up a proportion help you find the constant of proportionality in a relationship? Explain.

5. **Error Analysis** Assume 130 out of 150 students buy lunch each day. There are 180 school days in a year. A classmate writes an equation to find how many lunches will be sold in one school year. Is he correct? Explain.

$$\frac{130}{150} = \frac{x}{180}$$

Maps and Scale Drawings

Digital Resources

CCSS: 7.G.A.1: Solve problems involving scale drawings of geometric figures, including computing actual lengths and areas from a scale drawing and reproducing a scale drawing at a different scale.

Launch

MP2, MP3

A peculiar professor wants a perfectly proportioned poster of a photo of her pet paper cup. She brings the 4-inch by 6-inch photo to your store and says the poster must be at least three feet tall.

Identify the side lengths of two possible posters.

Reflect What will the pet paper cup look like if the poster is not proportional to the photo? Explain.

Got It?

PART 1 Got It

What is the actual distance between Jacksonville and Orlando?

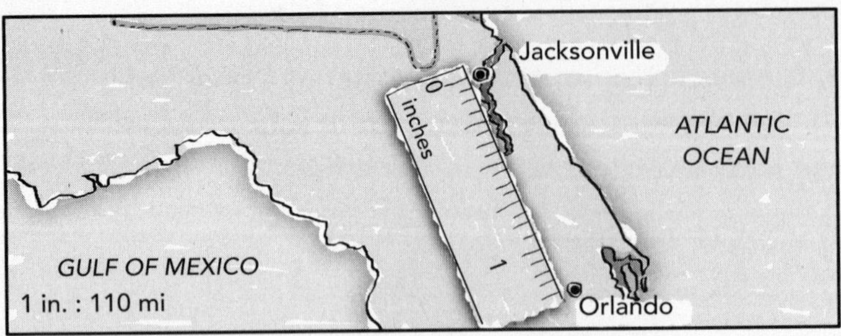

Discuss with a classmate

Maps contain lots of information.
Choose a piece of information provided on the map for this problem.
Explain what that piece of information tells you.
What pieces of information on the map were NOT needed to find the distance between Jacksonville and Orlando?

PART 2 Got It (1 of 2)

A state's driver's manual shows a scale drawing in the shape of a rectangular parking sign. The scale used is 1 in. : 0.5 ft. What is the area of the actual sign?

Got It?

PART 2 Got It (2 of 2)

A tennis court is 36 ft wide. A scale drawing of the court is $2\frac{1}{4}$ in. wide and $5\frac{1}{16}$ in. long. What was the scale used to make the scale drawing? Explain.

PART 3 Got It (1 of 2)

You are planning a neighborhood. The rectangle shown is a scale drawing of the roof of a rectangular building. You used a scale of
2 in. = 75 ft. What would be the dimensions of the roof in your drawing if you used a scale of 1 in. = 100 ft instead?

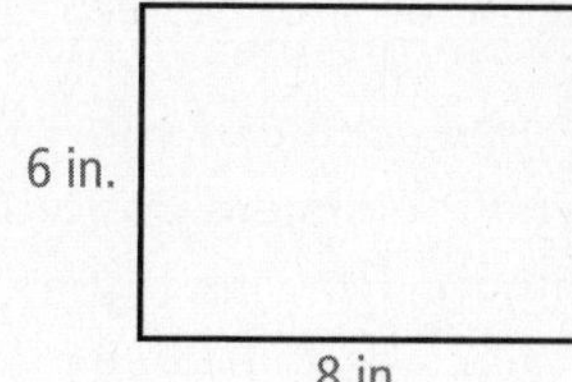

PART 3 Got It (2 of 2)

Consider two scale drawing of the same object. The drawings have scales of 1: 2 and 1: 3. Which drawing is larger? Explain.

Close and Check

Focus Question

MP4, MP7

How can you use proportional relationships to solve problems that involve maps and scale drawings?

Do you know HOW?

1. A replica of a popular car is built to a scale of 1 in. : 24 in. The length of the replica car is 5.6 inches. What is the length, in inches, of the actual car?

2. The official ratio of length to width of the U. S. flag is 1.9 : 1. If the width of a flag is 3 ft, what is the area of the flag?

3. A company designs a billboard to advertise their grand opening. They used a scale of 1 in. : 10 ft. What would be the dimensions of the billboard in the drawing if they use a scale of 2 in. : 25 ft instead?

10 in.

8 in.

Do you UNDERSTAND?

4. **Writing** Can understanding scale drawings help you make decisions? Explain.

5. **Compare and Contrast** How are scale and ratio related?

8-6 Additional Problem Solving

Digital Resources

CCSS: 7.G.A.1: Solve problems involving scale drawings of geometric figures, including computing actual lengths and areas from a scale drawing and reproducing a scale drawing at a different scale. Also, 7.RP.A.2, 7.RP.A.2a, 7.RP.A.2b, 7.RP.A.2c, and 7.RP.A.2d.

Launch

MP6, MP7

The peculiar professor plans a room addition for her pet paper cup and poster. The scale of the model is 1 in. = 3 ft.

Draw a net for the walls and ceiling of the room on the inch grid. Label the dimensions.

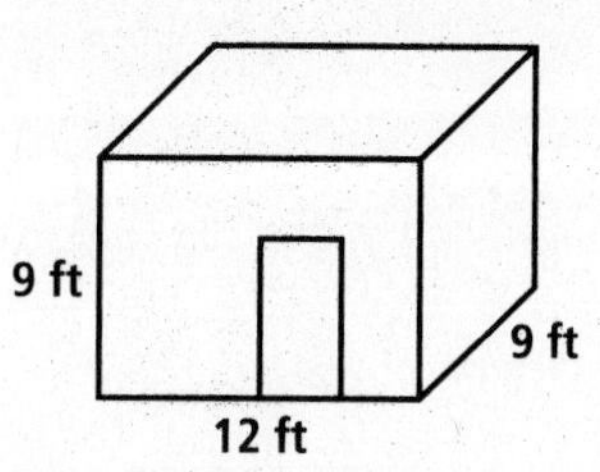

Reflect Is the ratio of the length to the width of the ceiling in the actual room the same as the ratio of the length to the width of the ceiling in the scale drawing? Explain.

Got It?

PART 1 Got It

Does the situation describe a proportional relationship?
A map is drawn using a scale of 1 in. = 75 mi.

PART 2 Got It

In the apartment, the walls are 9 ft high. You want to put a double coat of paint on the longest wall of the living room. A gallon of paint covers 350 ft^2. Will 1 gal of paint be enough? Explain.

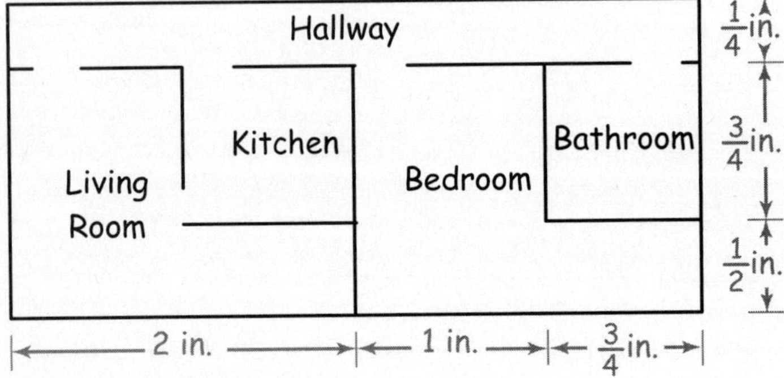

Scale 1 in. : 10 ft

Got It?

PART 3 Got It

You and your friend are each drawing a map of your neighborhood. The graph shows the scale that you used. Your friend's scale is represented by the equation $y = \frac{1}{12}x$, where x = the actual distance in feet and y = the distance on the scale drawing.

Your driveway is 180 feet long. On which map will the driveway be longer? And by how much?

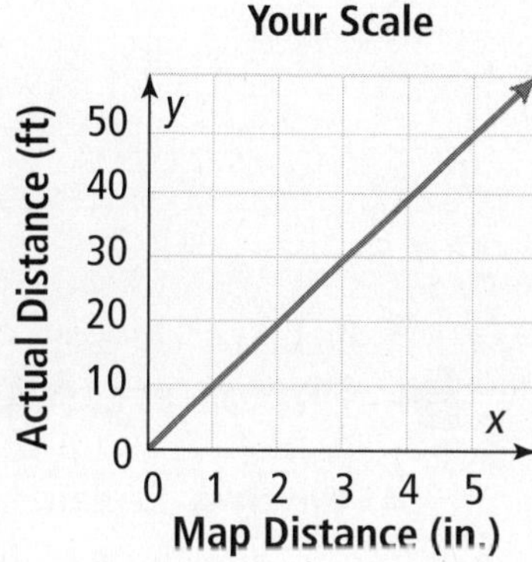

Close and Check

Focus Question

MP1, MP4

In this topic you have studied different ways to represent proportional relationships. In what ways can you represent proportional relationships? How can knowing how to represent proportional relationships in different ways be useful in solving problems?

Do you know HOW?

1. Circle the situation(s) that describes proportional relationships.

   A. The number of roller coaster riders is 12 more than the number of seats.

   B. There are 2 pieces of pizza for every friend.

   C. There are 3 times as many books as there are children.

2. An office is drawn to a scale of 3 in. : 10 ft. The drawing measures 4.5 in. by 7.5 in. How many square feet of carpet are needed to carpet the office?

3. The Statue of Liberty is 151 ft tall from the base to the top of the torch. You make a scale drawing of the monument using a scale of 1 in. : 20 ft. Your friend uses a scale of 1 in. : 25 ft.

   a. Whose drawing is larger?

   b. How much larger?

Do you UNDERSTAND?

4. **Writing** Explain how you decided which relationships were proportional in Exercise 1 and which ones were not.

5. **Reasoning** The scale drawing in Exercise 2 is redrawn to a scale of 4 in. : 9 ft. Is this second drawing larger or smaller than the first? Explain.

8-R

Topic Review

New Vocabulary: constant of proportionality, proportion, proportional relationship, scale, scale drawing
Review Vocabulary: equivalent ratios

Vocabulary Review

Identify two challenging vocabulary terms from this topic. Write one vocabulary term in the center oval, and fill in the surrounding boxes with details that will help you better understand the term.

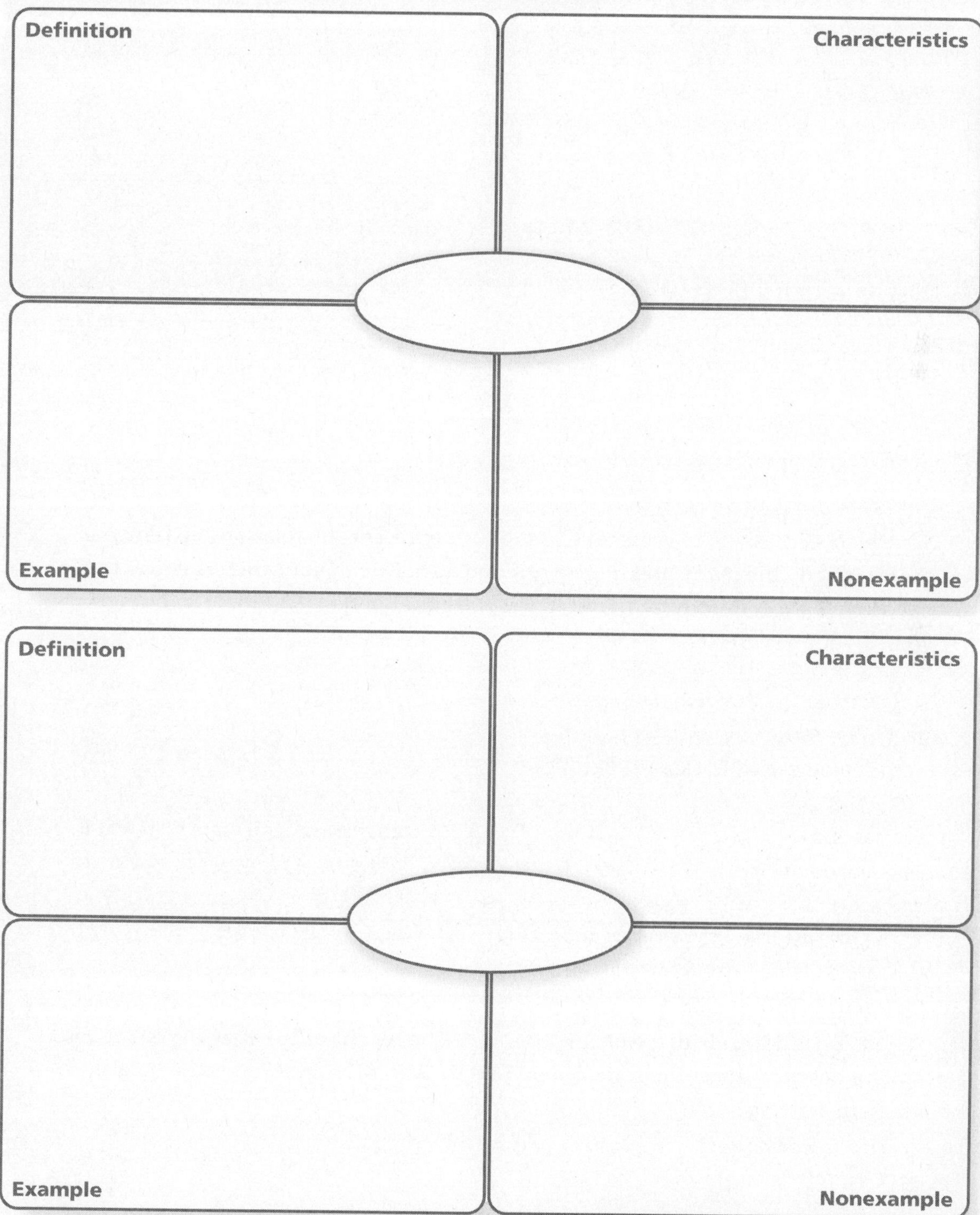

Pull It All Together

TASK 1

Can you use the information below to find how much a person who weighs 102 lb on Earth would weigh on the moon? Explain.

Earth: 174 lb
Moon: 29 lb

Earth: 126 lb
Moon: 21 lb

Earth: 249 lb
Moon: 41.5 lb

Your teacher asks you to write an equation to represent the relationship between the weight on the moon and the weight on Earth. One of your friends writes the equation $y = \frac{1}{6}x$. Your other friend writes the equation $y = 6x$. How can both of your friends be correct?

TASK 2

A building is drawn with a scale of 1 in. : 3 ft. The height of the drawing is 1 ft 2 in. After a design change, the scale is modified to be 1 in. : 4 ft. What is the height of the new drawing?

The Percent Equation

Digital Resources

CCSS: 7.RP.A.2b: Identify the constant of proportionality (unit rate) in tables, graphs, equations, diagrams, and verbal descriptions of proportional relationships. **7.RP.A.2c:** Represent proportional relationships by equations . . . . Also, **7.RP.A.2.**

Launch

MP3, MP4

A down-in-the-dumps drummer scours the internet for a new kit to improve his mood and swing. Based on buyers' reviews, which kit should he get? Show how you decided.

Kit 1: 9 of 13 buyers love this kit!

Kit 2: 15 of 21 buyers love this kit!

Reflect Do you like the method of showing buyers' reviews (e.g., 9 of 13)? Explain.

Got It?

PART 1 Got It

Is the question "190 is 10% of what number?" looking for the *part*, the *percent*, or the *whole*?

PART 2 Got It

Which of the following is/are true?

I. 7 is 50% of 14.
II. 28 is 14% of 200.
III. 6 is 40% of 14.
IV. 40% of 35 is 14.

PART 3 Got It

Suppose your friend has given you a gift certificate for a haircut. After the haircut, you want to leave an appropriate tip for the hairdresser. The receptionist says you should leave exactly $3 if you want to tip 20% of the price of the haircut. What was the price of the haircut?

Discuss with a classmate

What are gift certificates and how do they work?
What are tips and how do they work?

Close and Check

Focus Question

MP1, MP4

How do percents and the percent equation help describe things in the real world?

Do you know HOW?

1. Is the question "What percent of 8 is 5?" looking for the *part*, the *percent*, or the *whole*?

2. Read each statement. Write **T** if it is true or **F** if it is false.

   9 is 15% of 60.

   12% of 120 is 10.

   32 is 40% of 80.

   90% of 180 is 162.

3. A shoe store is having a closeout sale. All the prices are 80% of the original price. The shoes you want originally cost $40. Find the sale price of the shoes.

Do you UNDERSTAND?

4. **Writing** The total bill at a restaurant equals $65.38. The waiter typically receives a tip equal to 15% of the total bill. He is given a $13 tip. Should he be happy with the amount of the tip? Explain.

5. **Vocabulary** Explain how to solve "72 is 18% of what number?" by using the terms *part*, *percent*, and *whole*.

This page intentionally left blank.

9-2 Using the Percent Equation

Digital Resources

CCSS: 7.RP.A.2: Recognize and represent proportional relationships between quantities. **7.RP.A.3:** Use proportional relationships to solve … percent problems. Examples: … tax, gratuities and commissions … .

Launch

MP3, MP4

A movie studio sets two offers in front of a movie star to act in a blockbuster upcoming action flick. The star can choose only one offer.

Make a case for accepting each offer. Then explain which offer you would choose.

Reflect Which offer has a constant of proportionality? Explain.

Got It?

PART 1 Got It

Tips are calculated similarly to taxes. Suppose the team brought a total of $175 to pay for dinner. Do they have enough money to tip the waiter 18% of the subtotal? Explain.

The Diner

Item	Price
Hamburger (4)	$34.58
Spaghetti (5)	$40.09
Fries (4)	$17.00
Caesar Salad (2)	$16.57
Milkshake (11)	$33.76
Subtotal	$142.00
Meals Tax (5%)	$7.10
TOTAL	$149.10

Thank You!
Please Come Again 00310

Got It?

PART 2 Got It (1 of 2)

At a real estate agency, a real estate agent sold a house for $345,000. Her commission rate is 3%.

a. How much did the real estate agent earn on the house?
b. How much did the seller make on the house?

PART 2 Got It (2 of 2)

Suppose you are a car salesperson. Would you prefer to make a 6% commission on each car you sell, or would you prefer to get a flat fee of $1,500 per car? Explain.

Got It?

PART 3 Got It (1 of 2)

Jon has a new job at an electronics store. He has two options for how to be paid.

He plans to work 7 hours a day, 5 days a week. He also estimates that he can sell about $3,500 worth of electronics per week. Which option would give Jon more earnings per week? Explain.

Option A
Hourly wage of $16.00

Option B
16% commission on total sales

PART 3 Got It (2 of 2)

If you were Jon, which option would you choose if they both generate the same weekly pay based on his estimated work hours and sales predictions?

Option A
Hourly wage of $16.00

Option B
16% commission on total sales

Close and Check

Focus Question

MP1, MP6

In what situations are fixed numbers better than percents of an amount? In what situations are percents better than fixed numbers?

Do you know HOW?

1. You pay \$3.50 per gallon including taxes for 15 gallons of gas. Federal and state gas taxes make up 14% of the total cost. How much do you pay in gas taxes?

2. A new car depreciates (loses value) by 9% immediately after it is purchased and driven from the lot. If a new car costs \$28,400, how much is it worth right after it is driven off the car lot?

3. A company expects a new sales employee to work 40 hours per week. The company offers the employee either \$25 per hour or a salary of \$500 per week plus a 7% sales commission. Each sales employee averages \$7,800 in sales each week. Which offer pays more?

Do you UNDERSTAND?

4. **Error Analysis** A basketball player made 88% of 125 free throw attempts. Your friend calculates how many free throws the player made below. Explain her error and find the correct number.

$$\begin{aligned} \text{total} &= 88\% \cdot 125 \\ &= 88.0 \cdot 125 \\ &= 11{,}000 \end{aligned}$$

5. **Writing** Your uncle offers to sell your guitar at his auction. He offers you \$75 or 50% of the final selling price. How would you choose? Explain.

This page intentionally left blank.

9-3 Simple Interest

Digital Resources

CCSS: 7.RP.A.2: Recognize and represent proportional relationships between quantities. **7.RP.A.3:** Use proportional relationships to solve multistep … percent problems. Examples: simple interest … .

Launch

MP1, MP4

Two banks offer different incentives to make a deposit at their bank.
Bank A offers a $10 gift card for making a minimum initial deposit.
Bank B offers cash back equal to 2% of your deposit at the end of the year.

Tell which line represents each bank's offer. Explain your reasoning.

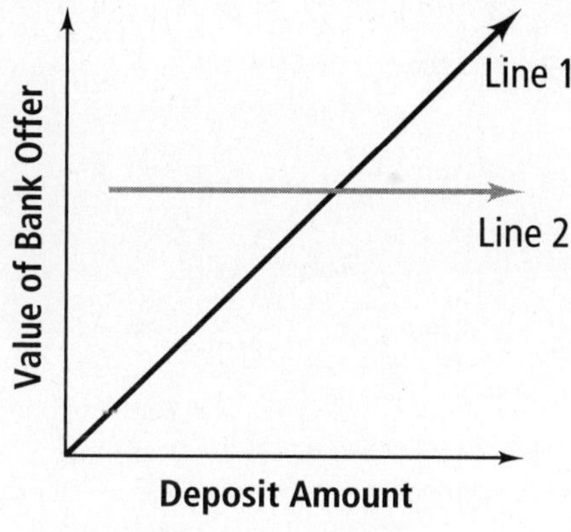

Reflect What would you need to know to decide which offer to choose? Explain.

Got It?

PART 1 Got It (1 of 2)

Suppose you deposit $500 in a bank account that earns simple interest at 1.2% per year. You keep it in the bank for two years. Which of the following is/are true?

I. $I = 12$ **II.** $p = 1.2\%$

III. $r = 500$ **IV.** $t = 2$

PART 1 Got It (2 of 2)

How does the formula for simple interest after one year relate to the percent equation?

Got It?

PART 2 Got It

A new bank customer with $5,000 to deposit looks at the manager's poster. The customer wants to open a CD to earn money for his retirement. If he wants to have $5,500 in the CD, how long does he need to keep the account?

If you deposit $2,500 at 3.5% annual interest...		
Time (years)	**Simple Interest Earned**	**New Account Balance**
0	$0.00	$2,500.00
1	$87.50	$2,587.50
2	$175.00	$2,675.00
3	$262.50	$2,762.50
4	$350.00	$2,850.00

Discuss with a classmate

Choose a row from the table.
Explain what the entries in Columns 1, 2, and 3 mean for the row that you selected.
Take turns until you have reviewed all the rows in the table.

Got It?

PART 3 Got It (1 of 2)

After 16 months, does Mia still have the higher balance? Explain.

Name on Account: Alex **Principal:** \$2,950 **Annual interest rate:** 4%	**Name on Account:** Mia **Principal:** \$3,000 **Annual interest rate:** 2.5%

Got It?

PART 3 Got It (2 of 2)

Suppose your friend has earned $5.51 in interest after 9 months. If the annual interest rate is 3%, how much is the principal in the account? Round to the nearest dollar.

Close and Check

Focus Question

MP1, MP7

Why is simple interest called "simple"? When would you use simple interest?

____

____

____

____

Do you know HOW?

1. U.S. savings bonds pay 1.4% interest. You purchase $750 in savings bonds and hold them for $2\frac{1}{2}$ years. Circle the true statement(s).

A. $I = 1.4\%$

B. $p = 750$

C. $r = 26.25$

D. $t = 2.5$

2. You buy $2,500 of savings bonds at 1.7% interest. How many years will it take for your investment to equal $3,000? Round your answer to the nearest whole year.

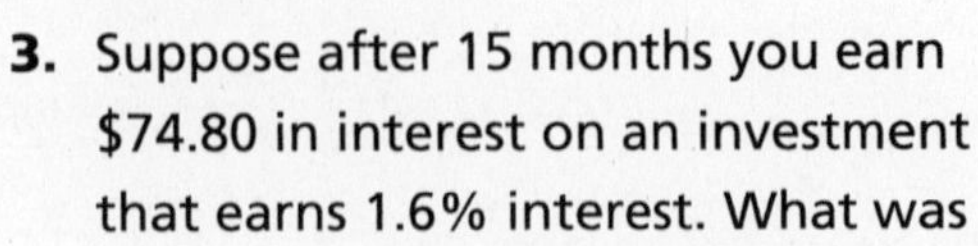

3. Suppose after 15 months you earn $74.80 in interest on an investment that earns 1.6% interest. What was your principal investment?

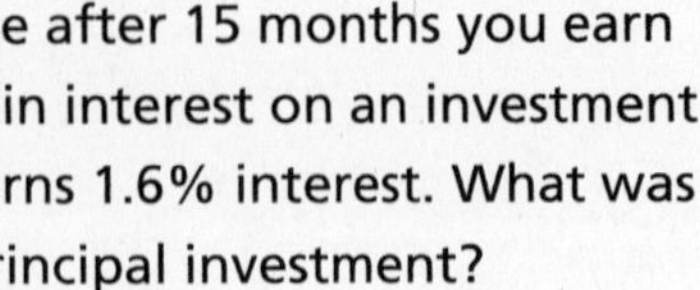

Do you UNDERSTAND?

4. Reasoning You and your friend both have savings accounts that pay 3.5% interest. Do you both earn the same amount of money in interest? Explain how you know.

____

____

____

5. Error Analysis Your friend says she has $75 in her savings account that pays 3.5% interest. She finds the amount of interest earned in one year. Is she correct? Explain.

I = 75 • 3.5 • 1
I = 262.50

____

____

____

____

____

9-4 Compound Interest

Digital Resources

CCSS: 7.NS.A.3: Solve real-world and mathematical problems involving the four operations with rational numbers.

Launch

MP1, MP3

A bank manager shows your friend a graph of different types of interest the bank can pay on her $100 deposit. The manager advises your friend to opt for 2% simple interest "because it's easy to compute and a good rate."

Tell which line represents simple interest. Explain whether your friend should listen to the bank manager.

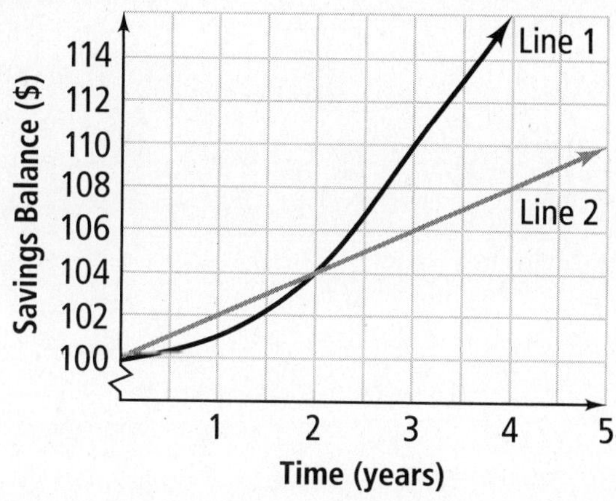

Reflect What makes simple interest simple? How is the other interest line different? Explain.

Got It?

PART 1 Got It (1 of 2)

Make a table and find the balance after two years.

principal = $500

annual interest rate = 3%, compounded annually

PART 1 Got It (2 of 2)

Which account balance grows faster, an account that earns simple interest or an account that earns compound interest? Explain.

Got It?

PART 2 Got It

A graduate student has kept money in a savings account since middle school. After 12 years earning 4% annual interest compounded once a year, the account balance is $2,560. What was his original deposit to the nearest ten dollars?

PART 3 Got It (1 of 2)

Suppose you used a credit card to purchase a bicycle. If there are no additional late fees, how much would you owe after a year of not paying off the balance? Round to the nearest dollar.

Your Credit Card This Month

Bicycle.................................... $150

Balance................... $150

Annual interest rate: 30%

Compound monthly

No late fees for a year!

Got It?

PART 3 Got It (2 of 2)

In the first Got It, you found the interest compounded monthly for a year. If the interest had been compounded annually instead, how much more or less would you owe after not paying off the balance for a year?

Your Credit Card This Month

Bicycle.................................... $150

Balance.................. $150

Annual interest rate: 30%

Compound monthly

No late fees for a year!

Close and Check

Focus Question

MP2, MP6

How is compound interest different from simple interest? When do you use each kind?

Do you know **HOW?**

1. You invest $750 in an account that earns 4.5%, compounded annually. Find the balance of the account after 2 years. Round your answer to the nearest cent.

2. A 10-year investment at 3.5%, compounded annually, totals $4,250. Find the amount of the original deposit to the nearest cent.

3. You qualify for a 5-year loan of $2,000. The interest rate is 9.5% with no late fees. How much more or less would you owe if interest is compounded quarterly rather than compounded annually?

Do you **UNDERSTAND?**

4. Writing Explain how you can use what you have learned about compound interest to develop a savings or investment plan.

5. Error Analysis Your friend can get a 3-year car loan for $3,700 at 7.5% annual interest compounded quarterly. Explain the error she makes in calculating the amount of interest.

$B = 3{,}700(1 + 0.01875)^4$

$= 3{,}985.40$

$I = 3{,}985.40 - 3{,}700$

$= 285.40$

This page intentionally left blank.

9-5 Percent Increase and Decrease

Digital Resources

CCSS: 7.RP.A.2: Recognize and represent proportional relationships between quantities. 7.RP.A.3: Use proportional relationships to solve multistep … percent problems. Examples: … percent increase and decrease … .

Launch

MP2, MP6

Two friends argue about which of their little town's populations grew the most between 2000 and 2009.

Write an argument to support each friend's point of view. Explain your reasoning.

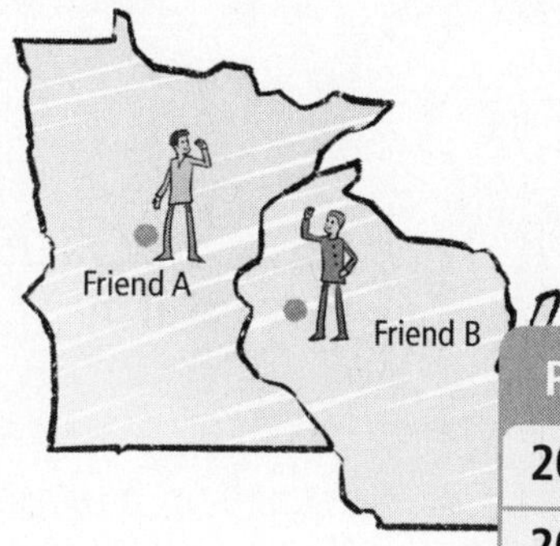

U.S. Census Bureau Data

Population data	Little Falls, MN	Little Falls, WI
2009 population	8,067	1,540
2000 population	7,719	1,334

Reflect Which do you think tells more about the growth of a town — percent increase in population or increase in number of people? Explain.

Got It?

PART 1 Got It (1 of 2)

A pet frog measures 51 mm in body length while sitting. Its body length extends to 89 mm while jumping. Find the approximate percent increase in body length of the frog from sitting to jumping.

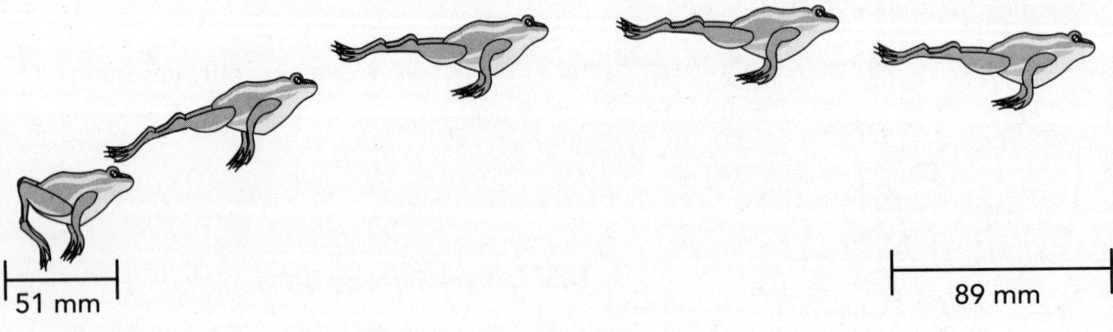

PART 1 Got It (2 of 2)

What does it mean for a quantity to increase by 100%? Explain.

Got It?

PART 2 Got It

Every 10 years, the U.S. government takes a census, or survey, of the population. One possible result of changes in population is that the number of U.S. representatives for a state may change. Find the approximate percent decrease in the number of representatives for Michigan.

Number of House Representatives for Michigan

In 2000	In 2010
15 representatives	14 representatives

PART 3 Got It

Estimate the percent of change.

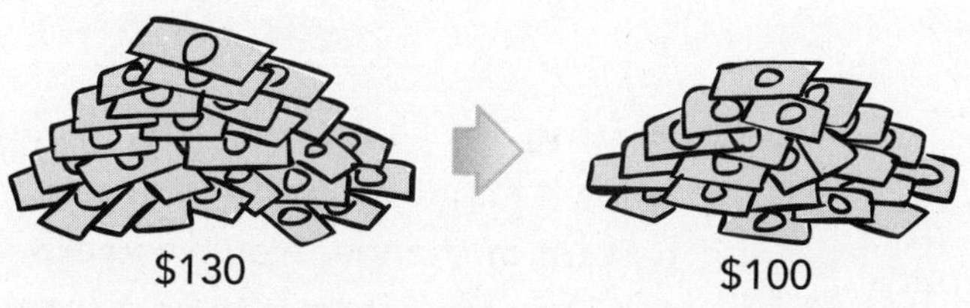

Close and Check

Focus Question

MP4, MP7

How can you use a percent to represent change?

Do you know HOW?

1. The banded ribbon worm is a carnivorous aquatic worm. It measures about 2.5 ft when contracted and up to 25 ft when expanded. Find the percent increase between the contracted and expanded length of a banded ribbon worm.

2. The oceans' tide levels vary based on the phases of the moon. Find the percent decrease in tide levels when high tide is 4.25 ft and low tide is 0.75 ft above sea level.

3. The national debt in 2000 was about $5.7 trillion. In 2010, the national debt had risen to about $13.6 trillion. Find the approximate percent of change in the national debt during that ten-year period.

Do you UNDERSTAND?

4. **Reasoning** Explain how you know whether a percent of change is a percent increase or a percent decrease.

5. **Writing** Give a real-world example of when it might be useful to calculate a percent of change. Would you expect the percent of change to be a percent increase or a percent decrease?

9-6 Markups and Markdowns

Digital Resources

CCSS: 7.RP.A.3: Use proportional relationships to solve multistep … percent problems. Examples: … markups and markdowns … .

Launch

MP1, MP4

A sporting goods store holds a storewide clearance sale. You comb the ads for boxing items.

Order the ads from best deal to worst deal. Explain your reasoning.

Reflect Should you always choose the item with the greatest change in price when shopping? Explain.

Got It?

PART 1 Got It (1 of 2)

Airlines usually increase the price of their plane tickets as the day of the flight gets closer. What is the percent markup for the plane ticket below?

Base cost: $310
Selling price: $550

PART 1 Got It (2 of 2)

Concert halls change the price for concert tickets depending on the performer. What is the selling price for the concert ticket below?

Base cost: $20
Percent markup: 90%

Got It?

PART 2 Got It

Each month at an electronics store, new televisions come in. The store manager puts older televisions on sale. What is the percent markdown on the television below?

Selling Price: $250
Sale Price: $200

PART 3 Got It

Relax Yoga Store negotiates to buy even more yoga mats from their seller if he can give them 35% off the original $15. If the seller gets the mats for $8.50, would he still make a profit on each mat with this deal? If so, how much of a profit?

Close and Check

Focus Question

MP1, MP6

When are percent markups and percent markdowns used? How are they similar? How are they different?

Do you know HOW?

1. A car dealership pays $26,215 for a new car. They sell the car for $28,265. Find the percent markup on the car.

2. A computer is purchased by a store for $756 and offered to the customer for $1,200. At the end of the year, the store discounts the computer for quick sale. Find the greatest percent markdown possible without losing money.

3. Gaming Unlimited buys a gaming system for $249. It sells the system for $385. This week the system is on sale for 30% off. Find the amount of profit made on each gaming system sold.

Do you UNDERSTAND?

4. **Reasoning** Does a seller make a profit if the percent markdown on an item is equal to the percent markup? Explain using an example.

5. **Vocabulary** A $70 jacket is marked down to $52.50. Your friend says the markdown is 25%. You say the markdown is $17.50. Explain how both of you can be correct.

9-7 Problem Solving

Digital Resources

CCSS: 7.RP.A.3: Use proportional relationships to solve multistep … percent problems. Examples: simple interest, tax, markups and markdowns, gratuities and commissions, fees, percent increase and decrease … .

Launch

MP2, MP6

Two friends agree to pay half each for their mostly excellent meatloaf dinner and most excellent 20% tip. Each friend has $8.50.

Do they have enough money to complete their excellent plan? If so, by how much? If not, tell what they should do.

Meatloaf House

Meatloaf Dinner	$5.50
Meatloaf Dinner	$5.50
Soda	$1.00
Soda	$1.00
Subtotal	$13.00
Tax	$1.30
Total	$14.30

Reflect How do you use percents in your life outside of school? Provide one example.

Got It?

PART 1 Got It

You bought three airplane tickets. Each ticket cost $110. If you paid a total of $353.10 including a processing fee, what is the fee as a percent rate?

PART 2 Got It (1 of 2)

Is Kit correct? Explain.

Got It?

PART 2 Got It (2 of 2)

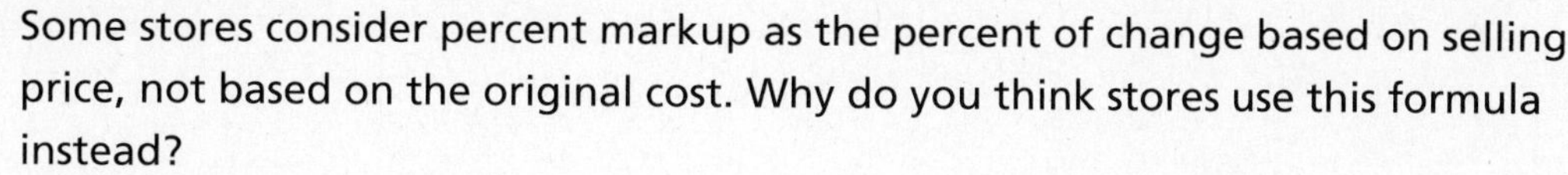

Some stores consider percent markup as the percent of change based on selling price, not based on the original cost. Why do you think stores use this formula instead?

percent markup $= \frac{\text{markup}}{\text{cost}}$

percent markup (in stores) $= \frac{\text{markup}}{\text{selling price}}$

PART 3 Got It

After buying a board, you have \$13 left. You decide to buy a surfboard leash, which prevents the surfboard from floating away from the surfer. Which leash(es) can you afford to buy after a 6.25% sales tax?

Leash A: Selling price \$14.99; $\rightarrow$ Sale $\frac{1}{5}$ off!
Leash B: Selling price \$17.99; $\rightarrow$ Our price 30% off!

Close and Check

Focus Question

MP1, MP3

How do percents help you compare, predict, and make decisions?

Do you know HOW?

1. You and 3 friends combine a snowboard purchase to save on shipping fees. Each board costs $82.50 after tax. The total bill is $392.70. Express the shipping fee as a percent rate to the nearest whole percent.

2. The number 450 is increased by 75%. The result is then decreased by 90%. What is the final number?

3. You receive a $50 gift card to your favorite store. If sales tax is 7.5%, what is the greatest amount you can spend without using any additional money?

Do you UNDERSTAND?

4. **Writing** A researcher finds that 11 out of 15 people work within 30 miles of their home. He says 73% of people work within 30 miles of their home. Which statement do you find more useful? Explain.

5. **Reasoning** A bookstore special-orders books for a fee of $1.50 per book. Online orders have a shipping charge of 10% of the total order. If 5 books cost $70.96, which is the better offer?

9-R Topic Review

New Vocabulary: balance, compound interest, interest, interest period, interest rate, markdown, markup, percent decrease, percent equation, percent increase, percent of change, principal, simple interest
Review Vocabulary: percent, ratio

Vocabulary Review

Identify two challenging vocabulary terms from this topic. Write one vocabulary term in the center oval, and fill in the surrounding boxes with details that will help you better understand the term.

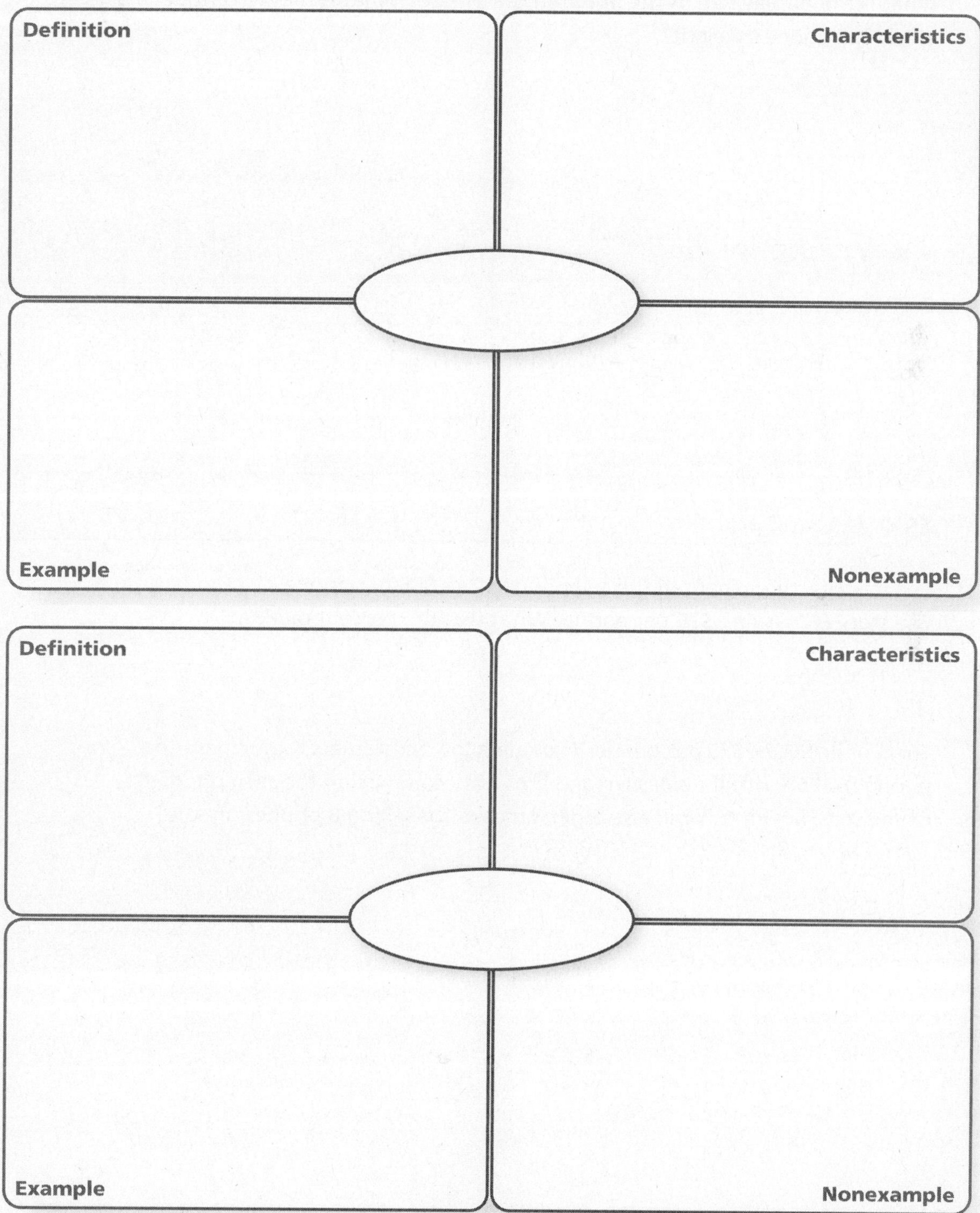

Pull It All Together

TASK 1

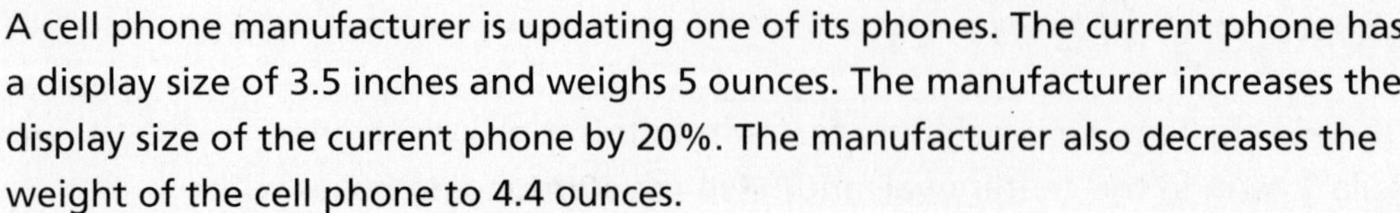

A cell phone manufacturer is updating one of its phones. The current phone has a display size of 3.5 inches and weighs 5 ounces. The manufacturer increases the display size of the current phone by 20%. The manufacturer also decreases the weight of the cell phone to 4.4 ounces.

What is the display size of the updated cell phone? What is the percent decrease in the cell phone's weight?

TASK 2

The manufacturer charged the cell phone store $35 per phone.
The store is charging $75 per phone. What was the percent markup?

The store charges $75 per phone. The sale allows customers to purchase the phone for 25% off. If a salesperson earns 20% commission for each phone he or she sells, how much will a salesperson earn for selling 6 phones on sale?

10-1 Expanding Algebraic Expressions

Digital Resources

CCSS: 7.EE.A.1: Apply properties of operations as strategies to add, subtract, factor, and expand linear expressions with rational coefficients. 7.EE.A.2: Understand that rewriting an expression in different forms in a problem context can shed light on the problem … .

Launch

MP2, MP7

Use the symbols, numbers, and a variable to make three equivalent expressions. Tell which properties (Commutative, Associative, and Distributive) you used. You can use each tile more than once.

( ) + • 7 −3 −21 *w*

Reflect Your expressions are equivalent, but are they different in any way? Explain.

Got It?

PART 1 Got It

Which expressions show a *sum* or *difference* equivalent to $-\frac{1}{5}(-5m + 10)$?

I. $-\frac{1}{5}(10 - 5m)$

II. $m - 2$

III. $-m + 2$

m-2

PART 2 Got It

Which expression can be expanded? Write the expression in its expanded form.

$(5 - x)(-y)$ $(5 - x) - y$

-5y +xy

Discuss with a classmate

What does it mean to expand something?
Give a non-math example of something being expanded.

Got It?

PART 3 Got It

For your birthday party, you plan to buy 2 cupcakes for each guest and 5 additional cupcakes to have as extras. Cupcakes cost $2.25 each. Let x represent the number of guests you invite to your party. Use the expression below.

$2.25(2x + 5)$

a. What does each factor of the expression represent? What does the expression represent?

b. Use the Distributive Property to expand the expression. What does each term of your new expression represent?

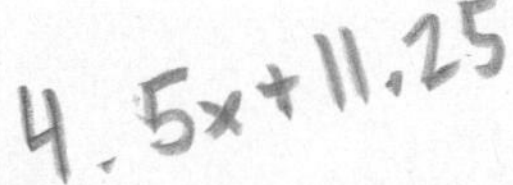

Close and Check

Focus Question

MP1, MP7

When would you want to expand an algebraic expression? What operation would you use? What does expanding an expression help you do?

Do you know HOW?

1. Circle the expression(s) that shows a sum or difference equivalent to $-0.9(3x - 2.6)$. $-2.7x - 2.34$

   A. $-2.7x - 2.34$ B. $-2.7x + 2.34$

   C. $-2.7x + 23.4$ D. $-27x - 23.4$

2. Write the expression in expanded form.

   $(4.2z)(-5y - 3)$

3. You charge $2.50 per hour for each child you babysit. You also earn an activity fee of $2.75 for each hour. You babysit an average of 10 hours a month. Write an expression using the product of two factors to find how much you will earn on average each month for any number of children c.

4. Simplify the expression you wrote in Exercise 3.

Do you UNDERSTAND?

5. **Writing** What does each factor in the expression in Exercise 3 represent? What does the expression itself represent?

6. **Error Analysis** A classmate says that the expression $-5r(6s)$ can be expanded to $-30r - 5rs$. Explain his error.

10-2 Factoring Algebraic Expressions

Digital Resources

CCSS: 7.EE.A.1: Apply properties of operations as strategies to add, subtract, factor, and expand linear expressions with rational coefficients. **7.EE.A.2:** Understand that rewriting an expression in different forms in a problem context can shed light on the problem … .

Launch

MP1, MP2

Your friends name five expressions—all using the same variable p—equivalent to the one shown. They say there's even more equality to be expressed.

What five equivalent expressions could they have named? Explain your reasoning.

$$12p + 3.6$$

Reflect Do you think there are only five expressions equivalent to $12p + 3.6$? Explain.

Got It?

PART 1 Got It

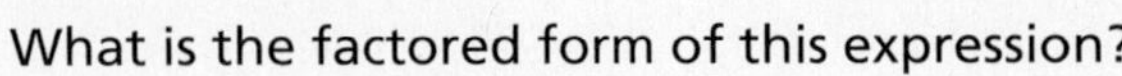

What is the factored form of this expression?

$12x - 42y - 3$

PART 2 Got It

Which expression has like terms? Combine the like terms.

$-x + 3.5x$ $\qquad$ $7 - 2x$

Got It?

PART 3 Got It (1 of 2)

The bakery manager at the grocery store decides to have a 15% off sale on all bread. Let b be the original price of a loaf of bread. Use this expression for the new price of a loaf of bread.

$$b - 0.15b$$

Write an equivalent expression by combining like terms. What does your equivalent expression tell you about how to find the new price of a loaf of bread?

PART 3 Got It (2 of 2)

A clothing store advertises a sale. Your friend says that you can find the sale price of a shirt by multiplying the shirt's original price by 0.7. Do you agree? Explain.

Discuss with a classmate

Read your explanation for this problem out loud to your classmate.
Is your explanation convincing? What key math terms and phrases did you include in your response?

Close and Check

Focus Question

MP1, MP7

How does a common factor help you rewrite an algebraic expression?

Do you know HOW?

1. Write the factored form of the algebraic expression.

$$54f - 9g + 27h$$

2. Combine the like terms.

$$-17tr + 12tr$$

3. A video game store sells games for various prices. Sales tax is 7.5%. Let g be the price of a game. Use the expression to find the total cost of a video game.

$$g + 0.075g$$

4. A store advertises a sale of 15% off the total purchase price. Let p be the purchase price. Use the expression to find the final price.

$$p - 0.15p$$

Do you UNDERSTAND?

5. **Writing** How are the results of factoring the following expressions different?

$2b + 6b$ $\quad$ $2b + 6$

6. **Error Analysis** A classmate says the expression cannot be rewritten because it does not contain any like terms. Do you agree? Explain.

$$3x + (4y - 2xy)$$

10-3 Adding Algebraic Expressions

Digital Resources

CCSS: 7.EE.A.1: Apply properties of operations as strategies to add, subtract, factor, and expand linear expressions with rational coefficients. **7.EE.A.2:** Understand that rewriting an expression in different forms in a problem context can shed light on the problem ... .

Launch

MP2, MP8

The twins hold a fundraiser for a local food pantry. People bring cash and food, so the twins struggle to state the total value of all items donated.

Write an expression to show the value of items donated. Explain your reasoning.

Reflect Could the twins find out how much money all the donated items are worth? Explain.

Got It?

PART 1 Got It

Identify the number of terms, the coefficients, and the constant term of this expression.

$6p - 7pc + 9c - 4$

PART 2 Got It

Which expressions are equivalent to $-6 + 5t$?

I. $(8t + 13) + (-3t + 7)$

II. $(t + 9) + (4t - 15)$

III. $5(-2 + t) + 4$

IV. $-1 + (2t + 3) + 2(t - 3)$

Got It?

PART 3 Got It

The width of the rectangle is one half of its length. Write and simplify an algebraic expression for the perimeter of the rectangle in terms of the rectangle's length ℓ.

ℓ

Close and Check

Focus Question

MP1, MP3

When would you want to add algebraic expressions? How do properties of operations help you add expressions?

Do you know HOW?

1. Identify the parts of the expression.

$14d - 9 + 21k - 7dk + 2$

A. number of terms

B. the coefficients

C. the constant terms

2. Circle the expressions that are equivalent to $12r - 4$.

A. $(9r + 6) - (-3r + 10)$

B. $-4(3r + 1)$

C. $(6r - 2) + (6r - 2)$

D. $-2(-6r - 2)$

3. The length of a box is 2.75 times greater than the width. Write and simplify an algebraic expression for the perimeter of the box in terms of the width w.

Do you UNDERSTAND?

4. Reasoning Is the coefficient of b in the expression below 2 or −2? Explain.

$$5c - 2b$$

5. Error Analysis A classmate simplifies the expression in Exercise 1. Is the expression he wrote equivalent to the original expression? Explain.

$$7dk(2 - 3 - 1) - 7$$

10-4 Subtracting Algebraic Expressions

Digital Resources

CCSS: **7.EE.A.1:** Apply properties of operations as strategies to add, subtract, factor, and expand linear expressions with rational coefficients. **7.EE.A.2:** Understand that rewriting an expression in different forms in a problem context can shed light on the problem and how the quantities in it are related.

Launch

MP4, MP7

Your twin friends store the fundraiser items in a shed. Three raccoons break in and steal some of the food and money.
Write an expression that shows the value of the remaining fundraiser items in the shed. Explain your reasoning.

Reflect How are adding and subtracting expressions alike? Explain.

Got It?

PART 1 Got It

Which expression(s) are equivalent to $(6y + 15) - (4 - 8y)$?

I. $6y + 15 - 4 - 8y$

II. $6y + 15 - 4 + 8y$

III. $6y + 15 + (-1)(4 - 8y)$

IV. $6y + 15 + (-4) - (-8y)$

PART 2 Got It

What is the correct order for the steps of simplifying the expression $(-9x + 15) - (2x - 1)$?

I. $-9x - 2x + 15 + 1$

II. $-11x + 16$

III. $-9x + 15 - 2x - (-1)$

IV. $-9x + 15 - 2x + 1$

Got It?

PART 3 Got It

Write and simplify an expression for the area of the shaded region.

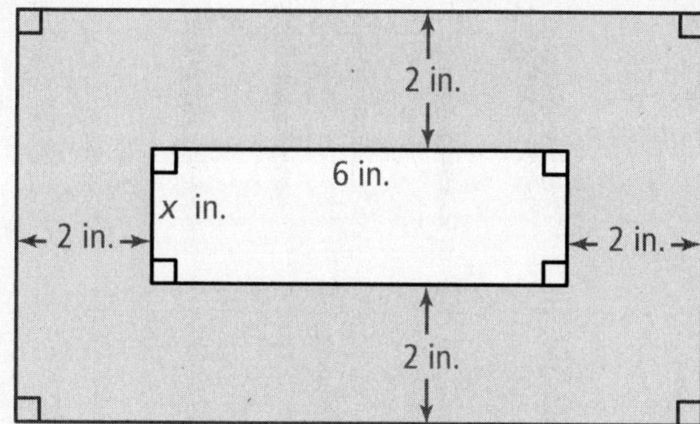

Close and Check

Focus Question

When would you want to subtract algebraic expressions? How do properties of operations help you subtract expressions?

Do you know HOW?

1. Rewrite the expression without parentheses.

$4t - 4(3r - 2)$

2. Number the steps of simplifying the expression in the correct order.

$-3(-r + s) - 2(4r - 7s)$

☐ $3r - 8r - 3s - (-14s)$

☐ $3r - 8r - 3s + 14s$

☐ $3r - 3s - 8r - (-14s)$

☐ $-5r + 11s$

3. One friend buys a pair of shoes for \$54.98 and 3 t-shirts. Another friend buys a sweatshirt for \$26.49 and 5 t-shirts. Using one variable write a simplified expression to represent how much more one friend spent.

☐

Do you UNDERSTAND?

4. Writing Explain a different method for simplifying the expression in Exercise 2 than the method shown.

5. Error Analysis A classmate says she prefers to remove the parentheses before solving the equation. Can she do that and still find the correct solution? Explain.

$(1.47a - 2.9) - (3.08a - 0.5)$

10-5 Problem Solving

Digital Resources

CCSS: **7.EE.A.1:** Apply properties of operations as strategies to add, subtract, factor, and expand linear expressions with rational coefficients. **7.EE.A.2:** Understand that rewriting an expression in different forms in a problem context can shed light on the problem … .

Launch

MP3, MP4

Two friends each write an expression to describe the total area, in square feet, of a three-panel mural. Each panel is a rectangle.

One friend wrote $6.7h + 12.4h + 5.9h$.

The other friend wrote $25h$.

Does one expression describe the area of the mural better than the other? Explain.

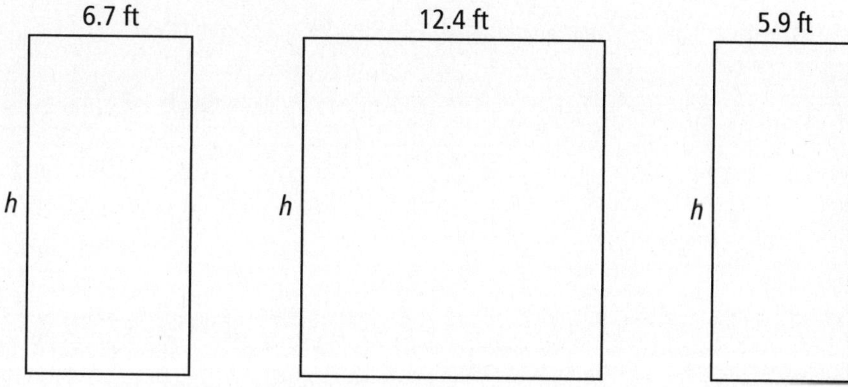

Reflect Does it help to show the equivalent expressions in different ways? Explain.

Got It?

PART 1 Got It

Write a difference of two products that is equivalent to $5x - 2y - 11$.

PART 2 Got It

A gardener plans to enlarge a small rectangular flower garden by x feet on all sides and then enclose the enlarged garden with a brick border. The border costs $2.30 per foot.

a. Write and simplify an expression for the cost, in dollars, of the brick border.

b. How much does the brick border cost if the gardener increases the length and width of the garden by 3.5 feet on each side?

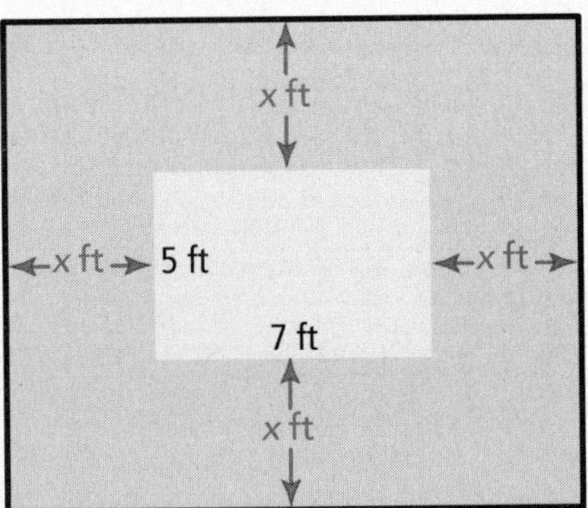

Close and Check

Focus Question

MP1, MP6

How do different forms of an algebraic expression help you solve a problem?

Do you know HOW?

1. Write a difference of two products that is equivalent to $3x - 7y - 13$.

2. Write a product of two factors that is equivalent to $35x - 21$.

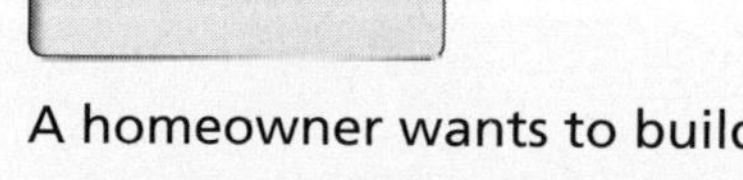

3. A homeowner wants to build a fence around her yard. Fencing costs $13.40 for each foot. Write and simplify an expression for the cost of the fencing.

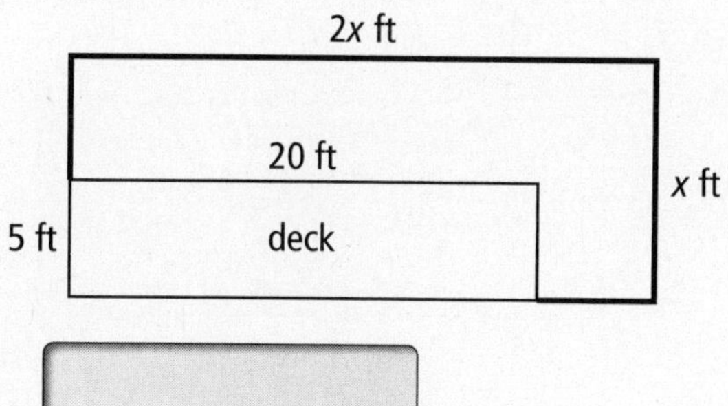

Do you UNDERSTAND?

4. **Reasoning** One student wrote an expression for Exercise 3 by using addition. Another student wrote an expression by using subtraction. Can both students be correct? Explain.

5. **Reasoning** If the dimensions of the yard in Exercise 3 were doubled, would the total cost of the fencing double? Explain.

This page intentionally left blank.

10-R

Topic Review

New Vocabulary: coefficient, constant, expand an algebraic expression, factor an algebraic expression, like terms, simplify an algebraic expression
Review Vocabulary: algebraic expression, Distributive Property, greatest common factor (GCF)

Vocabulary Review

Identify two challenging vocabulary terms from this topic. Write one vocabulary term in the center oval, and fill in the surrounding boxes with details that will help you better understand the term.

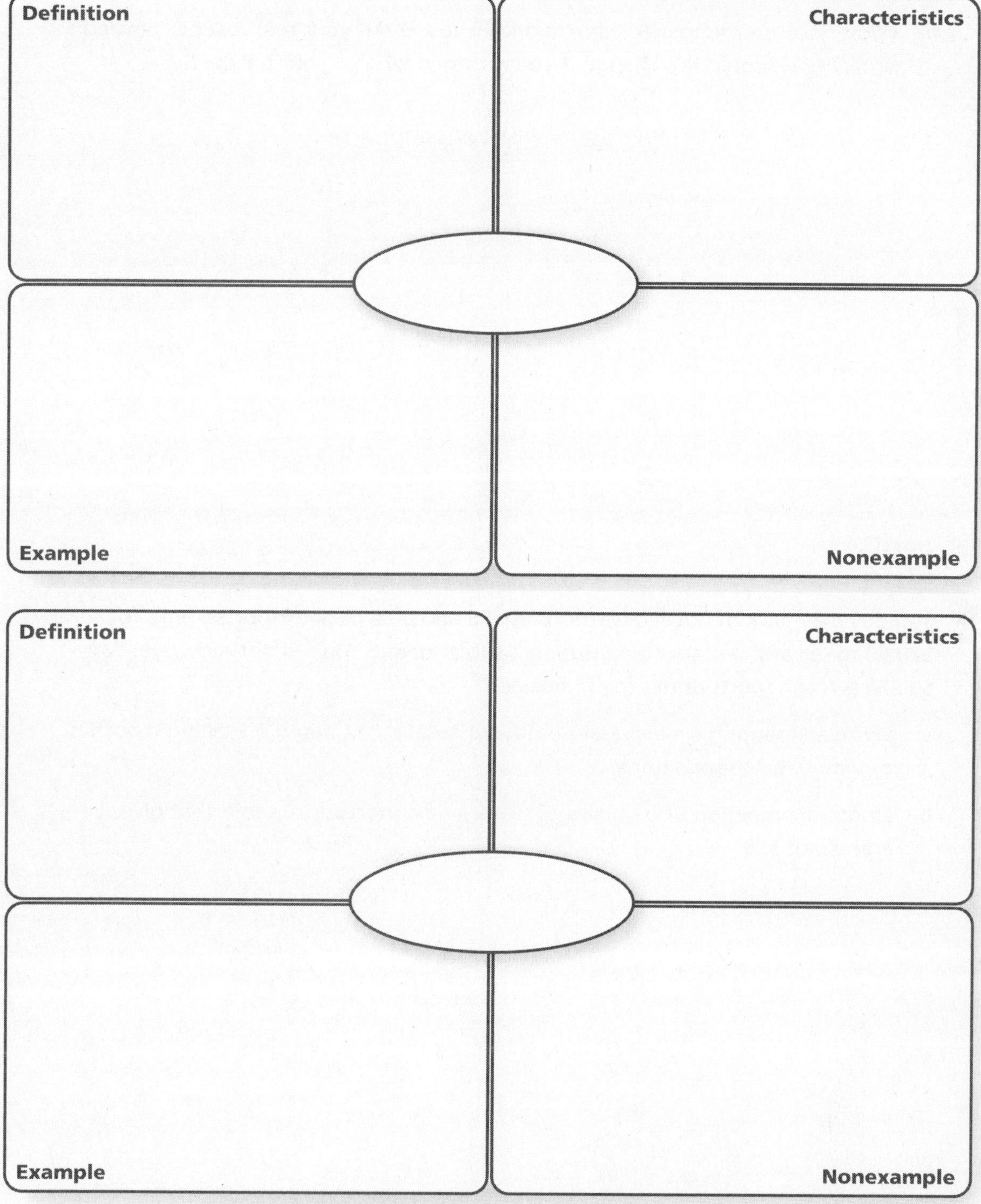

Pull It All Together

TASK 1

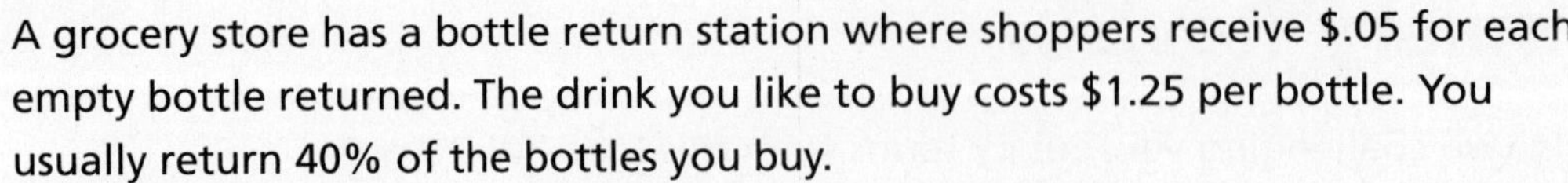

A grocery store has a bottle return station where shoppers receive $.05 for each empty bottle returned. The drink you like to buy costs $1.25 per bottle. You usually return 40% of the bottles you buy.

a. Write the simplify an expression to represent your final cost after you return 40% of the bottles you buy one month.

b. What does your simplified expression tell you about your real cost per bottled drink? How would this change if you returned 80% of your bottles?

TASK 2

You buy a 24-pack of bottled water for $4.25 and a 24-pack of sports drinks for $20.50 to sell at the snack stand during a soccer game. You sell bottled water for $1.25 each and sports drinks for $1.50 each.

a. Write and simplify an expression for your total profit based on selling b bottles of water and c sports drinks.

b. Find a combination of b bottles of water and c sports drinks sold that gives you a profit of $30.

11-1 # Solving Simple Equations

Digital Resources

CCSS: 7.EE.B.4: Use variables to represent quantities in a real-world or mathematical problem, and construct simple equations and inequalities to solve problems by reasoning about the quantities. Also, **7.EE.B.4a.**

Launch

MP1, MP7

A shaky egg bagel baker just wants to keep things equal. What should he charge for one bagel to match his cross-town rival?

Write and solve an equation to help him out. Explain your reasoning.

Reflect Can you represent this problem with more than one equation? Explain.

Got It?

PART 1 Got It

Solve the equation $b - 2 = -10$.

PART 2 Got It

Solve the equation $\frac{m}{0.5} = 11$. Check your answer.

PART 3 Got It

Which equation(s) have the same solution as $2.5a = 30$?

I. $\frac{4}{3}a = 16$

II. $a - 22.25 = -10.25$

Close and Check

Focus Question

 MP1, MP7

How can writing two equivalent expressions help you solve a problem?

Do you know HOW?

1. Solve the equation $g + 12 = 18$.

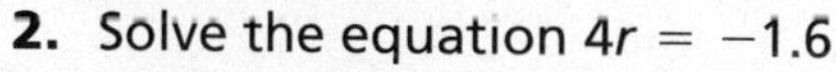

2. Solve the equation $4r = -1.6$.

3. Solve the equation $\frac{w}{2.5} = 9$.

4. Which equation(s) has the same solution as $\frac{d}{6} = 7.3$?

A. $d - 15.9 = 27.9$

B. $2d = 87.2$

C. $-49 + d = 5$

D. $\frac{d}{4} = 10.95$

Do you UNDERSTAND?

5. **Vocabulary** What does it mean to isolate the variable?

6. **Error Analysis** A classmate solves the equation shown below. Explain her error and find the correct solution.

$$5t = 65$$
$$5(5t) = 65(5)$$
$$t = 325$$

This page intentionally left blank.

11-2 Writing Two-Step Equations

Digital Resources

CCSS: 7.EE.B.4: Use variables to represent quantities in a real-world or mathematical problem, and construct simple equations and inequalities to solve problems by reasoning about the quantities. Also, **7.EE.B.4a.**

Launch

MP1, MP2

The shaky mini-cheese bagel baker can't figure out how to calculate the price of each bagel for bagels one to twelve.

Write an equation the bagel maker could use to calculate the cost of each of the first twelve bagels. Explain your reasoning.

Reflect Can you represent the value of the 13 bagels as $13 \cdot b$? Explain.

Got It?

PART 1 Got It

A zookeeper takes care of 5 mountain lions. The keeper orders 32.5 pounds of meat for them each day. Each mountain lion receives the same amount. What equation can you use to find how much meat each mountain lion eats in a day?

PART 2 Got It

You have a 125-pound calf that you are raising for a 4-H project. You expect the calf to gain 65 pounds per month. Write an equation to find how many months it will take for the calf to weigh 1,000 pounds.

PART 3 Got It

Write an equation to represent the following description.
Eight less than ten times a number is 36.

Discuss with a classmate
Divide the word sentence of the problem into three parts.
Read each part out loud.
Then show how you wrote each word phrase using math symbols.

Close and Check

Focus Question

MP1, MP6

What kinds of problems call for two operations?

Do you know HOW?

1. An animal shelter houses 32 cats. The workers use 24 cups of cat food each day. Write an equation to find how many cups of food per cat the shelter uses each day.

2. An apartment rents for $725 per month plus a security deposit. The total cost for the apartment is $9,300 for the first year. Write an equation to find the security deposit amount.

3. Write an equation to represent the following description.
   The difference of seven times a number and 15 is 41.

Do you UNDERSTAND?

4. **Writing** Describe your strategy for rewriting a word problem in the form of an equation.

5. **Reasoning** Is there more than one way to set up an equation based on a word problem? If so, give an example using Exercise 1, 2, or 3.

This page intentionally left blank.

11-3 Solving Two-Step Equations

Digital Resources

CCSS: 7.EE.B.3: Solve multi-step real-life and mathematical problems posed with positive and negative rational numbers … . **7.EE.B.4a:** Solve word problems leading to equations of the form $px + q = r$ … where p, q, and r are specific rational numbers … . Also, **7.EE.B.4.**

Launch

MP3, MP4

The shaky bagel baker decides to just divide by 13 to decide how much to charge for each bagel.

Does his method represent the per-bagel price his cross-town rival charges for bagels one to thirteen? Explain your reasoning.

Reflect What's the most important thing about solving equations? Explain.

Got It?

PART 1 Got It

Solve the equation $6x - 5 = 19$ using algebra tiles.

PART 2 Got It

Solve the equation $\frac{k}{2} + 7.3 = 29.3$.

PART 3 Got It

A boating club rents sail boats for $60 for the first hour and $20 for each additional hour. When you return your boat, your fee is $140. Write and solve an equation to find how many hours you kept the boat.

Close and Check

Focus Question

MP2, MP8

How is solving a two-step equation similar to solving a one-step equation?

Do you know HOW?

1. Write the modeled equation. Then solve it.

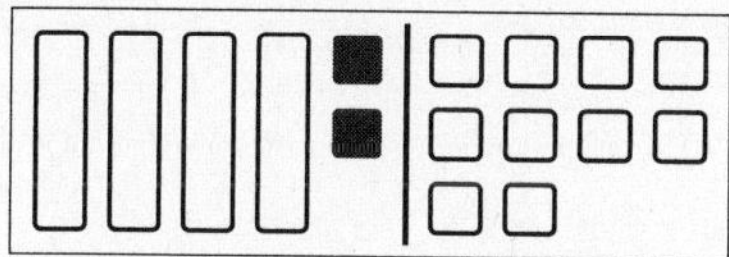

Equation:

Solution:

2. Solve the equation $24.8 = 6g + 10.4$.

Solution:

3. You open a savings account with \$30. You deposit an additional \$20 every week. Write and solve an equation to find how many weeks it will take you to save \$150.

Equation:

Solution:

Do you UNDERSTAND?

4. **Reasoning** Explain how to check the answer to Exercise 3.

5. **Error Analysis** Your friend says it will only take $4\frac{1}{2}$ weeks to save \$150 in the account from Exercise 3 because you have to subtract the original amount of the deposit, which is equal to $1\frac{1}{2}$ weeks. Do you agree? Explain.

This page intentionally left blank.

11-4

Solving Equations Using the Distributive Property

Digital Resources

CCSS: 7.EE.B.3: Solve multi-step real-life and mathematical problems posed with positive and negative rational numbers … . **7.EE.B.4a:** Solve word problems leading to equations of the form $px + q = r$ … where p, q, and r are specific rational numbers … . Also, **7.EE.B.4.**

Launch

MP2, MP4

The shaky bagel baker boldly decides to charge 5¢ more per bagel than his rival does for whole-wheat bagels.

Write an expression to show how he could figure out a per-dozen price. Explain your reasoning.

Expression

Reflect What is the difference between an expression and an equation?

Got It?

PART 1 Got It

Solve the equation $\frac{3}{4}(8b - 4) = -2$.

PART 2 Got It

Which equations require two or more operations to solve?

I. $\frac{4}{5}x = 20$ II. $-5(3x - 1) = 40$ III. $\frac{3}{5}x - 19 = 17$

Got It?

PART 3 Got It

You mailed 20 identical invitations weighing more than 1 ounce each. Mailing each invitation cost $.44 for the first ounce, plus $.17 for each additional ounce. The postage for all of the invitations cost $15.60. Write and solve an equation to find the weight of each invitation.

Close and Check

Focus Question

MP4, MP6

When is it useful to model a situation in two different ways?

Do you know HOW?

1. Solve the equation.
   $-3.2(5d - 7) = -17.6$

2. Circle the equation(s) that requires more than two operations to solve.

   A. $\frac{2}{3}x = -15$

   B. $3(5h + 9) = 57$

   C. $4(8s) - 6 = 218$

   D. $4.5(r + 1) = 27$

3. Three families each buy the same number of \$15 tickets to the zoo. Each family also pays \$5.50 for parking. The total cost is \$196.50. Write and solve an equation to find how many tickets each family buys.

   Equation:

   Solution:

Do you UNDERSTAND?

4. **Writing** Write a possible real-world problem to match the equation in Exercise 2, letter D.

5. **Error Analysis** A classmate says the first step to solve the equation $12(3g - 9) = 99$ is to add 9 to both sides. Do you agree? Explain.

11-5 Problem Solving

Digital Resources

CCSS: 7.EE.B.4: Use variables to represent quantities in a real-world or mathematical problem, and construct simple equations and inequalities to solve problems by reasoning about the quantities. Also, **7.EE.B.3** and **7.EE.B.4a.**

Launch

MP1, MP4

Use words to describe or a picture to model a real-world situation that relates to the equation shown. Your situation must somehow involve the secret ingredient, bagels. Go!

Reflect Does describing an equation with words or modeling it with a picture help you solve an equation? Explain.

Got It?

PART 1 Got It

A company is relocating their office to a larger office space. The manager rents a moving truck for $39.95 plus $.99 per mile. Before returning the truck, the manager fills the tank with gasoline, which costs $65.32. The total cost is $164.67. Make a bar diagram to find how many miles they drove the truck.

PART 2 Got It

Orcas swim at a rate of 704 feet per minute.

a. Solve the distance formula $d = rt$ for time t.

b. Find the time it will take for an orca to swim 26,400 feet.

PART 3 Got It

Write a baking problem that you can model with the equation $\frac{1}{2}r = 1\frac{2}{3}$.

Then solve the problem.

Close and Check

Focus Question

MP1, MP4

Real-world situations can be complicated or hard to understand. What can models and equations show better than words?

Do you know HOW?

1. At an arcade you buy 5 game cards and your friend buys 3 game cards. Your lunch costs $6 and your friend's lunch costs $4. Altogether, the two of you spend $50. Complete the bar diagram to find the cost of one game card.

2. How much does each game card cost?

3. A ruby-throated hummingbird flies 9 miles in 20 minutes. Use the formula to find its average speed in miles per hour.

$$d = rt$$

Do you UNDERSTAND?

4. **Writing** Explain how formulas are helpful in problem solving.

5. **Reasoning** A classmate solves Exercise 3 by using division. Is this a reasonable method? Explain.

This page intentionally left blank.

11-R Topic Review

New Vocabulary: Addition Property of Equality, Division Property of Equality, isolate a variable, Multiplication Property of Equality, Subtraction Property of Equality
Review Vocabulary: Distributive Property, equation, two-step equation

Vocabulary Review

Identify two challenging vocabulary terms from this topic. Write one vocabulary term in the center oval, and fill in the surrounding boxes with details that will help you better understand the term.

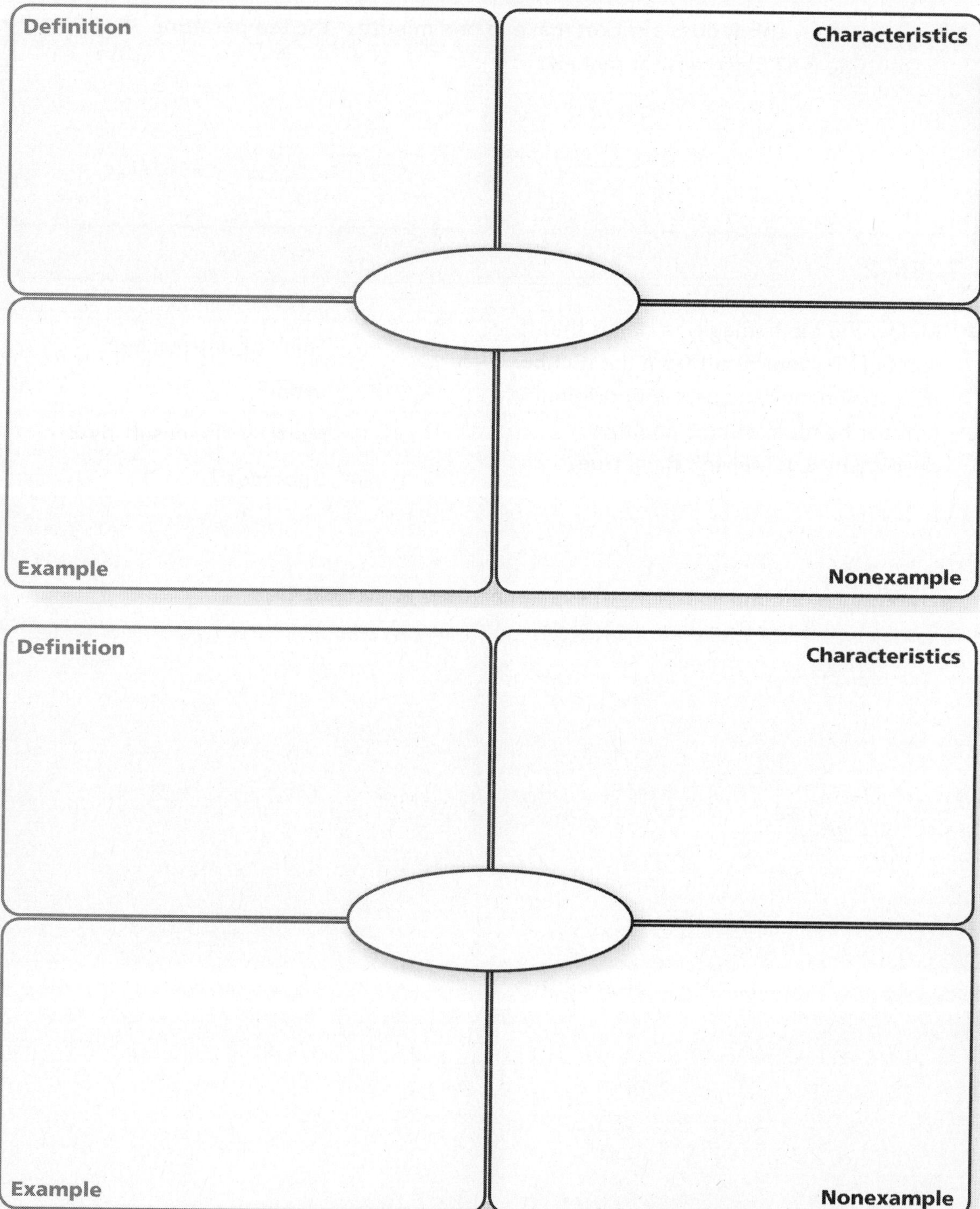

Pull It All Together

TASK 1

This formula relates temperature in degrees Fahrenheit (f), to the number of cricket chirps (n) in one minute.

$$f = 50 + \left(\frac{n - 40}{4}\right)$$

a. Solve the formula for n.

b. How many chirps does a cricket make in one minute if the temperature outside is 67.5 degrees Fahrenheit?

TASK 2

Melvin the Mathemagician claims that if you tell him your result from the number trick shown, he can guess your original number by subtracting 5 and then dividing by 2. Is Melvin's claim true?

Step 1 Think of any number.
Step 2 Add 3.
Step 3 Multiply the result by 2.
Step 4 Subtract 1.

Use expressions and equations to explain his "secret method."

12-1

Solving Two-Step Equations

Digital Resources

CCSS: 8.EE.C.7: Solve linear equations in one variable. **8.EE.C.7b:** Solve linear equations with rational number coefficients, including equations whose solutions require expanding expressions using the distributive property and collecting like terms.

Launch

MP2, MP4

Two friends shovel snow on a winter Saturday. Some people pay them their fee by handing them cash. Some give them their fee in an envelope. They split the money they make evenly.

What is their shoveling fee? Explain how you know.

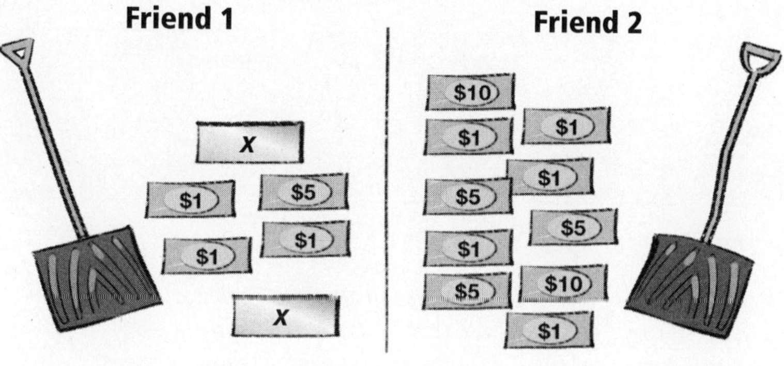

Reflect Could you write an equation for this problem? How might that help?

Got It?

PART 1 Got It

Solve $47 = -3 + 8y$.

PART 2 Got It

A family rents a moving van for $34.99 plus $.59 per mile. The bill is $148.86. Write and solve an equation to determine how many miles the family drove.

Discuss with a classmate

Compare the equations that you wrote for the problem.
How were they alike? How were they different?
Was one equation better than the other? What made it the better equation?

Got It?

PART 3 Got It

A plumber buys 20 feet of pipe in February and 35 feet of pipe in March. He spends a total of $384.45. What is the cost of the pipe, per foot?

Close and Check

Focus Question

MP7, MP8

What kinds of problems need two operations?

Do you know HOW?

1. Solve for x.

$$63 = 12x - 9$$

$x =$

2. A cell phone plan includes a monthly rate of \$19.95 plus \$0.55 per minute for international calls. The bill is \$95.30. Write and solve an equation to determine how many minutes were spent on international calls.

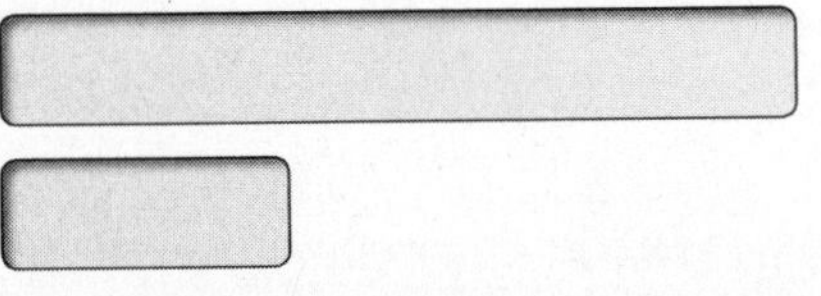

3. A family buys 132 ft^2 of carpet for the guest bedroom and 270 ft^2 of carpet for the family room. They spend \$1,201.98 on new carpet. What is the average cost per square foot for the new carpeting?

Do you UNDERSTAND?

4. Reasoning Which operation did you use first to solve Exercise 1? Explain.

5. Error Analysis A classmate solves the equation shown. Explain his error and tell how you would solve it.

$$1.25x + 7.4 = 10.4$$

$$100(1.25x) + 10(7.4) = 10(10.4)$$

$$125x + 74 = 104$$

$$125x = 30$$

$$x = 0.24$$

Writing and Solving Equations with Variables on Both Sides

Digital Resources

CCSS: 8.EE.C.7: Solve linear equations in one variable. **8.EE.C.7b:** Solve linear equations with rational number coefficients, including equations whose solutions require expanding expressions using the distributive property and collecting like terms.

Launch

MP2, MP4

Two friends mow lawns on a spring Saturday. Some people pay them their fee by handing them cash. Some people give them their fee in an envelope. They split the money they make evenly.

What is their lawn-mowing fee? Explain how you know.

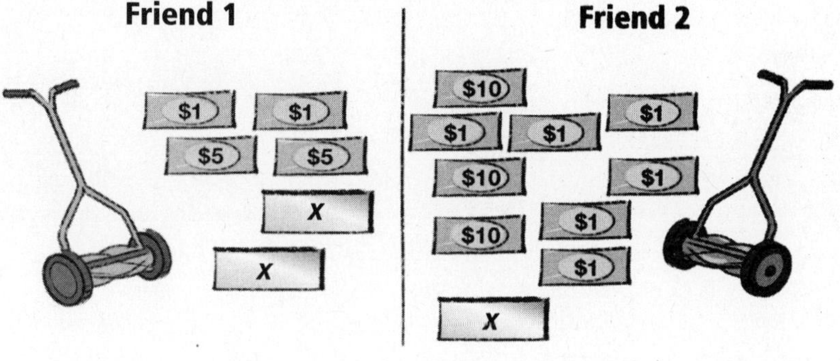

Reflect In the snow-shoveling problem in Lesson 12-1, only one friend had an envelope. The other friend had all cash. Was this problem more difficult because both friends had envelopes? Explain.

Got It?

PART 1 Got It

What is the value of x when the expression $12x + 7$ equals the expression $-8 + 13x$? Use algebra tiles to model the equation.

PART 2 Got It

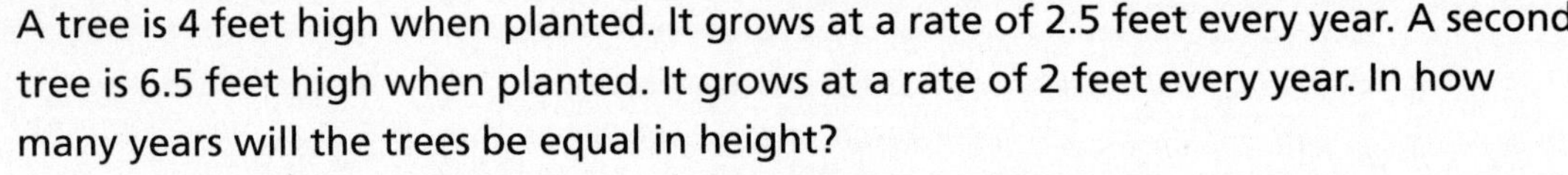

A tree is 4 feet high when planted. It grows at a rate of 2.5 feet every year. A second tree is 6.5 feet high when planted. It grows at a rate of 2 feet every year. In how many years will the trees be equal in height?

Got It?

PART 3 Got It

Solve $210t - 68 = 56t + 1{,}164$.

Close and Check

Focus Question

MP3, MP8

Why do some equations have the same variable on both sides?

Do you know HOW?

1. What is the value of x when the expression $3x + 6$ equals the expression $-15 + 6x$?

   $x =$ ☐

2. Two friends race. The first friend gets a head start and runs at a steady rate of 0.20 miles per minute. The second friend waits 1 minute and then runs at a steady rate of 0.25 miles per minute. How long will it take for the second runner to catch up with the first?

3. Solve $72x + 436 = -96x + 1108$.

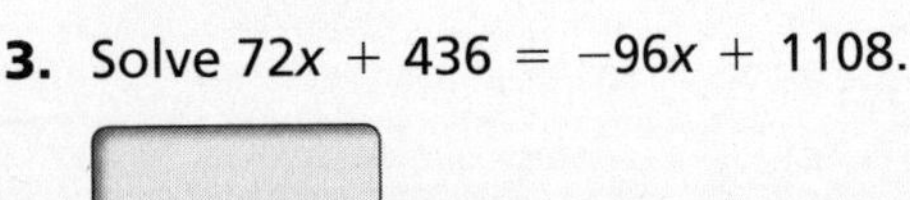

4. You have $12.50 in a savings account. You deposit $7.25 more each week. Your friend has $32.50 in a savings account. She deposits $5.25 more each week. In how many weeks will the amount of money in the accounts be equal?

 weeks

Do you UNDERSTAND?

5. **Reasoning** If the two friends in Exercise 2 race for 4 miles at their constant rates, who will win the race? Explain.

6. **Compare and Contrast** How is solving an equation with the variable on both sides of the equation the same as and different from solving an equation with the variable on one side of the equation?

12-3 Solving Equations Using the Distributive Property

Digital Resources

CCSS: 8.EE.C.7b: Solve linear equations with rational number coefficients, including equations whose solutions require expanding expressions using the distributive property and collecting like terms.

Launch

MP2, MP6

Match the equivalent expressions. Tell how you know your matches are correct.

$-3(-s + 5)$	$3s - 15$	$3(-s + 5)$
$-3(s - 5)$	$-3s + 15$	$3(s - 5)$

Reflect Which expressions were the simplest to match? Which were the hardest to match? Explain.

Got It?

PART 1 Got It

Use the Distributive Property to solve $3e - 8 = 2(e - 4)$.

PART 2 Got It

Describe and correct the error in the following student's work.

Student C

$$3 - \left(y + \frac{1}{2}\right) = 8$$

$$3 - 3 - \left(y + \frac{1}{2}\right) = 8 - 3$$

$$-y + \frac{1}{2} = 5$$

$$-y + \frac{1}{2} - \frac{1}{2} = 5 - \frac{1}{2}$$

$$-y = 4\frac{1}{2}$$

$$y = -4\frac{1}{2}$$

Got It?

PART 3 Got It

The length of a rectangle is 7 ft longer than its width. The perimeter of the rectangle is 26 ft. Write an equation to represent the perimeter in terms of its width w. What is the length of the rectangle?

Discuss with a classmate

Draw a diagram of the rectangle and label all the given information from the problem. Then explain what information you used to write the equation to solve the problem. If your equations don't agree, find the error in the reasoning for the equation that contains an error.

Close and Check

Focus Question

How can you model a problem with an equation that uses the Distributive Property?

Do you know HOW?

1. Use the Distributive Property to solve $3(11r - 13) = -7r + 57 + 32r$.

2. Circle the correct solution to the equation $\frac{7}{9}x - 6 = 17$.

A. $\frac{9}{7}\left(\frac{7}{9}x\right) - 6 = \frac{9}{7}(17)$

$x - 6 = \frac{153}{7}$

$x = \frac{153}{7} + \frac{42}{7}$

$x = \frac{195}{7}$

B. $\frac{7}{9}x = 17 + 6$

$\frac{9}{7}\left(\frac{7}{9}x\right) = \frac{9}{7}(23)$

$x = \frac{207}{7}$

3. The width of a rectangle is 17 yd shorter than the length. The perimeter of the rectangle is 126 yd. Find the width of the rectangle.

Do you UNDERSTAND?

4. Error Analysis Explain the error made in the incorrect solution in Exercise 2.

5. Reasoning Write an equation for the perimeter of the rectangle in Exercise 3 in terms of the length ℓ. How is this equation different than an equation for the perimeter in terms of the width w?

12-4

Solutions – One, None, or Infinitely Many

Digital Resources

CCSS: 8.EE.C.7: Solve linear equations in one variable. 8.EE.C.7a: Give examples of linear equations … with one solution, infinitely many solutions, or no solutions. Show which … is the case by successively transforming the given equation into simpler forms … .

Launch

MP2, MP7, MP8

Evaluate each expression using different values for s. Then, tell what you know about the expressions.

s	$3(4s + 8)$	$2(12 + 6s)$

Reflect Could you have reached the same conclusion about the expressions without trying different values for s? Explain.

Got It?

PART 1 Got It (1 of 2)

What should you conclude if, after solving an equation, the result is $\frac{1}{2} = \frac{2}{3}$?

PART 1 Got It (2 of 2)

a. Write a linear equation in one variable that has no solution.

b. Write a linear equation in one variable that has infinitely many solutions.

PART 2 Got It (1 of 2)

Solve $4(n - 2) - 1 = 5n - n + 9$.

Got It?

PART 2 Got It (2 of 2)

At what point in the solution below do you first recognize that the equation has no solution? Explain.

	$4(n - 2) - 1 = 5n - n + 9$
Use the Distributive Property.	$4n - 8 - 1 = 5n - n + 9$
Combine like terms.	$4n - 9 = 4n + 9$
Subtract $4n$ from each side.	$4n - 4n - 9 = 4n - 4n + 9$
Combine like terms.	$0 - 9 = 0 + 9$
Simplify.	$-9 \neq 9$

PART 3 Got It (1 of 2)

Solve $r = 5r - 3r - r$.

PART 3 Got It (2 of 2)

At what point in the solution below do you first recognize that the equation has no solution? Explain.

	$9 + 4p - 2 = p + 3p + 7$
Use the Commutative Property.	$9 - 2 + 4p = p + 3p + 7$
Combine like terms.	$7 + 4p = 4p + 7$
Subtract $4p$ from each side.	$7 + 4p - 4p = 4p - 4p + 7$
Combine like terms.	$7 = 7$

Close and Check

Focus Question

What does it mean if an equation is simplified to $0 = 0$? Do all problems have exactly one solution?

Do you know HOW?

1. Write *none, one,* or *many* to identify the number of solutions to each equation.

   $\frac{2}{3}x + 15 = \frac{4}{6}x + 15$

   $6 = 3^2$

   $2.7y - 9 = 18$

2. Solve $5(12 - d) + d = 2d - 6$.

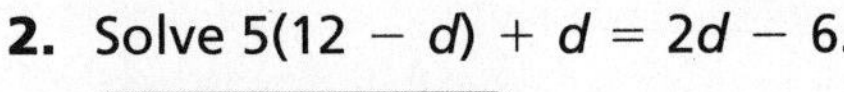

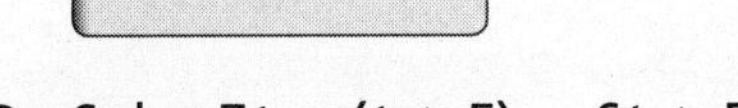

3. Solve $7t - (t + 5) = 6t + 5$.

4. Solve $\frac{2}{3}\left(9s - \frac{3}{2}\right) = s(0.45 + 5) + 1.2$.

Do you UNDERSTAND?

5. **Writing** Explain how to identify whether an equation has no solution, one solution, or infinitely many solutions.

6. **Error Analysis** A classmate solves the equation $8 + 2(8r - 2r) = 4(3r + 2)$. She says $r = 0$ is the only solution. Is she correct? Explain.

12-5 Problem Solving

Digital Resources

CCSS: 8.EE.C.7: Solve linear equations in one variable. 8.EE.C.7a: Give examples of linear equations in one variable with one solution, infinitely many solutions, or no solutions … .

Launch

MP3, MP4

Two friends argue over how much to bill for a two-hour raking job. They charge their normal hourly rate plus $2.75 for lawn bags.

Write and solve equations to show how each friend could be correct. Then tell who you think is right and why.

Reflect How did the money problem context affect the solution to this problem? Explain.

Got It?

PART 1 Got It

A small coffee distributor spends $7,860 per month on business expenses and $4.25 to produce each bag of coffee. It charges $12 for one bag of coffee. How many bags of coffee must the company sell in one month in order for its sales to equal its monthly costs?

PART 2 Got It

When you count by ones from any integer, you are counting consecutive integers. You can represent consecutive integers as x, $x + 1$, $x + 2$, $x + 3$, ...

The sum of three consecutive integers is -255. What are the three integers?

PART 3 Got It

Health Club A charges a $160 sign-up fee and $25 per month. Health Club B charges a $40 sign-up fee and $65 per month. In how many months will the total cost of membership at Club A be equal to the total cost of membership at Club B?

Close and Check

Focus Question

MP4, MP6

If you can describe a situation in two different ways, how do you use that information to solve a problem?

Do you know HOW?

1. A delivery driver earns $7.50 per hour and $2 per delivery. Each week, the driver spends $28 on vehicle maintenance and $86 on gas. If the driver works 40 hours per week, how many deliveries are needed each week to earn $300 a week after expenses?

☐ deliveries

2. The total cost, after additional fees, for three tickets to the dinner theater is $322.92. The fees include a 2% service charge and a 15% gratuity. What is the cost of one dinner theater ticket before the fees are added?

☐

3. Craft club members pay $39 a year plus $9 for each craft kit. Non-members can buy craft kits for $12 each. How many kits will have to be bought for the price of membership and non-membership to be equal?

☐ kits

Do you UNDERSTAND?

4. Writing Two students solve the equation. Can both students be correct? Explain.

$$5(3r - 6) = 10r - 10$$

Student A	Student B
$15r - 30 = 10r - 10$	$3r - 6 = 2r - 2$
$5r = 20$	$r = 4$
$r = 4$	

5. Reasoning Would Student B's method work if the equation were $5(3r - 6) = 11r - 14$? Explain.

This page intentionally left blank.

12-R Topic Review

New Vocabulary: infinitely many solutions, no solution
Review Vocabulary: Commutative Property, Distributive Property, least common multiple, order of operations, solution of an equation

Vocabulary Review

Identify two challenging vocabulary terms from this topic. Write one vocabulary term in the center oval, and fill in the surrounding boxes with details that will help you better understand the term.

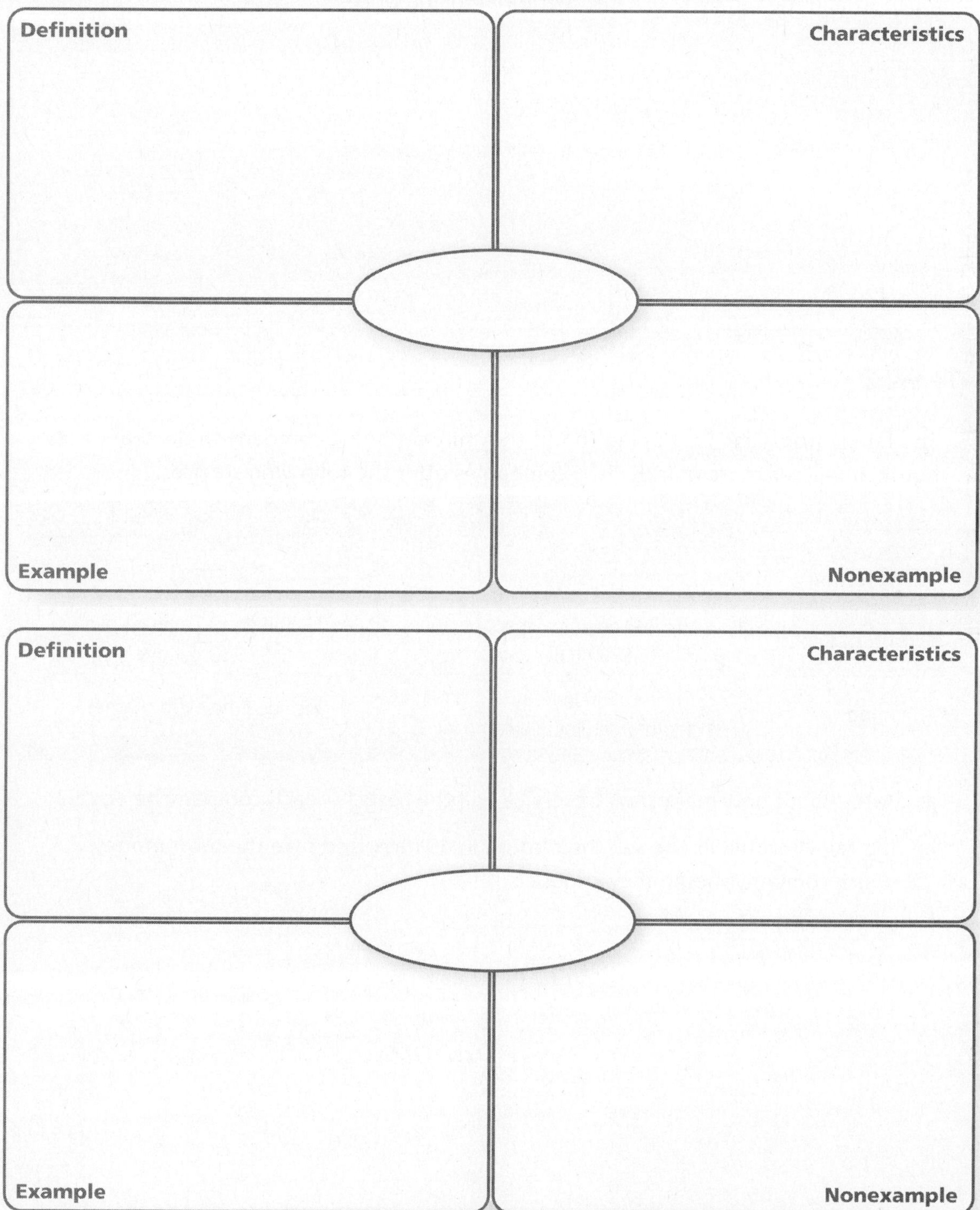

Pull It All Together

TASK 1

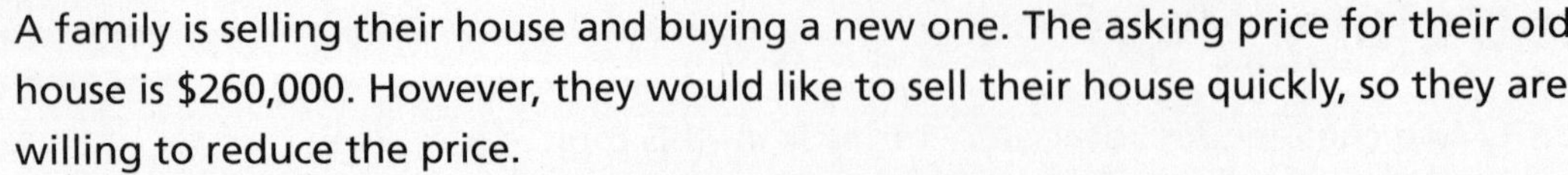

A family is selling their house and buying a new one. The asking price for their old house is $260,000. However, they would like to sell their house quickly, so they are willing to reduce the price.

20% of the new price must pay a $50,440 down payment on the new house. How much should the family take off the original selling price?

TASK 2

The family from Task 1 is hoping that if they hire a staging company to decorate their house, it will sell more quickly. Two companies offer the following services.

Service	Company A	Company B
Consultation	$600	$950
Furniture Rental	$1,200 down payment plus $26.66 per day	$1,350 down payment plus $23.33 per day
Cleaning	$30 per day (no charge first and last day)	Included (no extra charge)

a. After about how many days of service will the costs for each company be equal?

b. If a family would like to sell their house in 45 days, and save the most money, which company should they choose?

13-1

Solving Simple Inequalities

Digital Resources

CCSS: 7.EE.B.4: Use variables to represent quantities in a real-world or mathematical problem, and construct simple inequalities to solve problems by reasoning about the quantities. 7.EE.B.4b: … Graph the solution set of the inequality.

Launch

MP3, MP4

A superstar challenges a track team's top three runners to beat his 100-meter time. "You can take 5 seconds from your times and still not best it," he says. Two runners fail. One runner doesn't.

Show their possible times and how you know you're right.

9.95 sec

100 m

Runner 1:

Runner 2:

Runner 3:

Reflect How many possible times minus 5 seconds could beat the runner's record? Explain.

Got It?

PART 1 Got It

Write an inequality to represent the following statement.

You drank less than $2\frac{1}{2}$ cups of water today.

PART 2 Got It (1 of 2)

Solve $8 + r \leq 22.5$. Graph the solutions.

Got It?

PART 2 Got It (2 of 2)

Describe the error in the student's work in graphing the solution of $-3 < t + 3.6$.

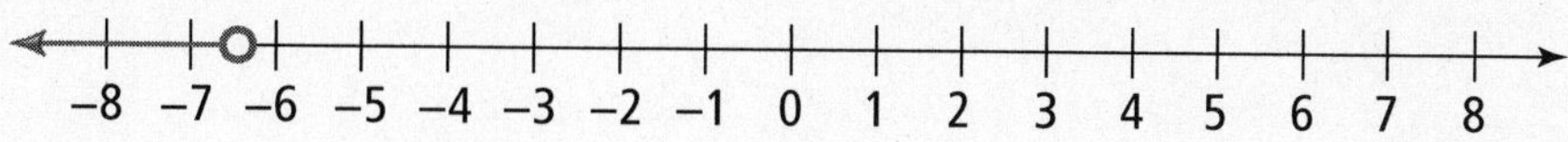

PART 3 Got It

A number minus $3\frac{2}{5}$ is more than 17. Write and solve an inequality. Check your answer.

Close and Check

Focus Question

MP2, MP3

How is the solution to an inequality different from the solution to an equation?

Do you know HOW?

1. Use the symbol, $<$, $\leq$, $>$, $\geq$, $=$, or $\neq$, that best represents the statement.

   I walked no more than 12 blocks.

   b  12

2. Solve $12.5 + c > 27.3$.

3. Graph $r \geq -3$.

   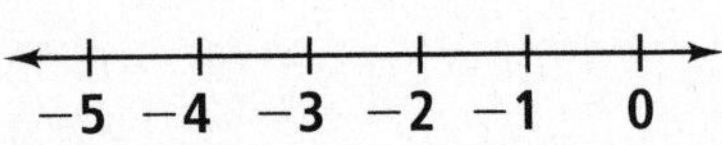

4. Write and solve an inequality to represent the statement.

   $14\frac{3}{5}$ is less than $3\frac{1}{5}$ fewer than a number.

   Inequality:

   Solution:

Do you UNDERSTAND?

5. **Reasoning** Can the solution to an inequality ever be equal to only one value? Explain.

6. **Error Analysis** A classmate solves and graphs the inequality $-7 + k \leq 3$. Is her work correct? Explain.

   $k \leq 10$

   7 8 9 10 11 12

13-2

Solving Inequalities Using Multiplication or Division

Digital Resources

CCSS: 7.EE.B.4: Use variables to represent quantities in a real-world or mathematical problem, and construct simple inequalities to solve problems by reasoning about the quantities. **7.EE.B.4b:** … Graph the solution set of the inequality.

Launch

MP1, MP4

The superstar runner says he can beat the track team's best 400 m time four straight times. "You can double my time each time I run, and I'll be fine," he says. The superstar succeeds three times and fails the fourth.

Show his possible times and how you know you're right.

Track Team Record

Run 1:

Run 2:

Run 3:

Run 4:

Reflect Did the superstar have to run a specific time to back his claim about beating the track team's time? Explain.

Got It?

PART 1 Got It

A mouse drinks at least 0.042 L of water a week. How many liters of water does a mouse drink in a day, on average?

Write and solve an inequality.

PART 2 Got It

Solve $-3.8g \geq 30.4$.

Got It?

PART 3 Got It (1 of 2)

What is the solution of $\frac{1}{12}b \leq \frac{1}{12}$?

PART 3 Got It (2 of 2)

If half of a number is less than 100, what is a possible value of the number?

Do not write and solve an inequality. Instead, make a conjecture about the solution.

Close and Check

Focus Question

MP6, MP7

The *concept of balance* plays a large role when you solve equations. What role does the *concept of balance* play when you solve inequalities?

Do you know HOW?

1. A rain forest receives up to 260 inches of rain each year. On average, how many inches of rain fall each month? Write and solve an inequality. Round your answer to the nearest tenth of an inch.

Inequality:

Solution:

Inches of Rain:

2. Solve $-3.7y \geq 9.62$.

3. Solve $\frac{s}{-4} < 14$.

4. Movie tickets cost at least $8. You want to buy as many tickets as possible with $36. Write and solve an inequality. Tell how many tickets you can buy.

Inequality:

Solution:

Tickets:

Do you UNDERSTAND?

5. Reasoning What values of x make the statement below false? Explain.

$$3x \geq 2x$$

6. Error Analysis A classmate solves the inequality $-5b > 40$. Her solution is shown below. Explain how to use substitution to determine if her solution is correct.

$$b > -8$$

13-3 Solving Two-Step Inequalities

Digital Resources

CCSS: 7.EE.B.4: Use variables to represent quantities … and construct simple inequalities … .
7.EE.B.4b: Solve problems leading to inequalities of the form $px + q > r$ or $px + q < r$, where p, q, and r are rational numbers. Graph the solution set … and interpret it in the context … .

Launch

MP3, MP4

The superstar runner challenges the track team to a bowling match. "You can each double your score and include 10 more, and I'll still top the top score," he says.

All three team members who try beat the runner using his scoring method. Show their possible scores and explain your reasoning.

Track Team Bowler 1:

Track Team Bowler 2:

Track Team Bowler 3:

Reflect Are there an infinite number of scores that could beat the superstar runner's boast? Explain.

Got It?

PART 1 Got It

Half of a number t plus 25.9 is at most 203.56.
Write an inequality that represents the situation.

PART 2 Got It (1 of 2)

The magician's assistant needs to rope off a rectangle for his most famous trick. The length of the rectangle must be exactly 7.5 ft, but he has at most 24 ft of rope to use. What are the possible widths of the rectangle?
Write, graph, and solve an inequality.

Got It?

PART 2 Got It (2 of 2)

The assistant is making a rectangle with a length of 7.5 ft and has at most 24 ft of rope to use. So the width w of the rectangle is $w \leq 4.5$ ft.
Do you think that all values that satisfy the inequality $w \leq 4.5$ ft are reasonable solutions? Explain your reasoning.

PART 3 Got It

What is the solution of $4f - 8 \geq -21$?

Close and Check

Focus Question

MP1, MP8

What kinds of problems call for two operations?

Do you know HOW?

1. You have \$54 to take yourself and some friends to the movies. Movie tickets cost \$8.50 each. Write and solve an inequality to find how many tickets you can buy if you also want to spend \$11.50 on snacks at the concession stand.

   Inequality:

   Solution:

2. Write and solve an inequality to represent 19 less than the product of −7 and a number is greater than or equal to 23.

   Inequality:

   Solution:

3. Write and solve an inequality to represent the difference of 3 times a number and 18 is less than 63.

   Inequality:

   Solution:

Do you UNDERSTAND?

4. **Writing** Explain how solving an inequality by multiplying or dividing by a negative value affects the solution. Why is the solution affected this way?

5. **Vocabulary** Explain how to solve an inequality by finding equivalent inequalities.

13-4 Solving Multi-Step Inequalities

Digital Resources

CCSS: **7.EE.B.4:** Use variables to represent quantities … and construct simple inequalities … .
7.EE.B.4b: Solve problems leading to inequalities of the form $px + q > r$ or $px + q < r$, where p, q, and r are rational numbers. Graph the solution set … and interpret it in the context … .

Launch

MP3, MP6

You and a friend spend Friday nights quizzing each other on math problems. Just as your friend races to show you the solution to $-2(x + 5.5) = 20$, you say, "I meant $-2(x + 5.5) > 20$."

Did your friend waste her time solving the equation? Explain.

Reflect How is solving an inequality alike and different from solving an equation? Explain.

Got It?

PART 1 Got It

Solve $56 > 231(q - 35)$ and graph the solution.

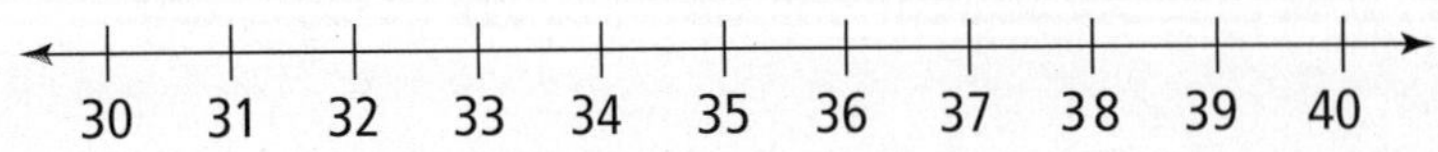

PART 2 Got It

Solve $3\frac{2}{5}w + 1\frac{4}{5}w \leq 26$.

Got It?

PART 3 Got It (1 of 2)

Find, describe, and correct the error in the student work shown.

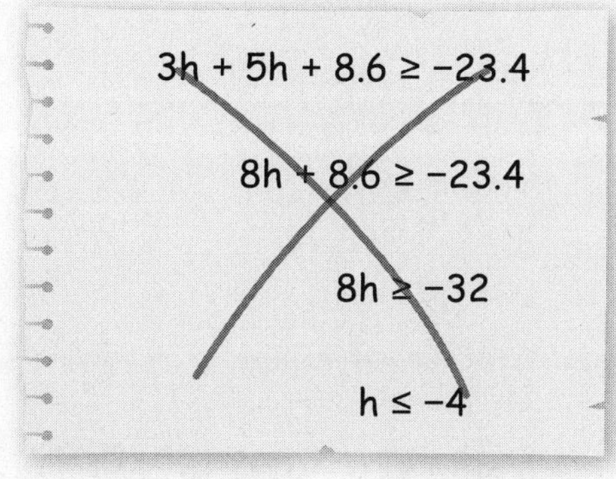
$3h + 5h + 8.6 \geq -23.4$

$8h + 8.6 \geq -23.4$

$8h \geq -32$

$h \leq -4$

PART 3 Got It (2 of 2)

Your friend says that the solution of $2(m + 3) < 10$ is $m > 2$. Give a counterexample to show that she is incorrect.

Close and Check

Focus Question

How is it possible for two different inequalities to describe the same situation? What does it mean for two inequalities to be equivalent?

Do you know HOW?

1. Solve $58 \leq 29(7 - r)$.

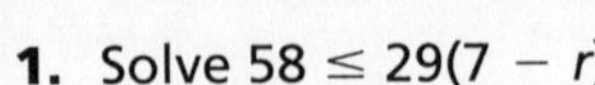

2. Graph the solution to Exercise 1.

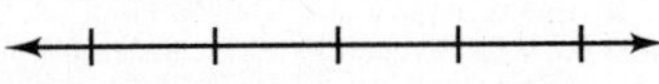

3. Solve $12.3g + 7.9g + 15.86 > 70.4$.

4. Graph the solution to Exercise 3.

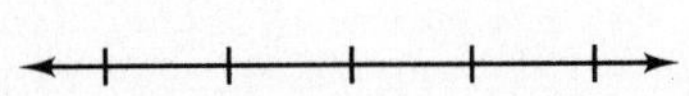

5. Your friend makes $15 each week babysitting. She makes $7.50 a week doing yard work. How many weeks will it take her to make more than $75?

 weeks

Do you UNDERSTAND?

6. **Writing** Explain how to check the solution to Exercise 1.

7. **Error Analysis** A classmate writes the solution to $-10r - 2r - 2 < 22$. Use a counterexample to show that she is incorrect, and explain her error.

$r < -2$

13-5 Problem Solving

Digital Resources

CCSS: 7.EE.B.4: Use variables to represent quantities in a real-world or mathematical problem, and construct simple inequalities to solve problems by reasoning about the quantities. **7.EE.B.4b:** Solve word problems leading to inequalities of the form $px + q > r$ or $px + q < r$ ... .

Launch

MP1, MP6

The Friday night math club wants to beat last year's fund drive of $40.25. The superstar runner shows his support by buying two club mugs.

Write and solve an inequality to show how many more mugs the club needs to sell to beat last year's total. Explain your reasoning.

Reflect Is an equation or an inequality better for solving this problem? Explain.

Got It?

PART 1 Got It

Write an inequality that has the solution $n \leq 8$.

PART 2 Got It

A salesperson has $375.80 in a savings account. Each week, she earns $865 and deposits 10% of the check into the account. After how many weeks will she have more than $1,000 in the account?

Got It?

PART 3 Got It

In the first quarter of the year, an applesauce company sells 721 units in the first month, 724 units in the second month, and 723 units in the third month.

How many units do they need to sell in the fourth month to average at least 724 units sold per month?

Close and Check

Focus Question

MP4, MP8

How can we describe problem situations that do not involve equal relationships?

Do you know **HOW?**

1. A credit card has a balance of $5,245 plus an interest of 13% of the balance. Write an inequality to find how much the cardholder will need to pay to bring the balance below $5,500.

2. For Exercise 1, what is the minimum amount the cardholder needs to pay to bring the balance below $5,500?

3. Write a 1-step inequality and a 2-step inequality that each have the solution $x > -12$.

   1-step:

   2-step:

4. The revenue from your lemonade stand is $R = 2(g - 10) + 50$ where g is the glasses of lemonade you sell. The cost to keep the stand running is $236. How many whole cups of lemonade do you have to sell to make a profit?

   Cups:

Do you **UNDERSTAND?**

5. **Writing** Give an example of how writing an inequality can help you make a decision in real life.

6. **Reasoning** The bank charges a low-balance fee to customers when their checking accounts fall below $100. A customer spends $27.50 at the grocery store. Can writing an inequality help the customer avoid the fee? Explain.

13-R Topic Review

New Vocabulary: equivalent inequalities, inequality, solution of an inequality
Review Vocabulary: Distributive Property, isolate a variable, negative number, positive number

Vocabulary Review

Identify two challenging vocabulary terms from this topic. Write one vocabulary term in the center oval, and fill in the surrounding boxes with details that will help you better understand the term.

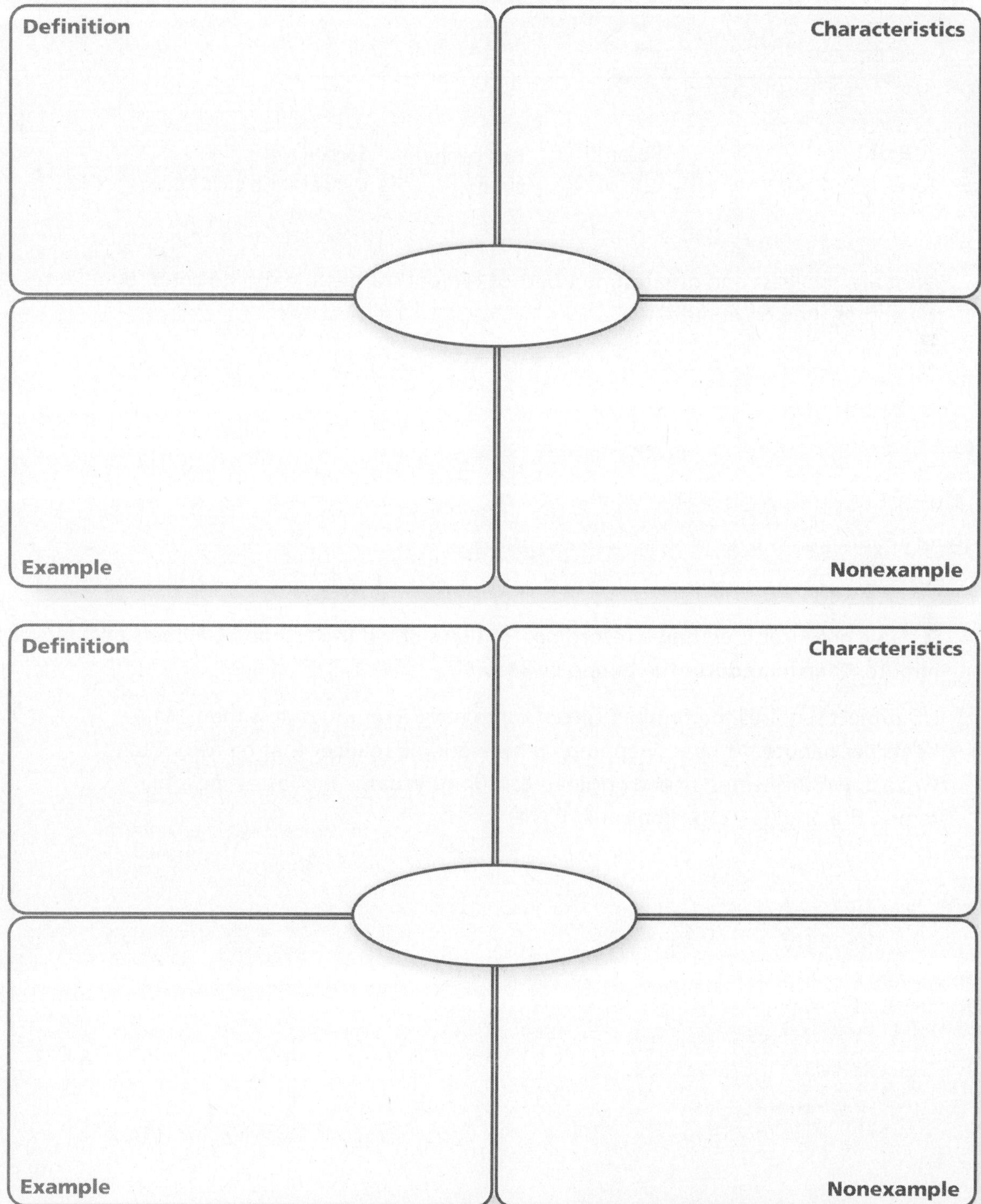

Pull It All Together

TASK 1

A *Moderato* piece of music has a tempo range of 66–126 beats per minute. A conductor is rehearsing the first minute of a *Moderato* piece. The diagram below shows how the conductor is going to monitor the beats for the piece. She counts the first 16 beats herself and then listens for the cymbal crashes (every 8 beats) for the remaining beats.

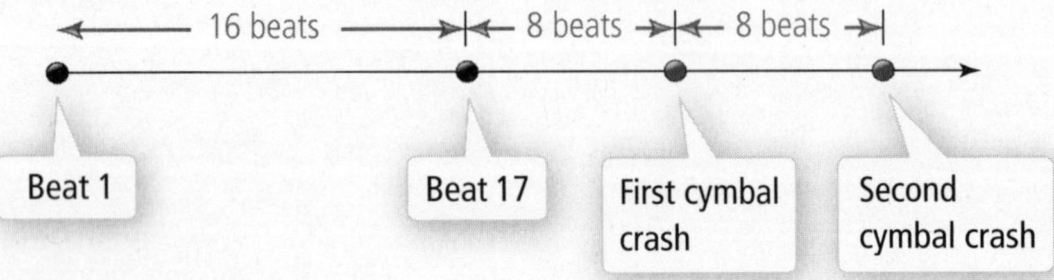

What are the least and greatest numbers of cymbal crashes she should count by the end of the first minute?

TASK 2

A music producer is editing a recording. He slows down the tempo by 8 beats per minute. Then he reduces the tempo by 15%.

His project requires the finished recording to have a tempo of less than 144.4 beats per minute. As he is wrapping up his work, he realizes that he forgot to write down the tempo of the original recording! What is the fastest possible tempo the original recording could have?

14-1

Graphing Proportional Relationships

Digital Resources

CCSS: 8.EE.B.5: Graph proportional relationships, interpreting the unit rate as the slope of the graph. Compare two different proportional relationships represented in different ways.

Launch

MP2, MP6

Make a graph based on the data in the table. Give the graph a title and label the axes so it's clear what the variables could represent.

Independent Variable	Dependent Variable
0	0
1	4
2	8
3	12
8	32

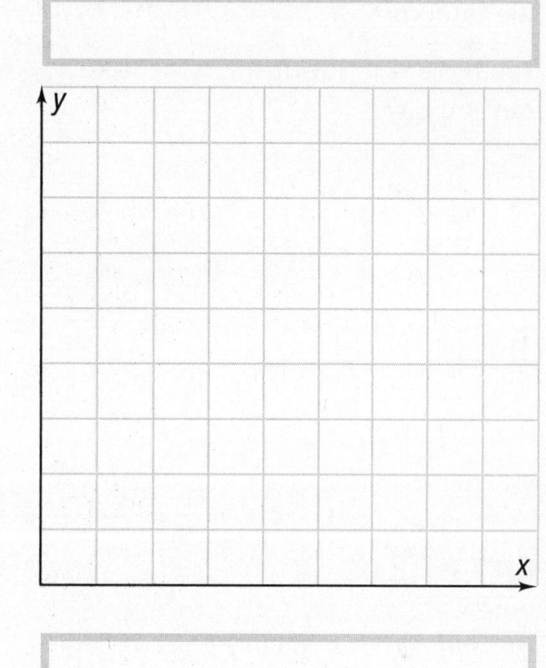

Reflect Does the table represent a proportional relationship? Explain.

Got It?

PART 1 Got It

Your school is selling raffle tickets as a fundraiser. The raffle tickets are sold in groups of 4 for $3. Draw a graph to model this situation where the horizontal axis is the number of raffle tickets purchased and the vertical axis is the total cost.

You have $21. How many raffle tickets can you buy?

PART 2 Got It

At some airports you pay a tax of 14% on the cost of a car rental. Draw a graph to model this situation where the horizontal axis is the cost of the car rental and the vertical axis is the amount of the tax. Is the amount you pay in tax proportional to the cost of your car rental? How do you know?

Got It?

PART 3 Got It

A drill makes a well by tunneling down into the ground. A certain drill can tunnel down 10 m every 8 h. Draw a graph to model this situation where the horizontal axis is time and the vertical axis is the position of the drill head relative to the surface.

Is the position of the drill head relative to the surface proportional to time? How do you know?

Close and Check

Focus Question

What does the graph of a proportional relationship look like? When and how can a graph of a proportional relationship be helpful?

Do you know HOW?

1. You earn $4 in Bonus Bucks for each $50 you spend. Complete the graph to model this situation.

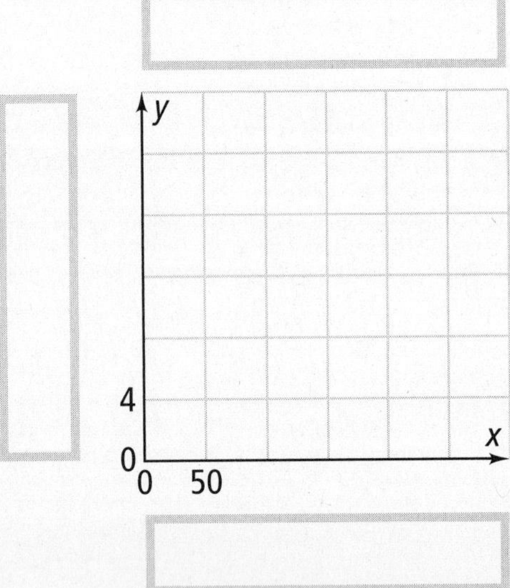

2. A scuba diver descends into the ocean from the surface at a rate of 65 feet per minute. Complete the table of the diver's position relative to the surface.

$$d = -65m$$

Minutes (m)	0	1	2
Depth (d)			

Do you UNDERSTAND?

3. Writing Based on the graph in Exercise 1, is the relationship between the amount spent and the amount of bonus bucks earned proportional? Explain.

4. Reasoning If the diver in Exercise 2 jumped off a boat into the ocean rather than descending from the surface of the ocean, would the relationship still be proportional?

14-2 Linear Equations: $y = mx$

Digital Resources

CCSS: 8.EE.B.5: Graph proportional relationships, interpreting the unit rate as the slope of the graph. Compare two different proportional relationships represented in different ways. **8.EE.B.6:** … derive the equation $y = mx$ for a line through the origin … .

Launch

MP3, MP7

How are the lines similar? How are they different? Explain.

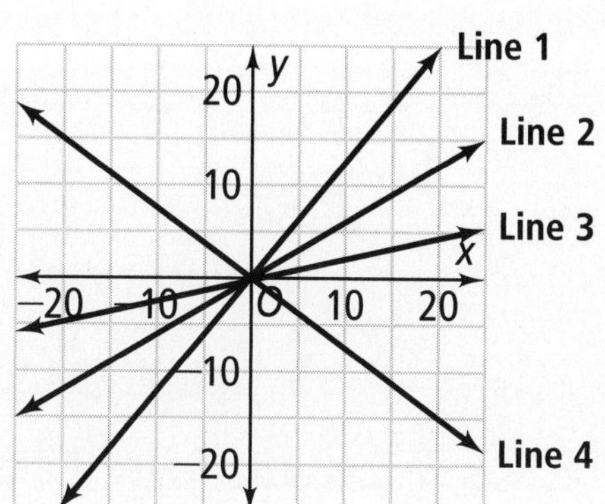

Similar:

Different:

Reflect Is one line more different than the others? Explain.

Got It?

PART 1 Got It

The graph shows the distance d a train travels in time t at a constant speed r. Write an equation in $d = rt$ form that models the situation shown.

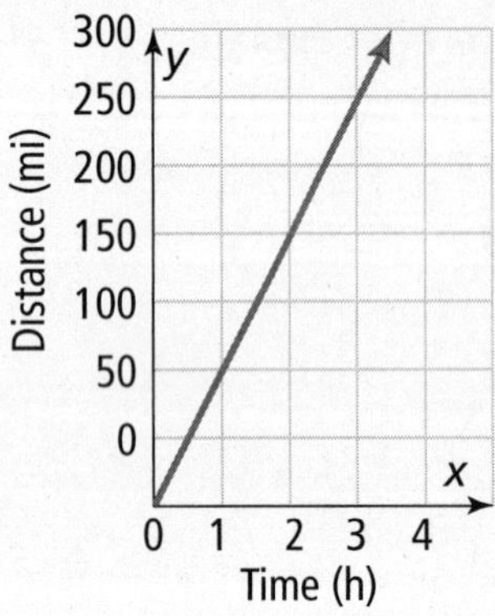

PART 2 Got It

Discuss with a classmate
Compare the equations you wrote for the problem.
Listen as you explain to each other how you determined the parts of the equation you wrote.

A hamburger made with a certain type of beef loses $\frac{1}{4}$ of its weight while cooking. Write an equation that models the weight of a cooked hamburger y based on the weight of the uncooked hamburger x.

Got It?

PART 3 Got It

The number of miles y a car travels in x hours can be modeled by the equation $y = 65x$. The graph shows the relationship between distance and time for a train. Which vehicle is traveling at a greater speed?

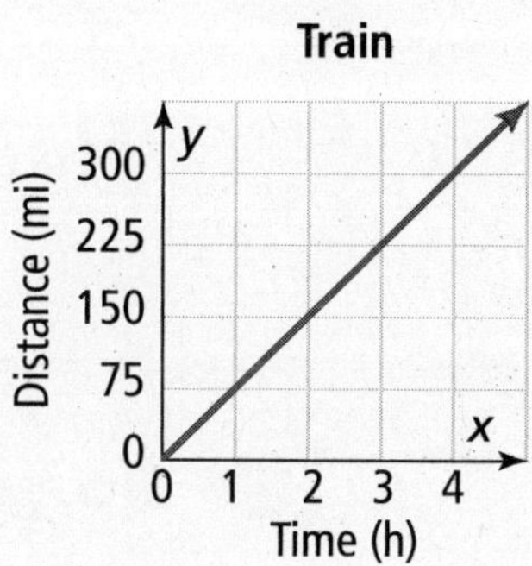

Close and Check

Focus Question

MP4, MP6

What does it mean for an equation to be linear? What kind of relationships can be modeled by equations in the form $y = mx$?

Do you know HOW?

1. The graph shows the earnings e of an airplane mechanic for a number of weeks w at a constant rate r. Write an equation to model the situation shown.

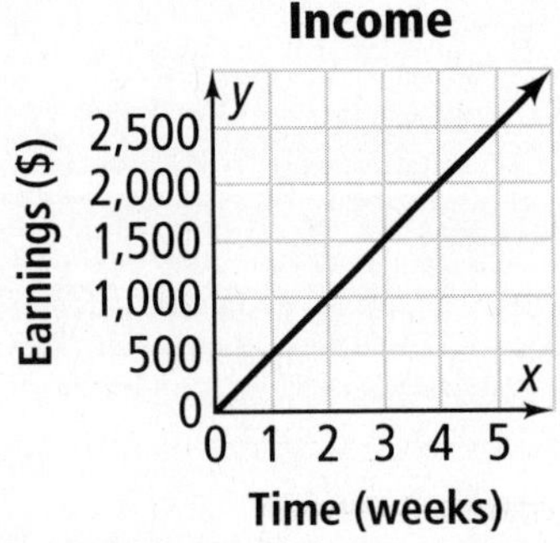

2. A machine manufactures a part in 11 minutes. A newer machine can manufacture the same part 1.5 minutes faster. Write an equation that models how many parts p each machine can manufacture in any number of minutes m.

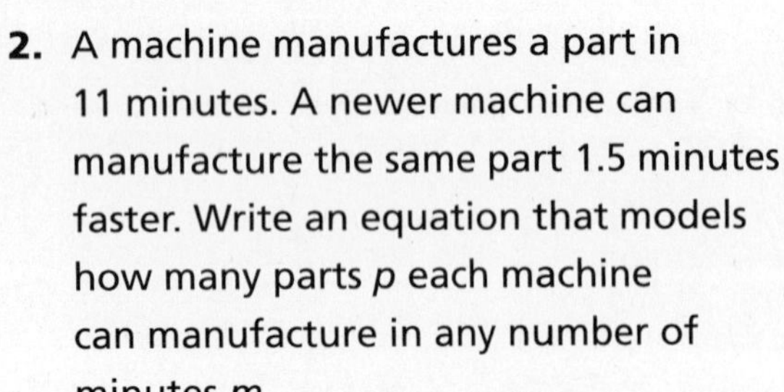

Old Machine:

New Machine:

Do you UNDERSTAND?

3. Writing A diesel mechanic's earnings can be represented by the equation $e = 475w$. Who earns more, the airplane mechanic in Exercise 1 or the diesel mechanic? Explain.

4. Reasoning Are all proportional equations linear? Are all linear equations proportional? Explain.

14-3 The Slope of a Line

Digital Resources

CCSS: 8.EE.B.5: Graph proportional relationships, interpreting the unit rate as the slope of the graph. Compare two different proportional relationships represented in different ways.

Launch

MP3, MP7

An architect diagrams a series of skyscrapers on a coordinate grid. Tell how they are alike and different.

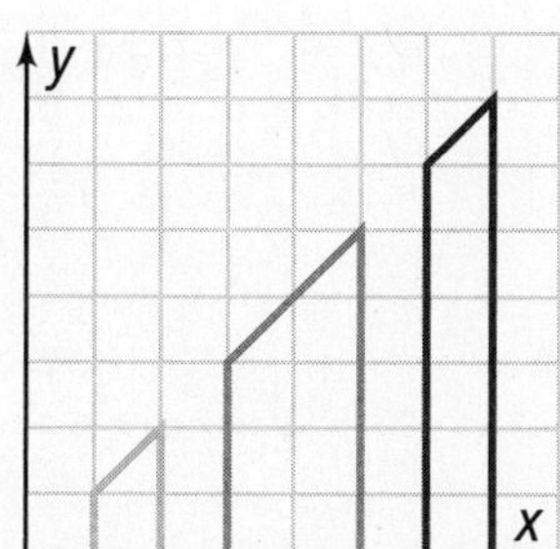

Alike:

Different:

Reflect Is one building more different than the others? Explain.

Got It?

PART 1 Got It (1 of 2)

What is the slope of the line?

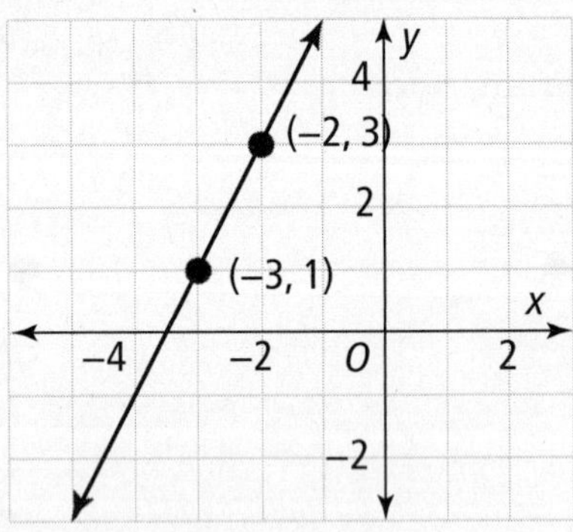

PART 1 Got It (2 of 2)

One of your friends describes the slope of a line: "as the *x*-coordinates increase by 2, the *y*-coordinates decrease by 5."
Your other friend describes the slope of a line: "as the *x*-coordinates decrease by 2, the *y*-coordinates increase by 5."
Is it possible for your friends to be describing the same line? Explain.

Got It?

PART 2 Got It (1 of 2)

What is the slope of the line that passes through the points (5, −3) and (−1, −2)?

PART 2 Got It (2 of 2)

The line shown has an *undefined* slope. Use the points shown to explain why.

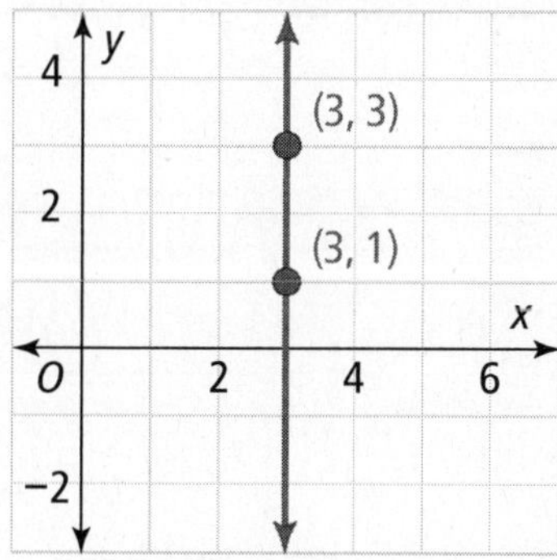

PART 3 Got It

Which roof is steeper: Roof A with a rise of 12 and a run of 7 or Roof B with a rise of 8 and a run of 4? How do you know?

Close and Check

Focus Question

What does the slope of a line tell you about the line?

Do you know HOW?

1. What is the slope of the line?

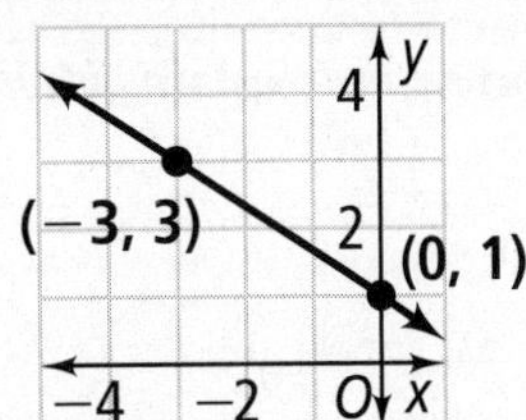

Slope:

2. What is the slope of the line that passes through the points (3, 3) and (1, −2)?

Slope:

3. Roof A has a rise of 11 and a run of 12. Roof B has a rise of 8 and a run of 9. Which roof is steeper?

4. Climber A climbs at a rate of 14 feet every 3 minutes. Climber B climbs 19 feet in 4 minutes. Which climber has the faster rate?

Do you UNDERSTAND?

5. **Reasoning** What is the slope of a horizontal line? Choose two points and show how you determined your solution.

6. **Error Analysis** A classmate finds the slope of a line containing the points (−7, 5) and (−3, 9). Explain the error she made in her calculations and find the correct slope.

$$\frac{9-5}{-7-(-3)} = \frac{4}{-4} = -1$$

14-4 Unit Rates and Slope

Digital Resources

CCSS: 8.EE.B.5: Graph proportional relationships, interpreting the unit rate as the slope of the graph. Compare two different proportional relationships represented in different ways.

Launch

MP4, MP6

The graph shows the results of a plant-growing contest among three friends at a local plant club.

Which friend's plant grew the fastest? Explain how you know.

Plant Club Contest

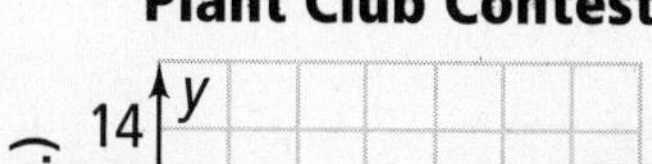
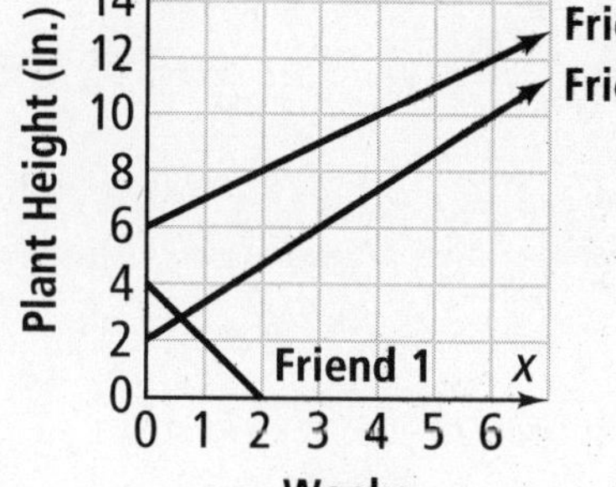

Reflect Is one line more different than the others? Explain.

Got It?

PART 1 Got It

The graph shows the amount of milk needed to make a quantity of butter. How many gallons of milk do you need per pound of butter?

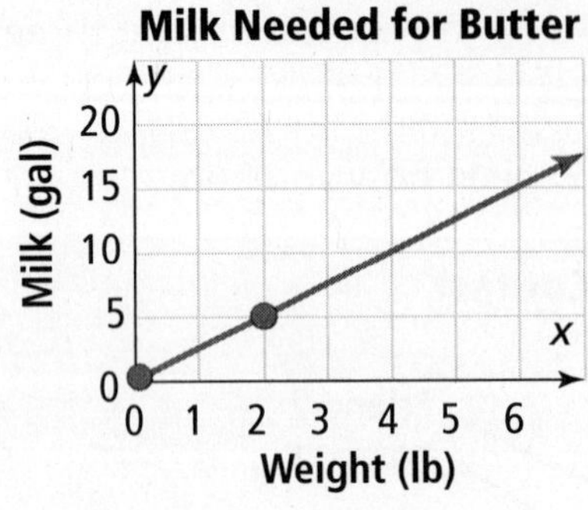

PART 2 Got It

There is a proportional relationship between fathoms and feet. A depth of 6 fathoms is equivalent to a depth of 36 feet.

a. What is the unit rate of feet per fathom?

b. Use the unit rate to draw a graph that models this situation where the horizontal axis shows depth in fathoms and the vertical axis shows depth in feet. What is the slope of the line?

Got It?

PART 3 Got It

You friend has an automatic fish food dispenser. The graph shows how much food is left in the feeder after x days. How much food is being dispensed per day?

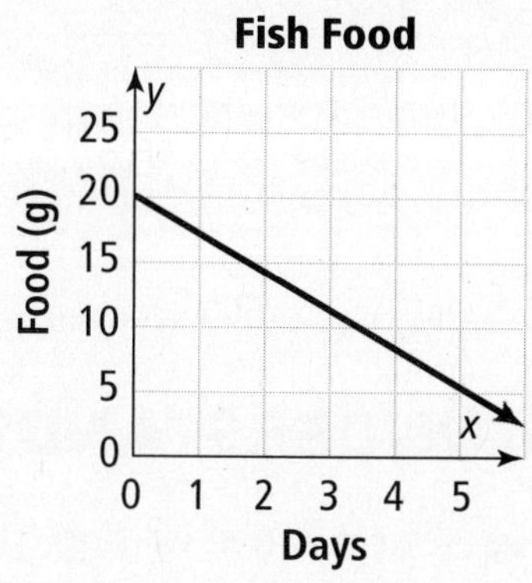

Close and Check

Focus Question

MP6, MP8

How are unit rates and slope related?

Do you know HOW?

1. A caterer is preparing meatloaf for a large party. She needs 3 eggs for 2 pounds of ground beef. Graph the ratio of eggs to ground beef.

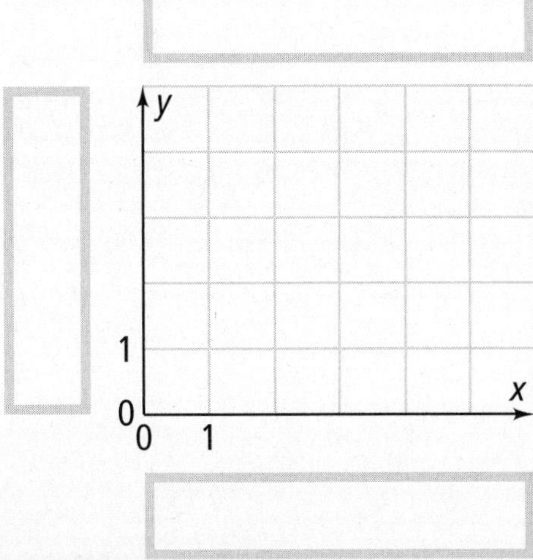

2. What is the slope of the line in the graph?

   Slope:

3. Write an equation for Exercise 1 to find the number of eggs y for any number of pounds of ground beef *x*. How many eggs will be needed for 18 pounds of ground beef?

   Equation:

   eggs

Do you UNDERSTAND?

4. **Reasoning** Your creative writing teacher says you will have 15 short stories due over the next 12 weeks. What is the slope of the graph of number of papers due? Explain whether the graph represents a proportional relationship.

5. **Writing** Explain how to graph a line if you only know one point on the line and the slope of the line.

14-5 The *y*-intercept of a Line

Digital Resources

CCSS: 8.EE.B.6: … derive the equation $y = mx$ for a line through the origin and the equation $y = mx + b$ for a line intercepting the vertical axis at b.

Launch

MP4, MP6

The graph shows the results of a plant-growing contest among three friends at a local plant club. The person with tallest plant after six weeks wins the contest.

Who won the contest? Do you think the contest was fair? Explain.

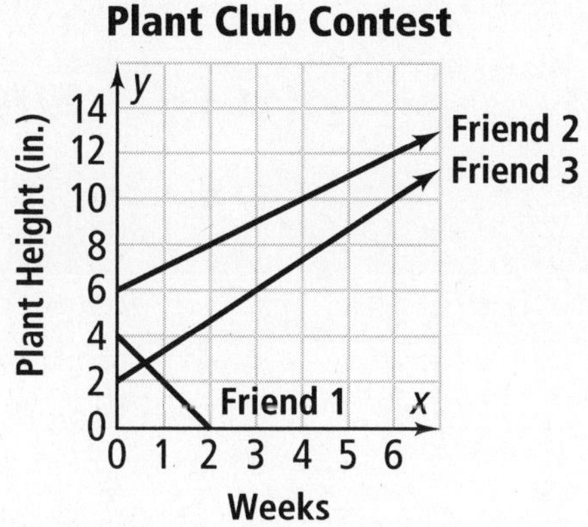

Reflect What do the lines all have in common?

Got It?

PART 1 Got It

What is the y-intercept of the graph of the equation $y = x + 6$?

PART 2 Got It (1 of 2)

What is the y-intercept of the graph of the equation $y = -5x - 1$?

Discuss with a classmate
What is the y-intercept of a graph?
How do you recognize the y-intercept when given an equation?

Got It?

PART 2 Got It (2 of 2)

Your friend says that the graph of every linear equation must cross the *y*-axis. Provide a counterexample to your friend's statement.

PART 3 Got It

A bottle of dish soap starts to leak. The line models the total amount of dish soap in the bottle.

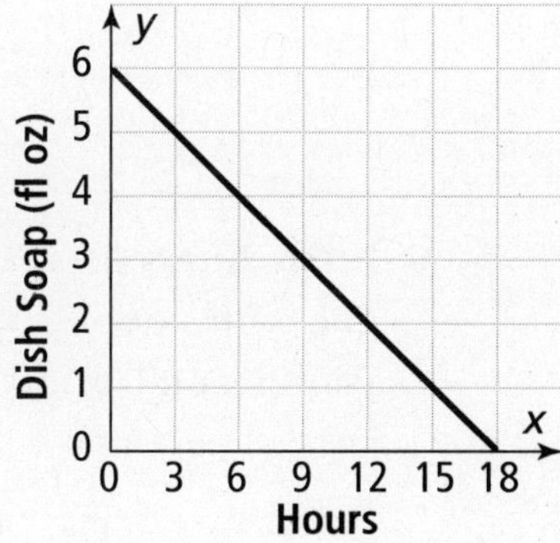

What is the *y*-intercept of the line? What does the *y*-intercept represent?

Close and Check

Focus Question

MP4, MP7

What is the y-intercept of a graph? What does the y-intercept tell you about the equation being graphed?

Do you know HOW?

1. You open a savings account with a $75 deposit. Then you deposit $25 each month. Complete the graph to model the situation.

y
50
0
0 1
x

2. What does the y-intercept represent?

3. What is the slope of the line?

Slope:

4. What does the slope represent?

Do you UNDERSTAND?

5. **Compare and Contrast** What about the graph in Exercise 1 would change if the initial deposit had been 0? What would stay the same? Explain.

6. **Error Analysis** A classmate says a line with slope = 0 does not have a y-intercept. Do you agree? Explain.

14-6 Linear Equations: $y = mx + b$

Digital Resources

CCSS: 8.EE.B.6: ... derive the equation $y = mx$ for a line through the origin and the equation $y = mx + b$ for a line intercepting the vertical axis at b.

Launch

MP2, MP5

Complete the table. Describe any patterns you see between the slope and y-intercept for each line and the equation.

Equation	Slope	y-intercept
$y = 2x + 1$		
$y = 2x + 3$		
$y = -\frac{1}{3}x + 6$		
$y = x$		
$y = 1$		

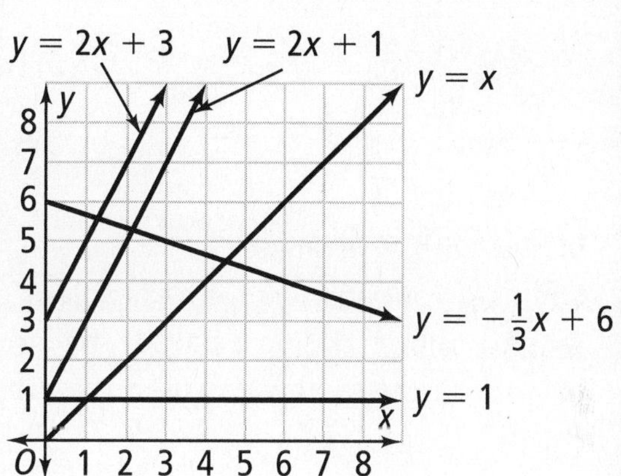

Reflect Is it easier to spot the slope and y-intercept of a line from the graph or the equation of the line? Explain.

Got It?

PART 1 Got It

Write an equation in slope-intercept form for the line.

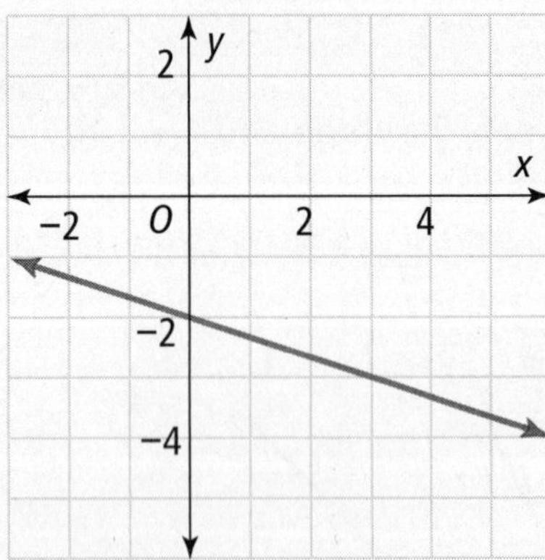

Discuss with a classmate
Compare your answers to the problem.
Take turns by choosing a part of the equation you wrote and explain to your classmate how you used the graph to find that value.

Got It?

PART 2 Got It

The Kelvin scale for measuring temperature is often used in scientific calculations. The line models the relationship between a temperature in degrees Celsius and a temperature in kelvins.

Write an equation for the line where x is the temperature in degrees Celsius and y is the temperature in kelvins.

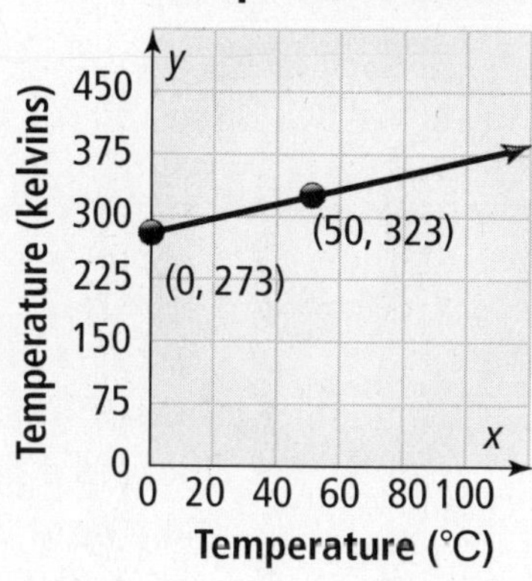

PART 3 Got It

What is the graph of the equation $y = -2x + 3$?

Close and Check

Focus Question

Previously you studied equations in the form $y = mx$. How are equations in the form $y = mx$ similar to equations in the form $y = mx + b$? How do you know when to use each form?

Do you know HOW?

Use the graph for Exercises 1–4.

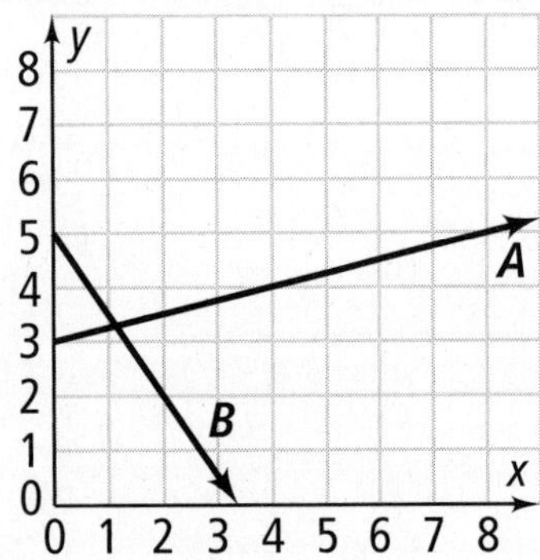

1. Write an equation in slope-intercept form for Line *A*.

2. Write an equation in slope-intercept form for Line *B*.

3. Graph and label Line *C* where $y = -\frac{2}{3}x + 7$.

4. Graph and label Line *D* where $y = \frac{7}{8}x + 1$.

Do you UNDERSTAND?

5. **Reasoning** You know the slope of a line and a point on the line that is not the *y*-intercept. Can you use a graph to write the equation of the line in slope-intercept form? Explain.

6. **Writing** Do the equations $y = \frac{5}{6}x + 2$ and $y = \frac{15}{18}x + 2$ represent two different lines? Explain.

14-7 Problem Solving

Digital Resources

CCSS: 8.EE.B.5: ... Compare two different proportional relationships represented in different ways.
8.EE.B.6: ... derive the equation $y = mx$ for a line through the origin and the equation $y = mx + b$ for a line intercepting the vertical axis at b.

Launch

MP4, MP6

Create your own graph and matching linear equation. Describe a situation that makes sense for each representation. Label your graph appropriately. Your situation must include the point (2, 4).

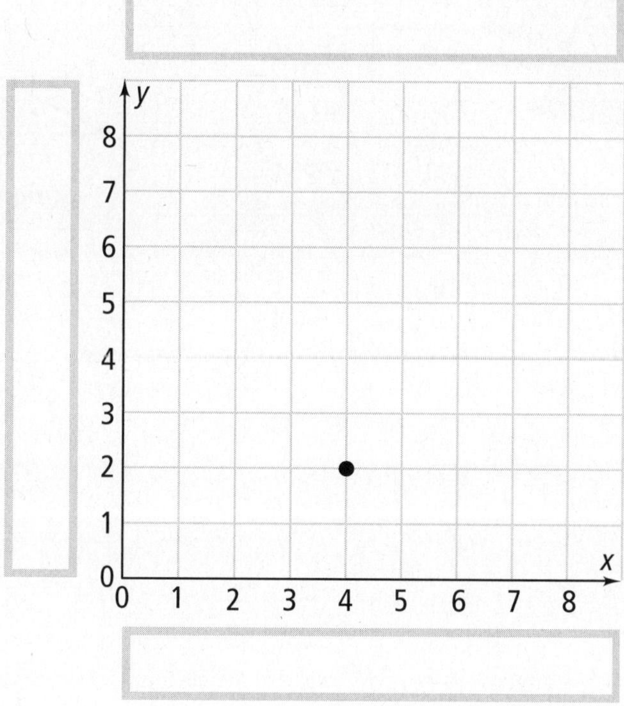

Equation:

Description of situation:

Reflect What did you do first—write an equation, complete the graph, or describe the situation? Why?

Got It?

PART 1 Got It

Three stores are having a sale. Each store advertises its sale in a different way. Which store is offering the greatest discount?

Store B

Original Price ($)	Sale Price ($)
30	25.50
50	42.50
75	63.75
90	76.50

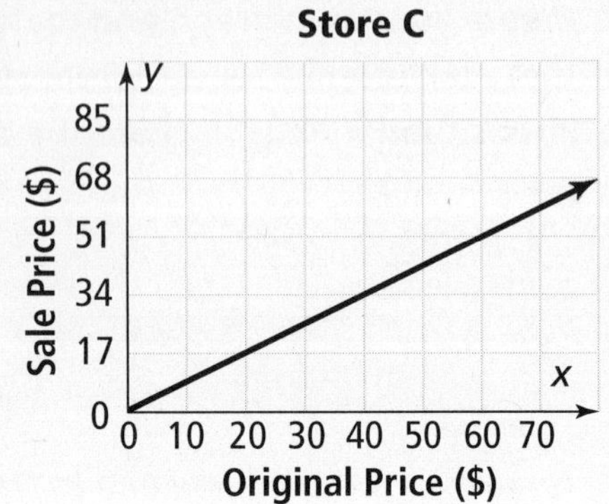

Got It?

PART 2 Got It

Stores offer different rewards programs.

Store A:
You earn 3 points for every dollar spent.

Store B:
You start with 100 points and then earn 1 point for every dollar spent.

Store C:
The equation $y = 2x + 50$ models the rewards program, where y is the total number of points and x is the total dollars spent.

At each store you need 240 points to receive your first reward.
At which store do you need to spend the least amount of money to earn your first reward?

Discuss with a classmate

Choose one of the Stores' rewards programs.
Read the description of the program out loud, and then show how much you would need to spend in order to earn your first reward.
If you do not understand any of the descriptions, circle the word or phrase that is not clear to you and ask your teacher to help you.

Close and Check

Focus Question

You have studied the relationship between linear equations and proportional relationships. How and when can you use linear equations to solve problems?

Do you know HOW?

1. To make a multi-age 800-meter race fair, Runner 1 gets a 100-meter head start. He runs 350 meters every 2 minutes. Represent on the graph how Runner 1 runs the race.

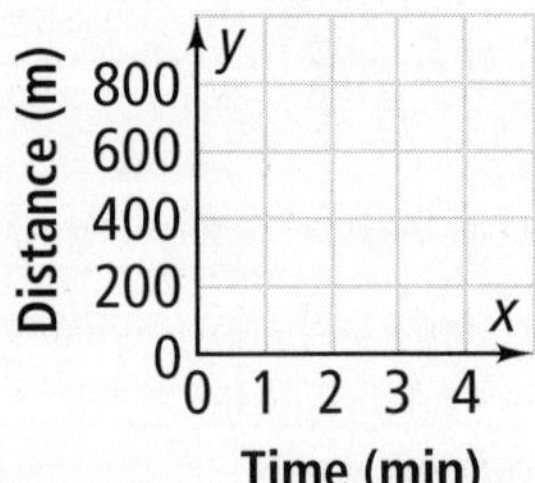

2. Runner 2 gets a 75-meter head start. Her rate is 210 meters per minute. Complete the table.

Time (min)	0	1	2	3	4
Distance (m)					

3. Runner 3 does not get a head start. He runs 750 meters every 3 minutes. Write an equation to represent Runner 3's distance y for x minutes.

Do you UNDERSTAND?

4. **Writing** Which runner from Exercises 1–3 is ahead after 1 minute? Will that runner win the race? Explain.

5. **Reasoning** Which is most helpful in problem solving, a graph, a table, or an equation? Explain.

14-R Topic Review

New Vocabulary: linear equation, slope, *y*-intercept
Review Vocabulary: constant of proportionality, proportional relationship, rate, unit rate

Vocabulary Review

Identify two challenging vocabulary terms from this topic. Write one vocabulary term in the center oval, and fill in the surrounding boxes with details that will help you better understand the term.

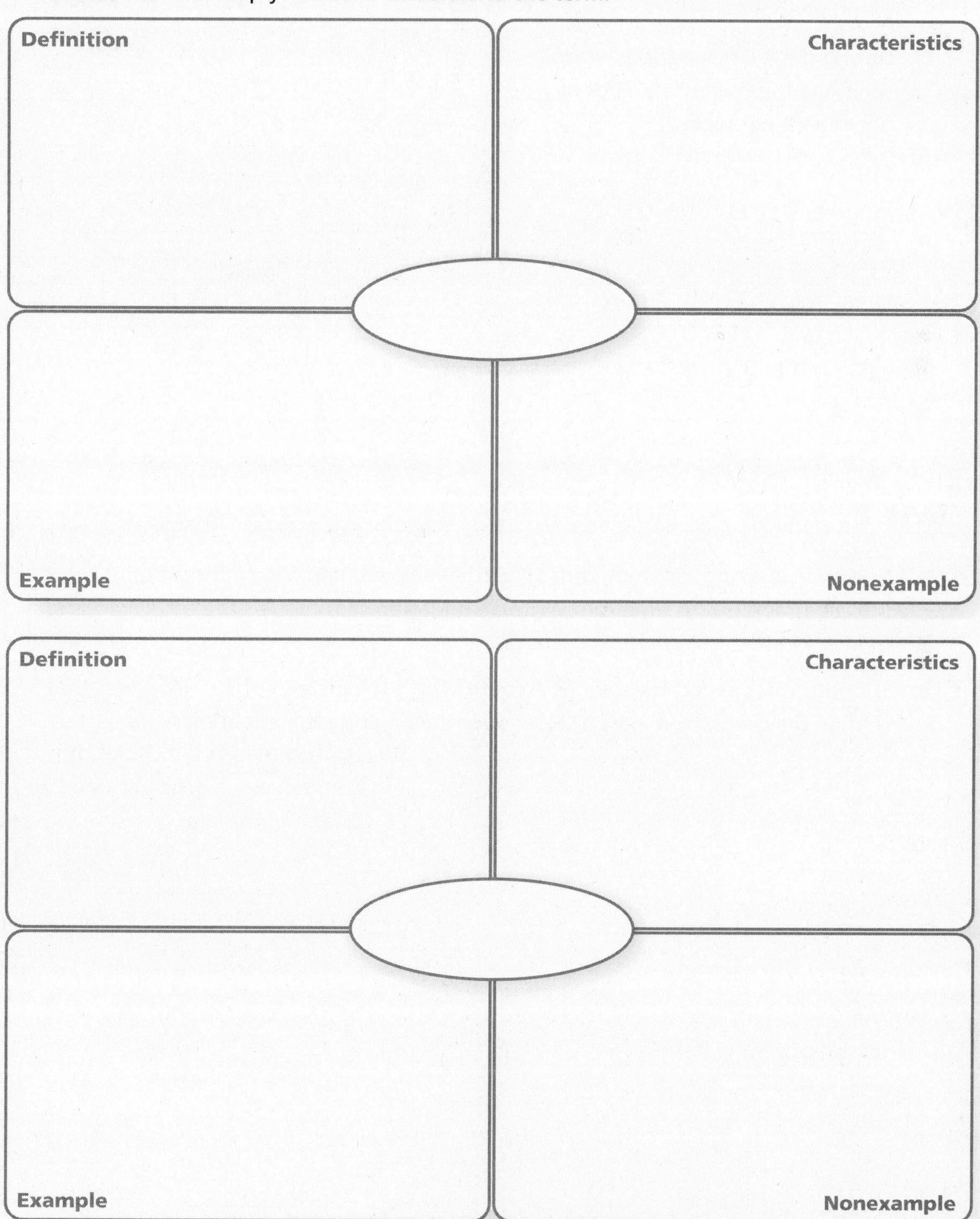

Pull It All Together

TASK 1

The graph shows the total number of downloads for three songs over a 4-week period.

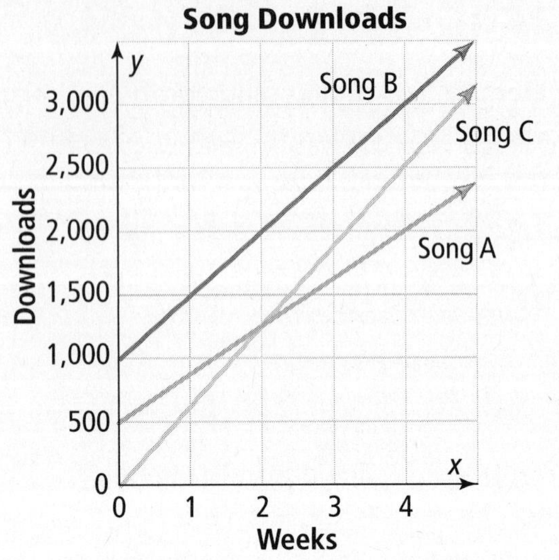

a. Write an equation to represent each line shown.

b. During the 4-week period, which song had the highest number of downloads per week?

TASK 2

a. You open a savings account with \$0. Each week you add \$25 to the account. Make a graph of the situation. Write an equation that models the total amount of money y in the account after x weeks.

b. Suppose you opened the savings account with \$100 instead of \$0. How does that change the graph from part a? How does that change the equation from part a?

English/Spanish Glossary

A

Absolute deviation from the mean Absolute deviation measures the distance that the data value is from the mean. You find the absolute deviation by taking the absolute value of the deviation of a data value. Absolute deviations are always nonnegative.

Desviación absoluta de la media La desviación absoluta mide la distancia a la que un valor se encuentra de la media. Para hallar la desviación absoluta, tomas el valor absoluto de la desviación de un valor. Las desviaciones absolutas siempre son no negativas.

Absolute value The absolute value of a number a is the distance between a and zero on a number line. The absolute value of a is written as $|a|$.

Valor absoluto El valor absoluto de un número a es la distancia entre a y cero en la recta numérica. El valor absoluto de a se escribe como $|a|$.

Accuracy The accuracy of an estimate or measurement is the degree to which it agrees with an accepted or actual value of that measurement.

Exactitud La exactitud de una estimación o medición es el grado de concordancia con un valor aceptado o real de esa medición.

Action In a probability situation, an action is a process with an uncertain result.

Acción En una situación de probabilidad, una acción es el proceso con un resultado incierto.

Acute angle An acute angle is an angle with a measure between 0° and 90°.

Ángulo agudo Un ángulo agudo es un ángulo que mide entre 0° y 90°.

Acute triangle An acute triangle is a triangle with three acute angles.

Triángulo acutángulo Un triángulo acutángulo es un triángulo que tiene tres ángulos agudos.

Addend Addends are the numbers that are added together to find a sum.

Sumando Los sumandos son los números que se suman para hallar un total.

English/Spanish Glossary

Additive inverses Two numbers that have a sum of 0.

Inversos de suma Dos números cuya suma es 0.

Adjacent angles Two angles are adjacent angles if they share a vertex and a side, but have no interior points in common.

Ángulos adyacentes Dos ángulos son adyacentes si tienen un vértice y un lado en común, pero no comparten puntos internos.

Algebraic expression An algebraic expression is a mathematical phrase that consists of variables, numbers, and operation symbols.

Expresión algebraica Una expresión algebraica es una frase matemática que consiste en variables, números y símbolos de operaciones.

Analyze To analyze is to think about and understand facts and details about a given set of information. Analyzing can involve providing a written summary supported by factual information, diagrams, charts, tables, or any combination of these.

Analizar Analizar es pensar en los datos y detalles de cierta información y comprenderlos. El análisis puede incluir la presentación de un resumen escrito sustentado por información objetiva, diagramas, tablas o una combinación de esos elementos.

Angle An angle is a figure formed by two rays with a common endpoint.

Ángulo Un ángulo es una figura formada por dos semirrectas que tienen un extremo en común.

Angle of rotation The angle of rotation is the number of degrees a figure is rotated.

Ángulo de rotación El ángulo de rotación es el número de grados que se rota una figura.

Annual salary The amount of money earned at a job in one year.

Salario annual La cantidad de dinero ganó en un trabajo en un año.

Area The area of a figure is the number of square units the figure encloses.

Área El área de una figura es el número de unidades cuadradas que ocupa.

English/Spanish Glossary

Area of a circle The formula for the area of a circle is $A = \pi r^2$, where A represents the area and r represents the radius of the circle.

Área de un círculo La fórmula del área de un círculo es $A = \pi r^2$, donde A representa el área y r representa el radio del círculo.

Area of a parallelogram The formula for the area of a parallelogram is $A = bh$, where A represents the area, b represents a base, and h is the corresponding height.

Área de un paralelogramo La fórmula del área de un paralelogramo es $A = bh$, donde A representa el área, b representa una base y h es la altura correspondiente.

Area of a rectangle The formula for the area of a rectangle is $A = bh$, where A represents the area, b represents the base, and h represents the height of the rectangle.

Área de un rectángulo La fórmula del área de un rectángulo es $A = bh$, donde A representa el área, b representa la base y h representa la altura del rectángulo.

Area of a square The formula for the area of a square is $A = s^2$, where A represents the area and s represents a side length.

Área de un cuadrado La fórmula del área de un cuadrado es $A = s^2$, donde A representa el área y l representa la longitud de un lado.

Area of a trapezoid The formula for the area of a trapezoid is $A = \frac{1}{2}h(b_1 + b_2)$, where A represents the area, b_1 and b_2 represent the bases, and h represents the height between the bases.

El área de un trapezoide La fórmula para el área de un trapezoide es $A = \frac{1}{2}h(b_1 + b_2)$, donde A representa el área, b_1 y b_2 representan las bases, y h representa la altura entre las bases.

Area of a triangle The formula for the area of a triangle is $A = \frac{1}{2}bh$, where A represents the area, b represents the length of a base, and h represents the corresponding height.

Área de un triángulo La fórmula del área de un triángulo es $A = \frac{1}{2}bh$, donde A representa el área, b representa la longitud de una base y h representa la altura correspondiente.

Asset An asset is money you have or property of value that you own.

Ventaja Una ventaja es dinero que tiene o la propiedad de valor que usted posee.

English/Spanish Glossary

Associative Property of Addition For any numbers a, b, and c: $(a + b) + c = a + (b + c)$

Propiedad asociativa de la suma Para los números cualesquiera a, b y c: $(a + b) + c = a + (b + c)$

Associative Property of Multiplication For any numbers a, b, and c: $(a \cdot b) \cdot c = a \cdot (b \cdot c)$

Propiedad asociativa de la multiplicación Para los números cualesquiera a, b y c: $(a \cdot b) \cdot c = a \cdot (b \cdot c)$

Average of two numbers The average of two numbers is the value that represents the middle of two numbers. It is found by adding the two numbers together and dividing by 2.

Promedio de dos números El promedio de dos números es el valor que está justo en el medio de esos dos números. Se halla sumando los dos números y dividiendo el resultado por 2.

B

Balance The balance in an account is the principal amount plus the interest earned.

Saldo El saldo de una cuenta es el capital más el interés ganado.

Balance of a checking account The balance of a checking account is the amount of money in the checking account.

El equilibrio de una Cuenta Corriente Bancaria El equilibrio de una cuenta corriente bancaria es la cantidad de dinero en la cuenta corriente bancaria.

Balance of a loan The balance of a loan is the remaining unpaid principal.

El equilibrio de un préstamo El equilibrio de un préstamo es el director impagado restante.

Bar diagram A bar diagram is a way to represent part to whole relationships.

Diagrama de barras Un diagrama de barras es una forma de representar una relación de parte a entero.

Base The base is the repeated factor of a number written in exponential form.

Base La base es el factor repetido de un número escrito en forma exponencial.

English/Spanish Glossary

Base area of a cone The base area of a cone is the area of a circle. Base Area $= \pi r^2$.

Área de la base de un cono El área de la base de un cono es el área de un círculo. El área de la base $= \pi r^2$.

Base of a cone The base of a cone is a circle with radius *r*.

Base de un cono La base de un cono es un círculo con radio *r*.

Base of a cylinder A base of a cylinder is one of a pair of parallel circular faces that are the same size.

Base de un cilindro Una base de un cilindro es una de dos caras circulares paralelas que tienen el mismo tamaño.

Base of a parallelogram A base of a parallelogram is any side of the parallelogram.

Base de un paralelogramo La base de un paralelogramo es cualquiera de los lados del paralelogramo.

Base of a prism A base of a prism is one of a pair of parallel polygonal faces that are the same size and shape. A prism is named for the shape of its bases.

Base de un prisma La base de un prisma es una de las dos caras poligonales paralelas que tienen el mismo tamaño y la misma forma. El nombre de un prisma depende de la forma de sus bases.

Base of a pyramid A base of a pyramid is a polygonal face that does not connect to the vertex.

Base de una pirámide La base de una pirámide es una cara poligonal que no se conecta con el vértice.

Base of a triangle The base of a triangle is any side of the triangle.

Base de un triángulo La base de un triángulo es cualquiera de los lados del triángulo.

Benchmark A benchmark is a number you can use as a reference point for other numbers.

Referencia Una referencia es un número que usted puede utilizar como un punto de referencia para otros números.

English/Spanish Glossary

Bias A bias is a tendency toward a particular perspective that is different from the overall perspective of the population.

Sesgo Un sesgo es una tendencia hacia una perspectiva particular que es diferente de la perspectiva general de la población.

Biased sample In a biased sample, the number of subjects in the sample with the trait that you are studying is not proportional to the number of members in the population with that trait. A biased sample does not accurately represent the population.

Muestra sesgada En una muestra sesgada, el número de sujetos de la muestra que tiene la característica que se está estudiando no es proporcional al número de miembros de la población que tienen esa característica. Una muestra sesgada no representa con exactitud la población.

Bivariate categorical data Bivariate categorical data pairs categorical data collected about two variables of the same population.

Datos bivariados por categorías Los datos bivariados por categorías agrupan pares de datos obtenidos acerca de dos variables de la misma población.

Bivariate data Bivariate data is comprised of pairs of linked observations about a population.

Datos bivariados Los datos bivariados se forman a partir de pares de observaciones relacionadas sobre una población.

Box plot A box plot is a statistical graph that shows the distribution of a data set by marking five boundary points where data occur along a number line. Unlike a dot plot or a histogram, a box plot does not show frequency.

Diagrama de cajas Un diagrama de cajas es un diagrama de estadísticas que muestra la distribución de un conjunto de datos al marcar cinco puntos de frontera donde se hallan los datos sobre una recta numérica. A diferencia del diagrama de puntos o el histograma, el diagrama de cajas no muestra la frecuencia.

Budget A budget is a plan for how you will spend your money.

Presupuesto Un presupuesto es un plan para cómo gastará su dinero.

English/Spanish Glossary

C

Categorical data Categorical data consist of data that fall into categories.

Datos por categorías Los datos por categorías son datos que se pueden clasificar en categorías.

Center of a circle The center of a circle is the point inside the circle that is the same distance from all points on the circle. Name a circle by its center.

Centro de un círculo El centro de un círculo es el punto dentro del círculo que está a la misma distancia de todos los puntos del círculo. Un círculo se identifica por su centro.

Center of a regular polygon The center of a regular polygon is the point that is equidistant from its vertices.

Centro de un polígono regular El centro de un polígono regular es el punto equidistante de todos sus vértices.

Center of rotation The center of rotation is a fixed point about which a figure is rotated.

Centro de rotación El centro de rotación es el punto fijo alrededor del cual se rota una figura.

Check register A record that shows all of the transactions for a bank account, including withdrawals, deposits, and transfers. It also shows the balance of the account after each transaction.

Verifique registro Un registro que muestra todas las transacciones para una cuenta bancaria, inclusive retiradas, los depósitos, y las transferencias. También muestra el equilibrio de la cuenta después de cada transacción.

Circle A circle is the set of all points in a plane that are the same distance from a given point, called the center.

Círculo Un círculo es el conjunto de todos los puntos de un plano que están a la misma distancia de un punto dado, llamado centro.

Circle graph A circle graph is a graph that represents a whole divided into parts.

Gráfica circular Una gráfica circular es una gráfica que representa un todo dividido en partes.

English/Spanish Glossary

Circumference of a circle The circumference of a circle is the distance around the circle. The formula for the circumference of a circle is $C = \pi d$, where C represents the circumference and d represents the diameter of the circle.

Circunferencia de un círculo La circunferencia de un círculo es la distancia alrededor del círculo. La fórmula de la circunferencia de un círculo es $C = \pi d$, donde C representa la circunferencia y d representa el diámetro del círculo.

Cluster A cluster is a group of points that lie close together on a scatter plot.

Grupo Un grupo es un conjunto de puntos que están agrupados en un diagrama de dispersión.

Coefficient A coefficient is the number part of a term that contains a variable.

Coeficiente Un coeficiente es la parte numérica de un término que contiene una variable.

Common denominator A common denominator is a number that is the denominator of two or more fractions.

Común denominador Un común denominador es un número que es el denominador de dos o más fracciones.

Common multiple A common multiple is a multiple that two or more numbers share.

Múltiplo común Un múltiplo común es un múltiplo que comparten dos o más números.

Commutative Property of Addition For any numbers a and b: $a + b = b + a$

Propiedad conmutativa de la suma Para los números cualesquiera a y b: $a + b = b + a$

Commutative Property of Multiplication For any numbers a and b: $a \cdot b = b \cdot a$

Propiedad conmutativa de la multiplicación Para los números cualesquiera a y b: $a \cdot b = b \cdot a$

Comparative inference A comparative inference is an inference made by interpreting and comparing two sets of data.

Inferencia comparativa Una inferencia comparativa es una inferencia que se hace al interpretar y comparar dos conjuntos de datos.

English/Spanish Glossary

Compare To compare is to tell or show how two things are alike or different.

Comparar Comparar es describir o mostrar en qué se parecen o en qué se diferencian dos cosas.

Compatible numbers Compatible numbers are numbers that are easy to compute mentally.

Números compatibles Los números compatibles son números fáciles de calcular mentalmente.

Complementary angles Two angles are complementary angles if the sum of their measures is 90°. Complementary angles that are adjacent form a right angle.

Ángulos complementarios Dos ángulos son complementarios si la suma de sus medidas es 90°. Los ángulos complementarios que son adyacentes forman un ángulo recto.

Complex fraction A complex fraction is a fraction $\frac{A}{B}$ where A and/or B are fractions and B is not zero.

Fracción compleja Una fracción compleja es una fracción $\frac{A}{B}$ donde A y/o B son fracciones y B es distinto de cero.

Compose a shape To compose a shape, join two (or more) shapes so that there is no gap or overlap.

Componer una figura Para componer una figura, debes unir dos (o más) figuras de modo que entre ellas no queden espacios ni superposiciones.

Composite figure A composite figure is the combination of two or more figures into one object.

Figura compuesta Una figura compuesta es la combinación de dos o más figuras en un objeto.

Composite number A composite number is a whole number greater than 1 with more than two factors.

Número compuesto Un número compuesto es un número entero mayor que 1 con más de dos factores.

Compound event A compound event is an event associated with a multi-step action. A compound event is composed of events that are the outcomes of the steps of the action.

Evento compuesto Un evento compuesto es un evento que se relaciona con una acción de varios pasos. Un evento compuesto se compone de eventos que son los resultados de los pasos de una acción.

Compound interest Compound interest is interest paid on both the principal and the interest earned in previous interest periods. To calculate compound interest, use the formula $B = p(1 + r)^n$, where B is the balance in the account, p is the principal, r is the annual interest rate, and n is the time in years that the account earns interest.

Interés compuesto El interés compuesto es el interés que se paga sobre el capital y el interés obtenido en períodos de interés anteriores. Para calcular el interés compuesto, usa la fórmula $B = c(1 + r)^n$ donde B es el saldo de la cuenta, c es el capital, r es la tasa de interés anual y n es el tiempo en años en que la cuenta obtiene un interés.

Cone A cone is a three-dimensional figure with one circular base and one vertex.

Cono Un cono es una figura tridimensional con una base circular y un vértice.

Congruent figures Two two-dimensional figures are congruent $\cong$ if the second can be obtained from the first by a sequence of rotations, reflections, and translations.

Figuras congruentes Dos figuras bidimensionales son congruentes $\cong$ si la segunda puede obtenerse a partir de la primera mediante una secuencia de rotaciones, reflexiones y traslaciones.

Conjecture A conjecture is a statement that you believe to be true but have not yet proved to be true.

Conjetura Una conjetura es un enunciado que crees que es verdadero, pero que todavía no has comprobado que sea verdadero.

Constant A constant is a term that only contains a number.

Constante Una constante es un término que solamente contiene un número.

Constant of proportionality In a proportional relationship, one quantity y is a constant multiple of the other quantity x. The constant multiple is called the constant of proportionality. The constant of proportionality is equal to the ratio $\frac{y}{x}$.

Constante de proporcionalidad En una relación proporcional, una cantidad y es un múltiplo constante de la otra cantidad x. El múltiplo constante se llama constante de proporcionalidad. La constante de proporcionalidad es igual a la razón $\frac{y}{x}$.

English/Spanish Glossary

Construct To construct is to make something, such as an argument, by organizing ideas. Constructing an argument can involve a written response, equations, diagrams, charts, tables, or a combination of these.

Construir Construir es hacer o crear algo, como se construye un argumento al organizar ideas. Para construir un argumento puede usarse una respuesta escrita, ecuaciones, diagramas, tablas o una combinación de esos elementos.

Convenience sampling Convenience sampling is a sampling method in which a researcher chooses members of the population that are convenient and available. Many researchers use this sampling technique because it is fast and inexpensive. It does not require the researcher to keep track of everyone in the population.

Muestra de conveniencia Una muestra de conveniencia es un método de muestreo en el que un investigador escoge miembros de la población que están convenientemente disponibles. Muchos investigadores usan esta técnica de muestreo porque es rápida y no es costosa. No requiere que el investigador lleve un registro de cada miembro de la población.

Cost of attendance The cost of attendance of one year of college is the sum of all of your expenses during the year.

El costo de asistencia El costo de asistencia de un año del colegio es la suma de todos sus gastos durante el año.

Cost of credit The cost of credit for a loan is the difference between the total cost and the principal.

El costo de crédito El costo de crédito para un préstamo es la diferencia entre el coste total y el director.

Converse of the Pythagorean Theorem If the sum of the squares of the lengths of two sides of a triangle equals the square of the length of the third side, then the triangle is a right triangle. If $a^2 + b^2 = c^2$, then the triangle is a right triangle.

Expresión recíproca del Teorema de Pitágoras Si la suma del cuadrado de la longitud de dos lados de un triángulo es igual al cuadrado de la longitud del tercer lado, entonces el triángulo es un triángulo rectángulo. $a^2 + b^2 = c^2$, entonces el triángulo es un triángulo rectángulo.

Conversion factor A conversion factor is a rate that equals 1.

Factor de conversión Un factor de conversión es una tasa que es igual a 1.

English/Spanish Glossary

Coordinate plane A coordinate plane is formed by a horizontal number line called the *x*-axis and a vertical number line called the *y*-axis.

Plano de coordenadas Un plano de coordenadas está formado por una recta numérica horizontal llamada eje de las *x* y una recta numérica vertical llamada eje de las *y*.

Corresponding angles Corresponding angles lie on the same side of a transversal and in corresponding positions.

Ángulos correspondientes Los ángulos correspondientes se ubican al mismo lado de una secante y en posiciones correspondientes.

Counterexample A counterexample is a specific example that shows that a conjecture is false.

Contraejemplo Un contraejemplo es un ejemplo específico que muestra que una conjetura es falsa.

Counting Principle If there are *m* possible outcomes of one action and *n* possible outcomes of a second action, then there are $m \cdot n$ outcomes of the first action followed by the second action.

Principio de conteo Si hay *m* resultados posibles de una acción y *n* resultados posibles de una segunda acción, entonces hay $m \cdot n$ resultados de la primera acción seguida de la segunda acción.

Coupon A coupon is part of a printed or online advertisement entitling the holder to a discount at checkout.

Cupón Un cupón forma parte de un anuncio impreso o en línea que permite al poseedor a un descuento en comprueba.

Credit card A credit card is a card issued by a lender that can be used to borrow money or make purchases on credit.

Tarjeta de crédito Una tarjeta de crédito es una tarjeta publicada por un prestamista que puede ser utilizado para pedir dinero prestado o compras de marca a cuenta.

Credit history A credit history shows how a consumer has managed credit in the past.

Acredite la historia Una historia del crédito muestra cómo un consumidor ha manejado crédito en el pasado.

Credit report A report that shows personal information about a consumer and details about the consumer's credit history.

Acredite reporte Un reporte que muestra información personal sobre un consumidor y detalles acerca de la historia del crédito del consumidor.

Critique A critique is a careful judgment in which you give your opinion about the good and bad parts of something, such as how a problem was solved.

Crítica Una crítica es una evaluación cuidadosa en la que das tu opinión acerca de las partes positivas y negativas de algo, como la manera en la que se resolvió un problema.

Cross section A cross section is the intersection of a three-dimensional figure and a plane.

Corte transversal Un corte transversal es la intersección de una figura tridimensional y un plano.

Cube A cube is a rectangular prism whose faces are all squares.

Cubo Un cubo es un prisma rectangular cuyas caras son todas cuadrados.

Cube root The cube root of a number, n, is a number whose cube equals n.

Raíz cúbica La raíz cúbica de un número, n, es un número que elevado al cubo es igual a n.

Cubic unit A cubic unit is the volume of a cube that measures 1 unit on each edge.

Unidad cúbica Una unidad cúbica es el volumen de un cubo en el que cada arista mide 1 unidad.

Cylinder A cylinder is a three-dimensional figure with two parallel circular bases that are the same size.

Cilindro Un cilindro es una figura tridimensional con dos bases circulares paralelas que tienen el mismo tamaño.

D

Data Data are pieces of information collected by asking questions, measuring, or making observations about the real world.

Datos Los datos son información reunida mediante preguntas, mediciones u observaciones sobre la vida diaria.

English/Spanish Glossary

Debit card A debit card is a card issued by a bank that is linked to a customer's bank account, normally a checking account. A debit card can normally be used to withdraw money from an ATM or to make a purchase.

Tarjeta de débito Una tarjeta de débito es una tarjeta publicada por un banco que es ligado la cuenta bancaria de un cliente, normalmente una cuenta corriente bancaria. Una tarjeta de débito puede ser utilizada normalmente retirar dinero de una ATM o para hacer una compra.

Decimal A decimal is a number with one or more places to the right of a decimal point.

Decimal Un decimal es un número que tiene uno o más lugares a la derecha del punto decimal.

Decimal places The digits after the decimal point are called decimal places.

Lugares decimales Los dígitos que están después del punto decimal se llaman lugares decimales.

Decompose a shape To decompose a shape, break it up to form other shapes.

Descomponer una figura Para descomponer una figura, debes separarla para formar otras figuras.

Deductive reasoning Deductive reasoning is a process of reasoning logically from given facts to a conclusion.

Razonamiento deductivo El razonamiento deductivo es un proceso de razonamiento lógico que parte de hechos dados hasta llegar a una conclusión.

Denominator The denominator is the number below the fraction bar in a fraction.

Denominador El denominador es el número que está debajo de la barra de fracción en una fracción.

Dependent events Two events are dependent events if the occurrence of the first event affects the probability of the second event.

Eventos dependientes Dos eventos son dependientes si el resultado del primer evento afecta la probabilidad del segundo evento.

Deposit A transaction that adds money to a bank account is a deposit.

Depósito Una transacción que agrega dinero a una cuenta bancaria es un depósito.

English/Spanish Glossary

Dependent variable A dependent variable is a variable whose value changes in response to another (independent) variable.

Variable dependiente Una variable dependiente es una variable cuyo valor cambia en respuesta a otra variable (independiente).

Describe To describe is to explain or tell in detail. A written description can contain facts and other information needed to communicate your answer. A diagram or a graph may also be included.

Describir Describir es explicar o indicar algo en detalle. Una descripción escrita puede incluir hechos y otra información necesaria para comunicar tu respuesta. También puede incluir un diagrama o una gráfica.

Design To design is to make using specific criteria.

Diseñar Diseñar es crear algo a partir de criterios específicos.

Determine To determine is to use the given information and any related facts to find a value or make a decision.

Determinar Determinar es usar la información dada y cualquier otro dato relacionado para hallar un valor o tomar una decisión.

Deviation from the mean Deviation indicates how far away and in which direction a data value is from the mean. Data values that are less than the mean have a negative deviation. Data values that are greater than the mean have a positive deviation.

Desviación de la media La desviación indica a qué distancia y en qué dirección un valor se aleja de la media. Los valores menores que la media tienen una desviación negativa. Los valores mayores que la media tienen una desviación positiva.

Diagonal A diagonal of a figure is a segment that connects two nonconsecutive vertices of the figure.

Diagonal La diagonal de una figura es un segmento que conecta dos vértices no consecutivos de la figura.

Diameter A diameter is a segment that passes through the center of a circle and has both endpoints on the circle. The term diameter can also mean the length of this segment.

Diámetro Un diámetro es un segmento que atraviesa el centro de un círculo y tiene sus dos extremos en el círculo. El término diámetro también puede referirse a la longitud de este segmento.

Difference The difference is the answer you get when subtracting two numbers.

Diferencia La diferencia es la respuesta que obtienes cuando restas dos números.

Dilation A dilation is a transformation that moves each point along the ray through the point, starting from a fixed center, and multiplies distances from the center by a common scale factor. If a vertex of a figure is the center of dilation, then the vertex and its image after the dilation are the same point.

Dilatación Una dilatación es una transformación que mueve cada punto a lo largo de la semirrecta a través del punto, a partir de un centro fijo, y multiplica las distancias desde el centro por un factor de escala común. Si un vértice de una figura es el centro de dilatación, entonces el vértice y su imagen después de la dilatación son el mismo punto.

Direct variation A linear relationship that can be represented by an equation in the form $y = kx$, where $x \neq 0$.

Dirija variación Una relación lineal que puede ser representada por una ecuación en la forma $y = kx$, donde x no iguale 0.

Distribution (of a data set) The distribution of a data set describes the way that its data values are spread out over all possible values. This includes describing the frequencies of each data value. The shape of a data display shows the distribution of a data set.

Distribución (de un conjunto de datos) La distribución de un conjunto de datos describe la manera en que sus valores se esparcen sobre todos los valores posibles. Eso incluye la descripción de las frecuencias de cada valor. La forma de una exhibición de datos muestra la distribución de un conjunto de datos.

Distributive Property Multiplying a number by a sum or difference gives the same result as multiplying that number by each term in the sum or difference and then adding or subtracting the corresponding products.
$a \cdot (b + c) = a \cdot b + a \cdot c$ and
$a \cdot (b - c) = a \cdot b - a \cdot c$

Propiedad distributiva Multiplicar un número por una suma o una diferencia da el mismo resultado que multiplicar ese mismo número por cada uno de los términos de la suma o la diferencia y después sumar o restar los productos obtenidos.
$a \cdot (b + c) = a \cdot b + a \cdot c$ and
$a \cdot (b - c) = a \cdot b - a \cdot c$

Dividend The dividend is the number to be divided.

Dividendo El dividendo es el número que se divide.

Divisible A number is divisible by another number if there is no remainder after dividing.

Divisible Un número es divisible por otro número si no hay residuo después de dividir.

Divisor The divisor is the number used to divide another number.

Divisor El divisor es el número por el cual se divide otro número.

Dot plot A dot plot is a statistical graph that shows the shape of a data set with stacked dots above each data value on a number line. Each dot represents one data value.

Diagrama de puntos Un diagrama de puntos es una gráfica estadística que muestra la forma de un conjunto de datos con puntos marcados sobre cada valor de una recta numérica. Cada punto representa un valor.

E

Earned wages Earned wages are the income you receive from an employer for doing a job. Earned wages are also called gross pay.

Sueldos ganados Los sueldos ganados son los ingresos que usted recibe de un empleador para hacer un trabajo. Los sueldos ganados también son llamados la paga bruta.

Easy-access loan The term easy-access loan refers to a wide variety of loans with a streamlined application process. Many easy-access loans are short-term loans of relatively small amounts of money. They often have high interest rates.

Préstamo de fácil-acceso El préstamo del fácil-acceso del término se refiere a una gran variedad de préstamos con un proceso simplificado de aplicación. Muchos préstamos del fácil-acceso son préstamos a corto plazo de cantidades relativamente pequeñas de dinero. Ellos a menudo tienen los tipos de interés altos.

Edge of a three-dimensional figure An edge of a three-dimensional figure is a segment formed by the intersection of two faces.

Arista de una figura tridimensional Una arista de una figura tridimensional es un segmento formado por la intersección de dos caras.

English/Spanish Glossary

Enlargement An enlargement is a dilation with a scale factor greater than 1. After an enlargement, the image is bigger than the original figure.

Aumento Un aumento es una dilatación con un factor de escala mayor que 1. Después de un aumento, la imagen es más grande que la figura original.

Equation An equation is a mathematical sentence that includes an equals sign to compare two expressions.

Ecuación Una ecuación es una oración matemática que incluye un signo igual para comparar dos expresiones.

Equilateral triangle An equilateral triangle is a triangle whose sides are all the same length.

Triángulo equilátero Un triángulo equilátero es un triángulo que tiene todos sus lados de la misma longitud.

Equivalent equations Equivalent equations are equations that have exactly the same solutions.

Ecuaciones equivalentes Las ecuaciones equivalentes son ecuaciones que tienen exactamente la misma solución.

Equivalent expressions Equivalent expressions are expressions that always have the same value.

Expresiones equivalentes Las expresiones equivalentes son expresiones que siempre tienen el mismo valor.

Equivalent fractions Equivalent fractions are fractions that name the same number.

Fracciones equivalentes Las fracciones equivalentes son fracciones que representan el mismo número.

Equivalent inequalities Equivalent inequalities are inequalities that have the same solution.

Desigualdades equivalentes Las desigualdades equivalentes son desigualdades que tienen la misma solución.

Equivalent ratios Equivalent ratios are ratios that express the same relationship.

Razones equivalentes Las razones equivalentes son razones que expresan la misma relación.

Estimate To estimate is to find a number that is close to an exact answer.

Estimar Estimar es hallar un número cercano a una respuesta exacta.

English/Spanish Glossary

Evaluate a numerical expression To evaluate a numerical expression is to follow the order of operations.

Evaluar una expresión numérica Evaluar una expresión numérica es seguir el orden de las operaciones.

Evaluate an algebraic expression To evaluate an algebraic expression, replace each variable with a number, and then follow the order of operations.

Evaluar una expresión algebraica Para evaluar una expresión algebraica, reemplaza cada variable con un número y luego sigue el orden de las operaciones.

Event An event is a single outcome or group of outcomes from a sample space.

Evento Un evento es un resultado simple o un grupo de resultados de un espacio muestral.

Expand an algebraic expression To expand an algebraic expression, use the Distributive Property to rewrite a product as a sum or difference of terms.

Desarrollar una expresión algebraica Para desarrollar una expresión algebraica, usa la propiedad distributiva para reescribir el producto como una suma o diferencia de términos.

Expected family contribution The amount of money a student's family is expected to contribute towards the student's cost of attendance for school.

Contribución familiar esperado La cantidad de dinero que la familia de un estudiante es esperada contribuir hacia el estudiante es costado de asistencia para la escuela.

Expense Money that a business or a person needs to spend to pay for or buy something.

Gasto El dinero que un negocio o una persona debe gastar para pagar por o comprar algo.

Experiment To experiment is to try to gather information in several ways.

Experimentar Experimentar es intentar reunir información de varias maneras.

English/Spanish Glossary

Experimental probability You find the experimental probability of an event by repeating an experiment many times and using this ratio: $P(\text{event}) = \frac{\text{number of times event occurs}}{\text{total number of trials}}$

Probabilidad experimental Para hallar la probabilidad experimental de un evento, debes repetir un experimento muchas veces y usar esta razón: $P(\text{evento}) = \frac{\text{número de veces que sucede el evento}}{\text{número total de pruebas}}$

Explain To explain is to give facts and details that make an idea easier to understand. Explaining can involve a written summary supported by a diagram, chart, table, or a combination of these.

Explicar Explicar es brindar datos y detalles para que una idea sea más fácil de comprender. Para explicar algo se puede usar un resumen escrito sustentado por un diagrama, una tabla o una combinación de esos elementos.

Exponent An exponent is a number that shows how many times a base is used as a factor.

Exponente Un exponente es un número que muestra cuántas veces se usa una base como factor.

Expression An expression is a mathematical phrase that can involve variables, numbers, and operations. See algebraic expression or numerical expression.

Expresión Una expresión es una frase matemática que puede tener variables, números y operaciones. Ver expresión algebraica o expresión numérica.

Exterior angle of a triangle An exterior angle of a triangle is an angle formed by a side and an extension of an adjacent side.

Ángulo externo de un triángulo Un ángulo externo de un triángulo es un ángulo formado por un lado y una extensión de un lado adyacente.

F

Face of a three-dimensional figure A face of a three-dimensional figure is a flat surface shaped like a polygon.

Cara de una figura tridimensional La cara de una figura tridimensional es una superficie plana con forma de polígono.

English/Spanish Glossary

Factor an algebraic expression To factor an algebraic expression, write the expression as a product.

Descomponer una expresión algebraica en factores Para descomponer una expresión algebraica en factores, escribe la expresión como un producto.

Factors Factors are numbers that are multiplied to give a product.

Factores Los factores son los números que se multiplican para obtener un producto.

False equation A false equation has values that do not equal each other on each side of the equals sign.

Ecuación falsa Una ecuación falsa tiene valores a cada lado del signo igual que no son iguales entre sí.

Financial aid Financial aid is any money offered to a student to assist with the cost of attendance.

Ayuda financiera La ayuda financiera es cualquier dinero ofreció a un estudiante para ayudar con el costo de asistencia.

Financial need A student's financial need is the difference between the student's cost of attendance and the student's expected family contribution.

Necesidad financiera Una necesidad financiera del estudiante es la diferencia entre el estudiante es costada de asistencia y la contribución esperado de familia de estudiante.

Find To find is to calculate or determine.

Hallar Hallar es calcular o determinar.

First quartile For an ordered set of data, the first quartile is the median of the lower half of the data set.

Primer cuartil Para un conjunto ordenado de datos, el primer cuartil es la mediana de la mitad inferior del conjunto de datos.

Fixed expenses Fixed expenses are expenses that do not change from one budget period to the next.

Gastos fijos Los gastos fijos son los gastos que no cambian de un período económico al próximo.

Fraction A fraction is a number that can be written in the form $\frac{a}{b}$, where a is a whole number and b is a positive whole number. A fraction is formed by a parts of size $\frac{1}{b}$.

Fracción Una fracción es un número que puede expresarse de forma $\frac{a}{b}$, donde a es un entero y b es un número entero positivo. La fracción está formada por a partes de tamaño $\frac{1}{b}$.

Frequency Frequency describes the number of times a specific value occurs in a data set.

Frecuencia La frecuencia describe el número de veces que aparece un valor específico en un conjunto de datos.

Function A function is a rule for taking each input value and producing exactly one output value.

Función Una función es una regla por la cual se toma cada valor de entrada y se produce exactamente un valor de salida.

G

Gap A gap is an area of a graph that contains no data points.

Espacio vacío o brecha Un espacio vacío o brecha es un área de una gráfica que no contiene ningún valor.

Grant A type of monetary award a student can use to pay for his or her education. The student does not need to repay this money.

Grant Un tipo de premio monetario que un estudiante puede utilizar para pagar por su educación. El estudiante no debe devolver este dinero.

Greater than $>$ The greater-than symbol shows a comparison of two numbers with the number of greater value shown first, or on the left.

Mayor que $>$ El símbolo de mayor que muestra una comparación de dos números con el número de mayor valor que aparece primero, o a la izquierda.

Greatest common factor The greatest common factor (GCF) of two or more whole numbers is the greatest number that is a factor of all of the numbers.

Máximo común divisor El máximo común divisor (M.C.D.) de dos o más números enteros no negativos es el número mayor que es un factor de todos los números.

English/Spanish Glossary

H

Height of a cone The height of a cone, *h*, is the length of a segment perpendicular to the base that joins the vertex and the base.

Altura de un cono La altura de un cono, *h*, es la longitud de un segmento perpendicular a la base que une el vértice y la base.

Height of a cylinder The height of a cylinder is the length of a perpendicular segment that joins the planes of the bases.

Altura de un cilindro La altura de un cilindro es la longitud de un segmento perpendicular que une los planos de las bases.

Height of a parallelogram A height of a parallelogram is the perpendicular distance between opposite bases.

Altura de un paralelogramo La altura de un paralelogramo es la distancia perpendicular que existe entre las bases opuestas.

Height of a prism The height of a prism is the length of a perpendicular segment that joins the bases.

Altura de un prisma La altura de un prisma es la longitud de un segmento perpendicular que une a las bases.

Height of a pyramid The height of a pyramid is the length of a segment perpendicular to the base that joins the vertex and the base.

Altura de una pirámide La altura de una pirámide es la longitud de un segmento perpendicular a la base que une al vértice con la base.

Height of a triangle The height of a triangle is the length of the perpendicular segment from a vertex to the base opposite that vertex.

Altura de un triángulo La altura de un triángulo es la longitud del segmento perpendicular desde un vértice hasta la base opuesta a ese vértice.

Hexagon A hexagon is a polygon with six sides.

Hexágono Un hexágono es un polígono de seis lados.

Histogram A histogram is a statistical graph that shows the shape of a data set with vertical bars above intervals of values on a number line. The intervals are equal in size and do not overlap. The height of each bar shows the frequency of data within that interval.

Histograma Un histograma es una gráfica de estadísticas que muestra la forma de un conjunto de datos con barras verticales encima de intervalos de valores en una recta numérica. Los intervalos tienen el mismo tamaño y no se superponen. La altura de cada barra muestra la frecuencia de los datos dentro de ese intervalo.

Hundredths One hundredth is one part of 100 equal parts of a whole.

Centésima Una centésima es 1 de las 100 partes iguales de un todo.

Hypotenuse In a right triangle, the longest side, which is opposite the right angle, is the hypotenuse.

Hipotenusa En un triángulo rectángulo, el lado más largo, que es opuesto al ángulo recto, es la hipotenusa.

I

Identify To identify is to match a definition or description to an object or to recognize something and be able to name it.

Identificar Identificar es unir una definición o una descripción con un objeto, o reconocer algo y poder nombrarlo.

Identity Property of Addition The sum of 0 and any number is that number. For any number n, $n + 0 = n$ and $0 + n = n$.

Propiedad de identidad de la suma La suma de 0 y cualquier número es ese número. Para cualquier número n, $n + 0 = n$ and $0 + n = n$.

Identity Property of Multiplication The product of 1 and any number is that number. For any number n, $n \cdot 1 = n$ and $1 \cdot n = n$.

Propiedad de identidad de la multiplicación El producto de 1 y cualquier número es ese número. Para cualquier número n, $n \cdot 1 = n$ and $1 \cdot n = n$.

Illustrate To illustrate is to show or present information, usually as a drawing or a diagram. You can also illustrate a point using a written explanation.

Ilustrar Ilustrar es mostrar o presentar información, generalmente en forma de dibujo o diagrama. También puedes usar una explicación escrita para ilustrar un punto.

English/Spanish Glossary

Image An image is the result of a transformation of a point, line, or figure.

Imagen Una imagen es el resultado de una transformación de un punto, una recta o una figura.

Improper fraction An improper fraction is a fraction in which the numerator is greater than or equal to its denominator.

Fracción impropia Una fracción impropia es una fracción en la cual el numerador es mayor que o igual a su denominador.

Included angle An included angle is an angle that is between two sides.

Ángulo incluido Un ángulo incluido es un ángulo que está entre dos lados.

Included side An included side is a side that is between two angles.

Lado incluido Un lado incluido es un lado que está entre dos ángulos.

Income Money that a business receives. The money that a person earns from working is also called income.

Ingresos El dinero que un negocio recibe. El dinero que una persona gana de trabajar también es llamado los ingresos.

Income tax Income tax is money collected by the government based on how much you earn.

Impuesto de renta El impuesto de renta es dinero completo por el gobierno basado en cuánto gana.

Independent events Two events are independent events if the occurrence of one event does not affect the probability of the other event.

Eventos independientes Dos eventos son eventos independientes cuando el resultado de un evento no altera la probabilidad del otro.

Independent variable An independent variable is a variable whose value determines the value of another (dependent) variable.

Variable independiente Una variable independiente es una variable cuyo valor determina el valor de otra variable (dependiente).

Indicate To indicate is to point out or show.

Indicar Indicar es señalar o mostrar.

English/Spanish Glossary

Indirect measurement Indirect measurement uses proportions and similar triangles to measure distances that would be difficult to measure directly.

Medición indirecta La medición indirecta usa proporciones y triángulos semejantes para medir distancias que serían difíciles de medir de forma directa.

Inequality An inequality is a mathematical sentence that uses $<$, $\leq$, $>$, $\geq$, or $\neq$ to compare two quantities.

Desigualdad Una desigualdad es una oración matemática que usa $<$, $\leq$, $>$, $\geq$, o $\neq$ para comparar dos cantidades.

Inference An inference is a judgment made by interpreting data.

Inferencia Una inferencia es una opinión que se forma al interpretar datos.

Infinitely many solutions A linear equation in one variable has infinitely many solutions if any value of the variable makes the two sides of the equation equal.

Número infinito de soluciones Una ecuación lineal en una variable tiene un número infinito de soluciones si cualquier valor de la variable hace que los dos lados de la ecuación sean iguales.

Initial value The initial value of a linear function is the value of the output when the input is 0.

Valor inicial El valor inicial de una función lineal es el valor de salida cuando el valor de entrada es 0.

Integers Integers are the set of positive whole numbers, their opposites, and 0.

Enteros Los enteros son el conjunto de los números enteros positivos, sus opuestos y 0.

Interest When you deposit money in a bank account, the bank pays you interest for the right to use your money for a period of time.

Interés Cuando depositas dinero en una cuenta bancaria, el banco te paga un interés por el derecho a usar tu dinero por un período de tiempo.

Interest period The length of time on which compound interest is based. The total number of interest periods that you keep the money in the account is represented by the variable n.

Período de interés La cantidad de tiempo sobre la que se calcula el interés compuesto. El número total de períodos de interés que mantienes el dinero en la cuenta se representa con la variable n.

Interest rate Interest is calculated based on a percent of the principal. That percent is called the interest rate (*r*).

Tasa de interés El interés se calcula con base en un porcentaje del capital. Ese porcentaje se llama tasa de interés, (*r*).

Interest rate for an interest period The interest rate for an interest period is the annual interest rate divided by the number of interest periods per year.

El tipo de interés por un período de interés El tipo de interés por un período de interés es el tipo de interés anual dividido por el número de períodos de interés por año.

Interquartile range The interquartile range (IQR) is the distance between the first and third quartiles of the data set. It represents the spread of the middle 50% of the data values.

Rango intercuartil El rango intercuartil es la distancia entre el primer y el tercer cuartil del conjunto de datos. Representa la ubicación del 50% del medio de los valores.

Interval An interval is a period of time between two points of time or events.

Intervalo Un intervalo es un período de tiempo entre dos puntos en el tiempo o entre dos sucesos.

Invalid inference An invalid inference is false about the population, or does not follow from the available data. A biased sample can lead to invalid inferences.

Inferencia inválida Una inferencia inválida es una inferencia falsa acerca de una población, o no se deduce a partir de los datos disponibles. Una muestra sesgada puede llevar a inferencias inválidas.

Inverse operations Inverse operations are operations that undo each other.

Operaciones inversas Las operaciones inversas son operaciones que se cancelan entre sí.

Inverse Property of Addition Every number has an additive inverse. The sum of a number and its additive inverse is zero.

Propiedad inversa de la suma Todos los números tienen un inverso de suma. La suma de un número y su inverso de suma es cero.

Irrational numbers An irrational number is a number that cannot be written in the form $\frac{a}{b}$, where a and b are integers and $b \neq 0$. In decimal form, an irrational number cannot be written as a terminating or repeating decimal.

Números irracionales Un número irracional es un número que no se puede escribir en la forma $\frac{a}{b}$ donde a y b, son enteros y $b \neq 0$. Los números racionales en forma decimal no son finitos y no son periódicos.

Isolate a variable When solving equations, to isolate a variable means to get a variable with a coefficient of 1 alone on one side of an equation. Use the properties of equality and inverse operations to isolate a variable.

Aislar una variable Cuando resuelves ecuaciones, aislar una variable significa poner una variable con un coeficiente de 1 sola a un lado de la ecuación. Usa las propiedades de igualdad y las operaciones inversas para aislar una variable.

Isosceles triangle An isosceles triangle is a triangle with at least two sides that are the same length.

Triángulo isósceles Un triángulo isósceles es un triángulo que tiene al menos dos lados de la misma longitud.

J

Justify To justify is to support your answer with reasons or examples. A justification may include a written response, diagrams, charts, tables, or a combination of these.

Justificar Justificar es apoyar tu respuesta con razones o ejemplos. Una justificación puede incluir una respuesta escrita, diagramas, tablas o una combinación de esos elementos.

L

Lateral area of a cone The lateral area of a cone is the area of its lateral surface. The formula for the lateral area of a cone is L.A. $= \pi r \ell$, where r represents the radius of the base and ℓ represents the slant height of the cone.

Área lateral de un cono El área lateral de un cono es el área de su superficie lateral. La fórmula del área lateral de un cono es A.L. $= \pi r \ell$, donde r representa el radio de la base y ℓ representa la altura inclinada del cono.

English/Spanish Glossary

Lateral area of a cylinder The lateral area of a cylinder is the area of its lateral surface. The formula for the lateral area of a cylinder is L.A. $= 2\pi rh$, where r represents the radius of a base and h represents the height of the cylinder.

Área lateral de un cilindro El área lateral de un cilindro es el área de su superficie lateral. La fórmula del área lateral de un cilindro es A.L. $= 2\pi rh$, donde r representa el radio de una base y h representa la altura del cilindro.

Lateral area of a prism The lateral area of a prism is the sum of the areas of the lateral faces of the prism. The formula for the lateral area, L.A., of a prism is L.A. $= ph$, where p represents the perimeter of the base and h represents the height of the prism.

Área lateral de un prisma El área lateral de un prisma es la suma de las áreas de las caras laterales del prisma. La fórmula del área lateral, A.L., de un prisma es A.L. $= ph$, donde p representa el perímetro de la base y h representa la altura del prisma.

Lateral area of a pyramid The lateral area of a pyramid is the sum of the areas of the lateral faces of the pyramid. The formula for the lateral area, L.A., of a pyramid is L.A. $= \frac{1}{2}p\ell$ where p represents the perimeter of the base and ℓ represents the slant height of the pyramid.

Área lateral de una pirámide El área lateral de una pirámide es la suma de las áreas de las caras laterales de la pirámide. La fórmula del área lateral, A.L., de una pirámide es A.L. $= \frac{1}{2}p\ell$ donde p representa el perímetro de la base y ℓ representa la altura inclinada de la pirámide.

Lateral face of a prism A lateral face of a prism is a face that joins the bases of the prism.

Cara lateral de un prisma La cara lateral de un prisma es la cara que une a las bases del prisma.

Lateral face of a pyramid A lateral face of a pyramid is a triangular face that joins the base and the vertex.

Cara lateral de una pirámide La cara lateral de una pirámide es una cara lateral que une a la base con el vértice.

Lateral surface of a cone The lateral surface of a cone is the curved surface that is not included in the base.

Superficie lateral de un cono La superficie lateral de un cono es la superficie curva que no está incluida en la base.

English/Spanish Glossary

Lateral surface of a cylinder The lateral surface of a cylinder is the curved surface that is not included in the bases.

Superficie lateral de un cilindro La superficie lateral de un cilindro es la superficie curva que no está incluida en las bases.

Least common multiple The least common multiple (LCM) of two or more numbers is the least multiple shared by all of the numbers.

Mínimo común múltiplo El mínimo común múltiplo (MCM) de dos o más números es el múltiplo menor compartido por todos los números.

Leg of a right triangle In a right triangle, the two shortest sides are legs.

Cateto de un triángulo rectángulo En un triángulo rectángulo, los dos lados más cortos son los catetos.

Less than $<$ The less-than symbol shows a comparison of two numbers with the number of lesser value shown first, or on the left.

Menor que $<$ El símbolo de menor que muestra una comparación de dos números con el número de menor valor que aparece primero, o a la izquierda.

Liability A liability is money that you owe.

Obligación Una obligación es dinero que usted debe.

Lifetime income The amount of money earned over a lifetime of working.

Ingresos para toda la vida La cantidad de dinero ganó sobre una vida de trabajar.

Like terms Terms that have identical variable parts are like terms.

Términos semejantes Los términos que tienen partes variables idénticas son términos semejantes.

Line of reflection A line of reflection is a line across which a figure is reflected.

Eje de reflexión Un eje de reflexión es una línea a través de la cual se refleja una figura.

Linear equation An equation is a linear equation if the graph of all of its solutions is a line.

Ecuación lineal Una ecuación es lineal si la gráfica de todas sus soluciones es una línea recta.

English/Spanish Glossary

Linear function A linear function is a function whose graph is a straight line. The rate of change for a linear function is constant.

Función lineal Una función lineal es una función cuya gráfica es una línea recta. La tasa de cambio en una función lineal es constante.

Linear function rule A linear function rule is an equation that describes a linear function.

Regla de la función lineal La ecuación que describe una función lineal es la regla de la función lineal.

Loan A loan is an amount of money borrowed for a period of time with the promise of paying it back.

Préstamo Un préstamo es una cantidad de dinero pedido prestaddo por un espacio de tiempo con la promesa de pagarlo apoya.

Loan length Loan length is the period of time set to repay a loan.

Preste longitud La longitud del préstamo es el conjunto de espacio de tiempo de devolver un préstamo.

Loan term The term of a loan is the period of time set to repay the loan.

Preste término El término de un préstamo es el conjunto de espacio de tiempo de devolver el préstamo.

Locate To locate is to find or identify a value, usually on a number line or coordinate graph.

Ubicar Ubicar es hallar o identificar un valor, generalmente en una recta numérica o en una gráfica de coordenadas.

Loss When a business's expenses are greater than the business's income, there is a loss.

Pérdida Cuando los gastos de un negocio son más que los ingresos del negocio, hay una pérdida.

M

Mapping diagram A mapping diagram describes a relation by linking the input values to the corresponding output values using arrows.

Diagrama de correspondencia Un diagrama de correspondencia describe una relación uniendo con flechas los valores de entrada con sus correspondientes valores de salida.

Markdown Markdown is the amount of decrease from the selling price to the sale price. The markdown as a percent decrease of the original selling price is called the percent markdown.

Rebaja La rebaja es la cantidad de disminución de un precio de venta a un precio rebajado. La rebaja como una disminución porcentual del precio de venta original se llama porcentaje de rebaja.

Markup Markup is the amount of increase from the cost to the selling price. The markup as a percent increase of the original cost is called the percent markup.

Margen de ganancia El margen de ganancia es la cantidad de aumento del costo al precio de venta. El margen de ganancia como un aumento porcentual del costo original se llama porcentaje del margen de ganancia.

Mean The mean represents the center of a numerical data set. To find the mean, sum the data values and then divide by the number of values in the data set.

Media La media representa el centro de un conjunto de datos numéricos. Para hallar la media, suma los valores y luego divide por el número de valores del conjunto de datos.

Mean absolute deviation The mean absolute deviation is a measure of variability that describes how much the data values are spread out from the mean of a data set. The mean absolute deviation is the average distance that the data values are spread around the mean. mean absolute deviation =

$$\frac{\text{sum of the absolute deviations of the data values}}{\text{total number of data values}}$$

Desviación absoluta media La desviación absoluta media es una medida de variabilidad que describe cuánto se alejan los valores de la media de un conjunto de datos. La desviación absoluta media es la distancia promedio que los valores se alejan de la media. desviación absoluta media =

$$\frac{\text{suma de las desviaciones absolutas de los valores}}{\text{número total de valores}}$$

English/Spanish Glossary

Measure of variability A measure of variability describes the spread of values in a data set. There may be more than one measure of variability for a data set.

Medida de variabilidad Una medida de variabilidad describe la distribución de los valores de un conjunto de datos. Puede haber más de una medida de variabilidad para un conjunto de datos.

Measurement data Measurement data consist of data that are measures.

Datos de mediciones Los datos de mediciones son datos que son medidas.

Measures of center A measure of center is a value that represents the middle of a data set. There may be more than one measure of center for a data set.

Medida de tendencia central Una medida de tendencia central es un valor que representa el centro de un conjunto de datos. Puede haber más de una medida de tendencia central para un conjunto de datos.

Median The median represents the center of a numerical data set. For an odd number of data values, the median is the middle value when the data values are arranged in numerical order. For an even number of data values, the median is the average of the two middle values when the data values are arranged in numerical order.

Mediana La mediana representa el centro de un conjunto de datos numéricos. Para un número impar de valores, la mediana es el valor del medio cuando los valores están organizados en orden numérico. Para un número par de valores, la mediana es el promedio de los dos valores del medio cuando los valores están organizados en orden numérico.

Median-median line The median-median line, or median trend line, is a method of finding a fit line for a scatter plot that suggests a linear association. This method involves dividing the data into three subgroups and using medians to find a summary point for each subgroup. The summary points are used to find the equation of the fit line.

Recta mediana-mediana La recta mediana-mediana es un método que se usa para hallar una línea de ajuste para un diagrama de dispersión que sugiere una asociación lineal. Este método implica dividir los datos en tres subgrupos y usar medianas para hallar un punto medio para cada subgrupo. Los puntos medios se usan para hallar la ecuación de la línea de ajuste.

Million Whole numbers in the millions have 7, 8, or 9 digits.

Millón Los números enteros no negativos que están en los millones tienen 7, 8 ó 9 dígitos.

Mixed number A mixed number combines a whole number and a fraction.

Número mixto Un número mixto combina un número entero no negativo con una fracción.

Mode The item, or items, in a data set that occurs most frequently.

Modo El artículo, o los artículos, en un conjunto de datos que ocurre normalmente.

Model To model is to represent a situation using pictures, diagrams, or number sentences.

Demostrar Demostrar es usar ilustraciones, diagramas o enunciados numéricos para representar una situación.

Monetary incentive A monetary incentive is an offer that might encourage customers to buy a product.

Estímulo monetario Un estímulo monetario es una oferta que quizás favorezca a clientes para comprar un producto.

Multiple A multiple of a number is the product of the number and a whole number.

Múltiplo El múltiplo de un número es el producto del número y un número entero no negativo.

N

Natural numbers The natural numbers are the counting numbers.

Números naturales Los números naturales son los números que se usan para contar.

Negative exponent property For every nonzero number a and integer n, $a^{-n} = \frac{1}{a^n}$.

Propiedad del exponente negativo Para todo número distinto de cero a y entero n, $a^{-n} = \frac{1}{a^n}$.

Negative numbers Negative numbers are numbers less than zero.

Números negativos Los números negativos son números menores que cero.

Net A net is a two-dimensional pattern that you can fold to form a three-dimensional figure. A net of a figure shows all of the surfaces of that figure in one view.

Modelo plano Un modelo plano es un diseño bidimensional que puedes doblar para formar una figura tridimensional. Un modelo plano de una figura muestra todas las superficies de la figura en una vista.

Net worth Net worth is the total value of all assets minus the total value of all liabilities.

Patrimonio neto El patrimonio neto es el valor total de todas las ventajas menos el valor total de todas las obligaciones.

Net worth statement Net worth is the total value of all assets minus the total value of all liabilities.

Declaración de patrimonio neto El patrimonio neto es el valor total de todas las ventajas menos el valor total de todas las obligaciones.

No solution A linear equation in one variable has no solution if no value of the variable makes the two sides of the equation equal.

Sin solución Una ecuación lineal en una variable no tiene solución si ningún valor de la variable hace que los dos lados de la ecuación sean iguales.

Nonlinear function A nonlinear function is a function that does not have a constant rate of change.

Función no lineal Una función no lineal es una función que no tiene una tasa de cambio constante.

Numerator The numerator is the number above the fraction bar in a fraction.

Numerador El numerador es el número que está arriba de la barra de fracción en una fracción.

Numerical expression A numerical expression is a mathematical phrase that consists of numbers and operation symbols.

Expresión numérica Una expresión numérica es una frase matemática que contiene números y símbolos de operaciones.

English/Spanish Glossary

O

Obtuse angle An obtuse angle is an angle with a measure greater than 90° and less than 180°.

Ángulo obtuso Un ángulo obtuso es un ángulo con una medida mayor que 90° y menor que 180°.

Obtuse triangle An obtuse triangle is a triangle with one obtuse angle.

Triángulo obtusángulo Un triángulo obtusángulo es un triángulo que tiene un ángulo obtuso.

Octagon An octagon is a polygon with eight sides.

Octágono Un octágono es un polígono de ocho lados.

Online payment system An online payment system allows money to be exchanged electronically between buyer and seller, usually using credit card or bank account information.

Sistema en línea de pago Un sistema en línea del pago permite dinero para ser cambiado electrónicamente entre comprador y vendedor, utilizando generalmente información de tarjeta de crédito o cuenta bancaria.

Open sentence An open sentence is an equation with one or more variables.

Enunciado abierto Un enunciado abierto es una ecuación con una o más variables.

Opposites Opposites are two numbers that are the same distance from 0 on a number line, but in opposite directions.

Opuestos Los opuestos son dos números que están a la misma distancia de 0 en la recta numérica, pero en direcciones opuestas.

Order of operations The order of operations is the order in which operations should be performed in an expression. Operations inside parentheses are done first, followed by exponents. Then, multiplication and division are done in order from left to right, and finally addition and subtraction are done in order from left to right.

Orden de las operaciones El orden de las operaciones es el orden en el que se deben resolver las operaciones de una expresión. Las operaciones que están entre paréntesis se resuelven primero, seguidas de los exponentes. Luego, se multiplica y se divide en orden de izquierda a derecha, y finalmente se suma y se resta en orden de izquierda a derecha.

Ordered pair An ordered pair identifies the location of a point in the coordinate plane. The *x*-coordinate shows a point's position left or right of the *y*-axis. The *y*-coordinate shows a point's position up or down from the *x*-axis.

Par ordenado Un par ordenado identifica la ubicación de un punto en el plano de coordenadas. La coordenada *x* muestra la posición de un punto a la izquierda o a la derecha del eje de las *y*. La coordenada *y* muestra la posición de un punto arriba o abajo del eje de las *x*.

Origin The origin is the point of intersection of the *x*- and *y*-axes on a coordinate plane.

Origen El origen es el punto de intersección del eje de las *x* y el eje de las *y* en un plano de coordenadas.

Outcome An outcome is a possible result of an action.

Resultado Un resultado es un desenlace posible de una acción.

Outlier An outlier is a piece of data that doesn't seem to fit with the rest of a data set.

Valor extremo Un valor extremo es un valor que parece no ajustarse al resto de los datos de un conjunto.

P

Parallel lines Parallel lines are lines in the same plane that never intersect.

Rectas paralelas Las rectas paralelas son rectas que están en el mismo plano y nunca se intersecan.

Parallelogram A parallelogram is a quadrilateral with both pairs of opposite sides parallel.

Paralelogramo Un paralelogramo es un cuadrilátero en el cual los dos pares de lados opuestos son paralelos.

Partial product A partial product is part of the total product. A product is the sum of the partial products.

Producto parcial Un producto parcial es una parte del producto total. Un producto es la suma de los productos parciales.

English/Spanish Glossary

Pay period Wages for many jobs are paid at regular intervals, such a weekly, biweekly, semimonthly, or monthly. The interval of time is called a pay period.

Pague el período Los sueldos para muchos trabajos son pagados con regularidad, tal semanal, quincenal, quincenal, o mensual. El intervalo de tiempo es llamado un período de la paga.

Payroll deductions Your employer can deduct your income taxes from your wages before you receive your paycheck. The amounts deducted are called payroll deductions.

Deducciones de nómina Su empleador puede descontar sus impuestos de renta de sus sueldos antes que reciba su cheque de pago. Las cantidades descontadas son llamadas nómina deducciones.

Percent A percent is a ratio that compares a number to 100.

Porcentaje Un porcentaje es una razón que compara un número con 100.

Percent bar graph A percent bar graph is a bar graph that shows each category as a percent of the total number of data items.

Gráfico de barras de por ciento Un gráfico de barras del por ciento es un gráfico de barras que muestra cada categoría como un por ciento del número total de artículos de datos.

Percent decrease When a quantity decreases, the percent of change is called a percent decrease. percent decrease = $\frac{\text{amount of decrease}}{\text{original quantity}}$

Disminución porcentual Cuando una cantidad disminuye, el porcentaje de cambio se llama disminución porcentual. disminución porcentual = $\frac{\text{cantidad de disminución}}{\text{cantidad original}}$

Percent equation The percent equation describes the relationship between a part and a whole. You can use the percent equation to solve percent problems. part = percent · whole

Ecuación de porcentaje La ecuación de porcentaje describe la relación entre una parte y un todo. Puedes usar la ecuación de porcentaje para resolver problemas de porcentaje. parte = por ciento · todo

Percent error Percent error describes the accuracy of a measured or estimated value compared to an actual or accepted value.

Error porcentual El error porcentual describe la exactitud de un valor medido o estimado en comparación con un valor real o aceptado.

Percent increase When a quantity increases, the percent of change is called a percent increase.

Aumento porcentual Cuando una cantidad aumenta, el porcentaje de cambio se llama aumento porcentual.

Percent of change Percent of change is the percent something increases or decreases from its original measure or amount. You can find the percent of change by using the equation: percent of change $= \frac{\text{amount of change}}{\text{original quantity}}$

Porcentaje de cambio El porcentaje de cambio es el porcentaje en que algo aumenta o disminuye en relación a la medida o cantidad original. Puedes hallar el porcentaje de cambio con la siguiente ecuación: porcentaje de cambio $= \frac{\text{cantidad de cambio}}{\text{cantidad original}}$

Perfect cube A perfect cube is the cube of an integer.

Cubo perfecto Un cubo perfecto es el cubo de un entero.

Perfect square A perfect square is a number that is the square of an integer.

Cuadrado perfecto Un cuadrado perfecto es un número que es el cuadrado de un entero.

Perimeter Perimeter is the distance around a figure.

Perímetro El perímetro es la distancia alrededor de una figura.

Period A period is a group of 3 digits in a number. Periods are separated by a comma and start from the right of a number.

Período Un período es un grupo de 3 dígitos en un número. Los períodos están separados por una coma y empiezan a la derecha del número.

Periodic savings plan A periodic savings plan is a method of saving that involves making deposits on a regular basis.

Plan de ahorros periódico Un plan de ahorros periódico es un método de guardar que implica depósitos que hace con regularidad.

Perpendicular lines Perpendicular lines intersect to form right angles.

Rectas perpendiculares Las rectas perpendiculares se intersecan para formar ángulos rectos.

Pi Pi (π) is the ratio of a circle's circumference, *C*, to its diameter, *d*.

Pi Pi (π) es la razón de la circunferencia de un círculo, *C*, a su diámetro, *d*.

Place value Place value is the value given to an individual digit based on its position within a number.

Valor posicional El valor posicional es el valor asignado a determinado dígito según su posición en un número.

Plane A plane is a flat surface that extends indefinitely in all directions.

Plano Un plano es una superficie plana que se extiende indefinidamente en todas direcciones.

Polygon A polygon is a closed figure formed by three or more line segments that do not cross.

Polígono Un polígono es una figura cerrada compuesta por tres o más segmentos que no se cruzan.

Population A population is the complete set of items being studied.

Población Una población es todo el conjunto de elementos que se estudian.

Positive numbers Positive numbers are numbers greater than zero.

Números positivos Los números positivos son números mayores que cero.

Power A power is a number expressed using an exponent.

Potencia Una potencia es un número expresado con un exponente.

Predict To predict is to make an educated guess based on the analysis of real data.

Predecir Predecir es hacer una estimación informada según el análisis de datos reales.

Prime factorization The prime factorization of a composite number is the expression of the number as a product of its prime factors.

Descomposición en factores primos La descomposición en factores primos de un número compuesto es la expresión del número como un producto de sus factores primos.

English/Spanish Glossary

Prime number A prime number is a whole number greater than 1 with exactly two factors, 1 and the number itself.

Número primo Un número primo es un número entero mayor que 1 con exactamente dos factores, 1 y el número mismo.

Principal The original amount of money deposited or borrowed in an account.

Capital La cantidad original de dinero que se deposita o se pide prestada en una cuenta.

Prism A prism is a three-dimensional figure with two parallel polygonal faces that are the same size and shape.

Prisma Un prisma es una figura tridimensional con dos caras poligonales paralelas que tienen el mismo tamaño y la misma forma.

Probability model A probability model consists of an action, its sample space, and a list of events with their probabilities. The events and probabilities in the list have these characteristics: each outcome in the sample space is in exactly one event, and the sum of all of the probabilities must be 1.

Modelo de probabilidad Un modelo de probabilidad consiste en una acción, su espacio muestral y una lista de eventos con sus probabilidades. Los eventos y las probabilidades de la lista tienen estas características: cada resultado del espacio muestral está exactamente en un evento, y la suma de todas las probabilidades debe ser 1.

Probability of an event The probability of an event is a number from 0 to 1 that measures the likelihood that the event will occur. The closer the probability is to 0, the less likely it is that the event will happen. The closer the probability is to 1, the more likely it is that the event will happen. You can express probability as a fraction, decimal, or percent.

Probabilidad de un evento La probabilidad de un evento es un número de 0 a 1 que mide la probabilidad de que suceda el evento. Cuanto más se acerca la probabilidad a 0, menos probable es que suceda el evento. Cuanto más se acerca la probabilidad a 1, más probable es que suceda el evento. Puedes expresar la probabilidad como una fracción, un decimal o un porcentaje.

Product A product is the value of a multiplication or an expression showing multiplication.

Producto Un producto es el valor de una multiplicación o una expresión que representa la multiplicación.

Profit When a business's expenses are less than the business's income, there is a profit.

Ganancia Cuando los gastos de un negocio son menos que los ingresos del negocio, hay una ganancia.

Proof A proof is a logical, deductive argument in which every statement of fact is supported by a reason.

Comprobación Una comprobación es un argumento lógico y deductivo en el que cada enunciado de un hecho está apoyado por una razón.

Proper fraction A proper fraction has a numerator that is less than its denominator.

Fracción propia Una fracción propia tiene un numerador que es menor que su denominador.

Proportion A proportion is an equation stating that two ratios are equal.

Proporción Una proporción es una ecuación que establece que dos razones son iguales.

Proportional relationship Two quantities x and y have a proportional relationship if y is always a constant multiple of x. A relationship is proportional if it can be described by equivalent ratios.

Relación de proporción Dos cantidades x y y tienen una relación de proporción si y es siempre un múltiplo constante de x. Una relación es de proporción si se puede describir con razones equivalentes.

Pyramid A pyramid is a three-dimensional figure with a base that is a polygon and triangular faces that meet at a vertex. A pyramid is named for the shape of its base.

Pirámide Una pirámide es una figura tridimensional con una base que es un polígono y caras triangulares que se unen en un vértice. El nombre de la pirámide depende de la forma de su base.

Pythagorean Theorem In any right triangle, the sum of the squares of the lengths of the legs equals the square of the length of the hypotenuse. If a triangle is a right triangle, then $a^2 + b^2 = c^2$, where a and b represent the lengths of the legs, and c represents the length of the hypotenuse.

Teorema de Pitágoras En cualquier triángulo rectángulo, la suma del cuadrado de la longitud de los catetos es igual al cuadrado de la longitud de la hipotenusa. Si un triángulo es un triángulo rectángulo, entonces $a^2 + b^2 = c^2$, donde a y b representan la longitud de los catetos, y c representa la longitud de la hipotenusa.

Q

Quadrant The x- and y-axes divide the coordinate plane into four regions called quadrants.

Cuadrante Los ejes de las x y de las y dividen el plano de coordenadas en cuatro regiones llamadas cuadrantes.

Quadrilateral A quadrilateral is a polygon with four sides.

Cuadrilátero Un cuadrilátero es un polígono de cuatro lados.

Quarter circle A quarter circle is one fourth of a circle.

Círculo cuarto Un círculo cuarto es la cuarta parte de un círculo.

Quartile The quartiles of a data set divide the data set into four parts with the same number of data values in each part.

Cuartil Los cuartiles de un conjunto de datos dividen el conjunto de datos en cuatro partes que tienen el mismo número de valores cada una.

Quotient The quotient is the answer to a division problem. When there is a remainder, "quotient" sometimes refers to the whole-number portion of the answer.

Cociente El cociente es el resultado de una división. Cuando queda un residuo, "cociente" a veces se refiere a la parte de la solución que es un número entero.

R

Radius A radius of a circle is a segment that has one endpoint at the center and the other endpoint on the circle. The term radius can also mean the length of this segment.

Radio Un radio de un círculo es un segmento que tiene un extremo en el centro y el otro extremo en el círculo. El término radio también puede referirse a la longitud de este segmento.

Radius of a sphere The radius of a sphere, r, is a segment that has one endpoint at the center and the other endpoint on the sphere.

Radio de una esfera El radio de una esfera, r, es un segmento que tiene un extremo en el centro y el otro extremo en la esfera.

Random sample In a random sample, each member in the population has an equal chance of being selected.

Muestra aleatoria En una muestra aleatoria, cada miembro en la población tiene una oportunidad igual de ser seleccionado.

Range The range is a measure of variability of a numerical data set. The range of a data set is the difference between the greatest and least values in a data set.

Rango El rango es una medida de la variabilidad de un conjunto de datos numéricos. El rango de un conjunto de datos es la diferencia que existe entre el mayor y el menor valor del conjunto.

Rate A rate is a ratio involving two quantities measured in different units.

Tasa Una tasa es una razón que relaciona dos cantidades medidas con unidades diferentes.

Rate of change The rate of change of a linear function is the ratio $\frac{\text{vertical change}}{\text{horizontal change}}$ between any two points on the graph of the function.

Tasa de cambio La tasa de cambio de una función lineal es la razón del $\frac{\text{cambio vertical}}{\text{cambio horizontal}}$ que existe entre dos puntos cualesquiera de la gráfica de la función.

Ratio A ratio is a relationship in which for every x units of one quantity there are y units of another quantity.

Razón Una razón es una relación en la cual por cada x unidades de una cantidad hay y unidades de otra cantidad.

Rational numbers A rational number is a number that can be written in the form $\frac{a}{b}$ or $-\frac{a}{b}$, where a is a whole number and b is a positive whole number. The rational numbers include the integers.

Números racionales Un número racional es un número que se puede escribir como $\frac{a}{b}$ or $-\frac{a}{b}$, donde a es un número entero no negativo y b es un número entero positivo. Los números racionales incluyen los enteros.

Real numbers The real numbers are the set of rational and irrational numbers.

Números reales Los números reales son el conjunto de los números racionales e irracionales.

Reason To reason is to think through a problem using facts and information.

Razonar Razonar es usar hechos e información para estudiar detenidamente un problema.

Rebate A rebate returns part of the purchase price of an item after the buyer provides proof of purchase through a mail-in or online form.

Reembolso Un reembolso regresa la parte del precio de compra de un artículo después de que el comprador proporcione comprobante de compra por un correo-en o forma en línea.

Recall To recall is to remember a fact quickly.

Recordar Recordar es traer a la memoria un hecho rápidamente.

Reciprocals Two numbers are reciprocals if their product is 1. If a nonzero number is named as a fraction, $\frac{a}{b}$, then its reciprocal is $\frac{b}{a}$.

Recíprocos Dos números son recíprocos si su producto es 1. Si un número distinto de cero se expresa como una fracción, $\frac{a}{b}$, entonces su recíproco es $\frac{b}{a}$.

Rectangle A rectangle is a quadrilateral with four right angles.

Rectángulo Un rectángulo es un cuadrilátero que tiene cuatro ángulos rectos.

Rectangular prism A rectangular prism is a prism with bases in the shape of a rectangle.

Prisma rectangular Un prisma rectangular es un prisma cuyas bases tienen la forma de un rectángulo.

English/Spanish Glossary

Reduction A reduction is a dilation with a scale factor less than 1. After a reduction, the image is smaller than the original figure.

Reducción Una reducción es una dilatación con un factor de escala menor que 1. Después de una reducción, la imagen es más pequeña que la figura original.

Reflection A reflection, or flip, is a transformation that flips a figure across a line of reflection.

Reflexión Una reflexión, o inversión, es una transformación que invierte una figura a través de un eje de reflexión.

Regular polygon A regular polygon is a polygon with all sides of equal length and all angles of equal measure.

Polígono regular Un polígono regular es un polígono que tiene todos los lados de la misma longitud y todos los ángulos de la misma medida.

Relate To relate two different things, find a connection between them.

Relacionar Para relacionar dos cosas diferentes, halla una conexión entre ellas.

Relation Any set of ordered pairs is called a relation.

Relación Todo conjunto de pares ordenados se llama relación.

Relative frequency relative frequency of an event $= \frac{\text{number of times event occurs}}{\text{total number of trials}}$

Frecuencia relativa frecuencia relativa de un evento $= \frac{\text{número de veces que sucede el evento}}{\text{número total de pruebas}}$

Relative frequency table A relative frequency table shows the ratio of the number of data in each category to the total number of data items. The ratio can be expressed as a fraction, decimal, or percent.

Mesa relativa de frecuencia Una mesa relativa de la frecuencia muestra la proporción del número de datos en cada categoría al número total de artículos de datos. La proporción puede ser expresada como una fracción, el decimal, o el por ciento.

Remainder In division, the remainder is the number that is left after the division is complete.

Residuo En una división, el residuo es el número que queda después de terminar la operación.

English/Spanish Glossary

Remote interior angles Remote interior angles are the two nonadjacent interior angles corresponding to each exterior angle of a triangle.	**Ángulos internos no adyacentes** Los ángulos internos no adyacentes son los dos ángulos internos de un triángulo que se corresponden con el ángulo externo que está más alejado de ellos.
Repeating decimal A repeating decimal has a decimal expansion that repeats the same digit, or block of digits, without end.	**Decimal periódico** Un decimal periódico tiene una expansión decimal que repite el mismo dígito, o grupo de dígitos, sin fin.
Represent To represent is to stand for or take the place of something else. Symbols, equations, charts, and tables are often used to represent particular situations.	**Representar** Representar es sustituir u ocupar el lugar de otra cosa. A menudo se usan símbolos, ecuaciones y tablas para representar determinadas situaciones.
Representative sample A representative sample is a sample of a population in which the number of subjects in the sample with the trait that you are studying is proportional to the number of members in the population with that trait. A representative sample accurately represents the population and does not have bias.	**Muestra representativa** Una muestra representativa es una muestra de una población en la que el número de sujetos de la muestra que tiene la característica que se estudia es proporcional al número de miembros de la población que tienen esa característica. Una muestra representativa representa la población con exactitud y no está sesgada.
Rhombus A rhombus is a parallelogram whose sides are all the same length.	**Rombo** Un rombo es un paralelogramo que tiene todos sus lados de la misma longitud.
Right angle A right angle is an angle with a measure of 90°.	**Ángulo recto** Un ángulo recto es un ángulo que mide 90°.
Right cone A right cone is a cone in which the segment representing the height connects the vertex and the center of the base.	**Cono recto** Un cono recto es un cono en el que el segmento que representa la altura une el vértice y el centro de la base.

English/Spanish Glossary

Right cylinder A right cylinder is a cylinder in which the height joins the centers of the bases.

Cilindro recto Un cilindro recto es un cilindro en el que la altura une los centros de las bases.

Right prism In a right prism, all lateral faces are rectangles.

Prisma recto En un prisma recto, todas las caras laterales son rectángulos.

Right pyramid In a right pyramid, the segment that represents the height intersects the base at its center.

Pirámide recta En una pirámide recta, el segmento que representa la altura interseca la base en el centro.

Right triangle A right triangle is a triangle with one right angle.

Triángulo rectángulo Un triángulo rectángulo es un triángulo que tiene un ángulo recto.

Rigid motion A rigid motion is a transformation that changes only the position of a figure.

Movimiento rígido Un movimiento rígido es una transformación que sólo cambia la posición de una figura.

Rotation A rotation is a rigid motion that turns a figure around a fixed point, called the center of rotation.

Rotación Una rotación es un movimiento rígido que hace girar una figura alrededor de un punto fijo, llamado centro de rotación.

Rounding Rounding a number means replacing the number with a number that tells about how much or how many.

Redondear Redondear un número significa reemplazar ese número por un número que indica más o menos cuánto o cuántos.

S

Sale A sale is a discount offered by a store. A sale does not require the customer to have a coupon.

Venta Una venta es un descuento ofreció por una tienda. Una venta no requiere al cliente a tener un cupón.

Sales tax A tax added to the price of goods and services.

Las ventas tasan Un impuesto añadió al precio de bienes y servicios.

Sample of a population A sample of a population is part of the population. A sample is useful when you want to find out about a population but you do not have the resources to study every member of the population.

Muestra de una población Una muestra de una población es una parte de la población. Una muestra es útil cuando quieres saber algo acerca de una población, pero no tienes los recursos para estudiar a cada miembro de esa población.

Sample space The sample space for an action is the set of all possible outcomes of that action.

Espacio muestral El espacio muestral de una acción es el conjunto de todos los resultados posibles de esa acción.

Sampling method A sampling method is the method by which you choose members of a population to sample.

Método de muestreo Un método de muestreo es el método por el cual escoges miembros de una población para muestrear.

Savings Savings is money that a person puts away for use at a later date.

Ahorros Los ahorros son dinero que una persona guarda para el uso en una fecha posterior.

Scale A scale is a ratio that compares a length in a scale drawing to the corresponding length in the actual object.

Escala Una escala es una razón que compara una longitud en un dibujo a escala con la longitud correspondiente en el objeto real.

Scale drawing A scale drawing is an enlarged or reduced drawing of an object that is proportional to the actual object.

Dibujo a escala Un dibujo a escala es un dibujo ampliado o reducido de un objeto que es proporcional al objeto real.

Scale factor The scale factor is the ratio of a length in the image to the corresponding length in the original figure.

Factor de escala El factor de escala es la razón de una longitud de la imagen a la longitud correspondiente en la figura original.

Scalene triangle A scalene triangle is a triangle in which no sides have the same length.

Triángulo escaleno Un triángulo escaleno es un triángulo que no tiene lados de la misma longitud.

Scatter plot A scatter plot is a graph that uses points to display the relationship between two different sets of data. Each point can be represented by an ordered pair.

Diagrama de dispersión Un diagrama de dispersión es una gráfica que usa puntos para mostrar la relación entre dos conjuntos de datos diferentes. Cada punto se puede representar con un par ordenado.

Scholarship A type of monetary award a student can use to pay for his or her education. The student does not need to repay this money.

Beca Un tipo de premio monetario que un estudiante puede utilizar para pagar por su educación. El estudiante no debe devolver este dinero.

Scientific notation A number in scientific notation is written as the product of two factors, one greater than or equal to 1 and less than 10, and the other a power of 10.

Notación científica Un número en notación científica está escrito como el producto de dos factores, uno mayor que o igual a 1 y menor que 10, y el otro una potencia de 10.

Segment A segment is part of a line. It consists of two endpoints and all of the points on the line between the endpoints.

Segmento Un segmento es una parte de una recta. Está formado por dos extremos y todos los puntos de la recta que están entre los extremos.

Semicircle A semicircle is one half of a circle.

Semicírculo Un semicírculo es la mitad de un círculo.

Similar figures A two-dimensional figure is similar (~) to another two-dimensional figure if you can map one figure to the other by a sequence of rotations, reflections, translations, and dilations.

Figuras semejantes Una figura bidimensional es semejante (~) a otra figura bidimensional si puedes hacer corresponder una figura con otra mediante una secuencia de rotaciones, reflexiones, traslaciones y dilataciones.

Simple interest Simple interest is interest paid only on an original deposit. To calculate simple interest, use the formula $I = prt$ where I is the simple interest, p is the principal, r is the annual interest rate, and t is the number of years that the account earns interest.

Interés simple El interés simple es el interés que se paga sobre un depósito original solamente. Para calcular el interés simple, usa la fórmula $I = crt$ donde I es el interés simple, c es el capital, r es la tasa de interés anual y t es el número de años en que la cuenta obtiene un interés.

Simple random sampling Simple random sampling is a sampling method in which every member of the population has an equal chance of being chosen for the sample.

Muestreo aleatorio simple El muestreo aleatorio simple es un método de muestreo en el que cada miembro de la población tiene la misma probabilidad de ser seleccionado para la muestra.

Simpler form A fraction is in simpler form when it is equivalent to a given fraction and has smaller numbers in the numerator and denominator.

Forma simplificada Una fracción está en su forma simplificada cuando es equivalente a otra fracción dada, pero tiene números más pequeños en el numerador y el denominador.

Simplest form A fraction is in simplest form when the only common factor of the numerator and denominator is one.

Mínima expresión Una fracción está en su mínima expresión cuando el único factor común del numerador y el denominador es 1.

Simplify an algebraic expression To simplify an algebraic expression, combine the like terms of the expression.

Simplificar una expresión algebraica Para simplificar una expresión algebraica, combina los términos semejantes de la expresión.

English/Spanish Glossary

Simulation A simulation is a model of a real-world situation that is used to find probabilities.

Simulación Una simulación es un modelo de una situación de la vida diaria que se usa para hallar probabilidades.

Sketch To sketch a figure, draw a rough outline. When a sketch is asked for, it means that a drawing needs to be included in your response.

Bosquejo Para hacer un bosquejo, dibuja un esquema simple. Si se pide un bosquejo, tu respuesta debe incluir un dibujo.

Slant height of a cone The slant height of a cone, ℓ, is the length of its lateral surface from base to vertex.

Altura inclinada de un cono La altura inclinada de un cono, ℓ, es la longitud de su superficie lateral desde la base hasta el vértice.

Slant height of a pyramid The slant height of a pyramid is the height of a lateral face.

Altura inclinada de una pirámide La altura inclinada de una pirámide es la altura de una cara lateral.

Slope Slope is a ratio that describes steepness.

$$\text{slope} = \frac{\text{vertical change}}{\text{horizontal change}} = \frac{\text{rise}}{\text{run}}$$

Pendiente La pendiente es una razón que describe la inclinación.

$$\text{pendiente} = \frac{\text{cambio vertical}}{\text{cambio horizontal}}$$

$$= \frac{\text{distancia vertical}}{\text{distancia horizontal}}.$$

Slope of a line slope =

$$\frac{\text{change in } y\text{-coordinates}}{\text{change in } x\text{-coordinates}} = \frac{\text{rise}}{\text{run}}$$

Pendiente de una recta pendiente =

$$\frac{\text{cambio en las coordenadas } y}{\text{cambio en las coordenadas } x}$$

$$= \frac{\text{distancia vertical}}{\text{distancia horizontal}}$$

Slope-intercept form An equation written in the form $y = mx + b$ is in slope-intercept form. The graph is a line with slope m and y-intercept b.

Forma pendiente-intercepto Una ecuación escrita en la forma $y = mx + b$ está en forma de pendiente-intercepto. La gráfica es una línea recta con pendiente m e intercepto en y b.

English/Spanish Glossary

Solution of a system of linear equations A solution of a system of linear equations is any ordered pair that makes all the equations of that system true.

Solución de un sistema de ecuaciones lineales Una solución de un sistema de ecuaciones lineales es cualquier par ordenado que hace que todas las ecuaciones de ese sistema sean verdaderas.

Solution of an equation A solution of an equation is a value of the variable that makes the equation true.

Solución de una ecuación Una solución de una ecuación es un valor de la variable que hace que la ecuación sea verdadera.

Solution of an inequality The solutions of an inequality are the values of the variable that make the inequality true.

Solución de una desigualdad Las soluciones de una desigualdad son los valores de la variable que hacen que la desigualdad sea verdadera.

Solution set A solution set contains all of the numbers that satisfy an equation or inequality.

Conjunto solución Un conjunto solución contiene todos los números que satisfacen una ecuación o desigualdad.

Solve To solve a given statement, determine the value or values that make the statement true. Several methods and strategies can be used to solve a problem, including estimating, isolating the variable, drawing a graph, or using a table of values.

Resolver Para resolver un enunciado dado, determina el valor o los valores que hacen que ese enunciado sea verdadero. Para resolver un problema se pueden usar varios métodos y estrategias, como estimar, aislar la variable, dibujar una gráfica o usar una tabla de valores.

Sphere A sphere is the set of all points in space that are the same distance from a center point.

Esfera Una esfera es el conjunto de todos los puntos en el espacio que están a la misma distancia de un punto central.

Square A square is a quadrilateral with four right angles and all sides the same length.

Cuadrado Un cuadrado es un cuadrilátero que tiene cuatro ángulos rectos y todos los lados de la misma longitud.

Square root A square root of a number is a number that, when multiplied by itself, equals the original number.

Raíz cuadrada La raíz cuadrada de un número es un número que, cuando se multiplica por sí mismo, es igual al número original.

Square unit A square unit is the area of a square that has sides that are 1 unit long.

Unidad cuadrada Una unidad cuadrada es el área de un cuadrado en el que cada lado mide 1 unidad de longitud.

Standard form A number written using digits and place value is in standard form.

Forma estándar Un número escrito con dígitos y valor posicional está escrito en forma estándar.

Statistical question A statistical question is a question that investigates an aspect of the real world and can have variety in the responses.

Pregunta estadística Una pregunta estadística es una pregunta que investiga un aspecto de la vida diaria y puede tener varias respuestas.

Statistics Statistics is the study of collecting, organizing, graphing, and analyzing data to draw conclusions about the real world.

Estadística La estadística es el estudio de la recolección, organización, representación gráfica y análisis de datos para sacar conclusiones sobre la vida diaria.

Stem-and-leaf plot A stem-and-leaf plot is a graph that uses the digits of each number to show the data distribution. Each data item is broken into a stem and into a leaf. The leaf is the last digit of the data value. The stem is the other digit or digits of the data value.

Complot de tallo y hoja Un complot del tallo y la hoja es un gráfico que utiliza los dígitos de cada número para mostrar la distribución de datos. Cada artículo de datos es roto en un tallo y en una hoja. La hoja es el último dígito de los datos valora. El tallo es el otro dígito o los dígitos de los datos valoran.

Stored-value card A stored-value card is a prepaid card electronically coded to be worth a specified amount of money.

Tarjeta de almacenado-valor Una tarjeta del almacenado-valor es una tarjeta pagada por adelantado codificó electrónicamente valer una cantidad especificado de dinero.

Straight angle A straight angle is an angle with a measure of 180°.

Ángulo llano Un ángulo llano es un ángulo que mide 180°.

Student loan A student loan provides money to a student to pay for college. The student needs to repay the loan after leaving college. Often the student will need to pay interest on the amount of the loan.

Crédito personal para estudiantes Un crédito personal para estudiantes le proporciona dinero a un estudiante para pagar por el colegio. El estudiante debe devolver el préstamo después de dejar el colegio. A menudo el estudiante deberá pagar interés en la cantidad del préstamo.

Subject Each member in a sample is a subject.

Sujeto Cada miembro de una muestra es un sujeto.

Sum The sum is the answer to an addition problem.

Suma o total La suma o total es el resultado de una operación de suma.

Summarize To summarize an explanation or solution, go over or review the most important points.

Resumir Para resumir una explicación o solución, revisa o repasa los puntos más importantes.

Supplementary angles Two angles are supplementary angles if the sum of their measures is 180°. Supplementary angles that are adjacent form a straight angle.

Ángulos suplementarios Dos ángulos son suplementarios si la suma de sus medidas es 180°. Los ángulos suplementarios que son adyacentes forman un ángulo llano.

Surface area of a cone The surface area of a cone is the sum of the lateral area and the area of the base. The formula for the surface area of a cone is S.A. = L.A. + B.

Área total de un cono El área total de un cono es la suma del área lateral y el área de la base. La fórmula del área total de un cono es A.T. = A.L. + B.

English/Spanish Glossary

Surface area of a cube The surface area of a cube is the sum of the areas of the faces of the cube. The formula for the surface area, S.A., of a cube is S.A. $= 6s^2$, where s represents the length of an edge of the cube.

Área total de un cubo El área total de un cubo es la suma de las áreas de las caras del cubo. La fórmula del área total, A.T., de un cubo es A.T. $= 6s^2$, donde s representa la longitud de una arista del cubo.

Surface area of a cylinder The surface area of a cylinder is the sum of the lateral area and the areas of the two circular bases. The formula for the surface area of a cylinder is S.A. = L.A. + $2B$, where L.A. represents the lateral area of the cylinder and B represents the area of a base of the cylinder.

Área total de un cilindro El área total de un cilindro es la suma del área lateral y las áreas de las dos bases circulares. La fórmula del área total de un cilindro es A.T. = A.L. + $2B$, donde A.L. representa el área lateral del cilindro y B representa el área de una base del cilindro.

Surface area of a pyramid The surface area of a pyramid is the sum of the areas of the faces of the pyramid. The formula for the surface area, S.A., of a pyramid is S.A. = L.A. + B, where L.A. represents the lateral area of the pyramid and B represents the area of the base of the pyramid.

Área total de una pirámide El área total de una pirámide es la suma de las áreas de las caras de la pirámide. La fórmula del área total, A.T., de una pirámide es A.T. = A.L. + B, donde A.L. representa el área lateral de la pirámide y B representa el área de la base de la pirámide.

Surface area of a sphere The surface area of a sphere is equal to the lateral area of a cylinder that has the same radius, r, and height $2r$. The formula for the surface area of a sphere is S.A. $= 4\pi r^2$, where r represents the radius of the sphere.

Área total de una esfera El área total de una esfera es igual al área lateral de un cilindro que tiene el mismo radio, r, y una altura de $2r$. La fórmula del área total de una esfera es A.T. $= 4\pi r^2$, donde r representa el radio de la esfera.

Surface area of a three-dimensional figure The surface area of a three-dimensional figure is the sum of the areas of its faces. You can find the surface area by finding the area of the net of the three-dimensional figure.

Área total de una figura tridimensional El área total de una figura tridimensional es la suma de las áreas de sus caras. Puedes hallar el área total si hallas el área del modelo plano de la figura tridimensional.

English/Spanish Glossary

System of linear equations A system of linear equations is formed by two or more linear equations that use the same variables.

Sistema de ecuaciones lineales Un sistema de ecuaciones lineales está formado por dos o más ecuaciones lineales que usan las mismas variables.

Systematic sampling Systematic sampling is a sampling method in which you choose every nth member of the population, where *n* is a predetermined number. A systematic sample is useful when the researcher is able to approach the population in a systematic, or methodical, way.

Muestreo sistemático El muestreo sistemático es un método de muestreo en el que se escoge cada enésimo miembro de la población, donde *n* es un número predeterminado. Una muestra sistemática es útil cuando el investigador puede enfocarse en la población de manera sistemática o metódica.

T

Taxable wages For federal income tax purposes, your taxable wages are the difference between your earned wages and your withholding allowance. Your employer divides your withholding allowance equally among the pay periods of one year.

Sueldos imponibles Para propósitos federales de impuesto de renta, sus sueldos imponibles son la diferencia entre sus sueldos ganados y su concesión que retienen. Su empleador divide su concesión que retiene igualmente entre los períodos de paga de un año.

Tenths One tenth is one out of ten equal parts of a whole.

Décimas Una décima es 1 de 10 partes iguales de un todo.

Term A term is a number, a variable, or the product of a number and one or more variables.

Término Un término es un número, una variable o el producto de un número y una o más variables.

Terminating decimal A terminating decimal has a decimal expansion that terminates in 0.

Decimal finito Un decimal finito tiene una expansión decimal que termina en 0.

English/Spanish Glossary

Terms of a ratio The terms of a ratio are the quantities *x* and *y* in the ratio.

Términos de una razón Los términos de una razón son la cantidad *x* y la cantidad *y* de la razón.

Theorem A theorem is a conjecture that is proven.

Teorema Un teorema es una conjetura que se ha comprobado.

Theoretical probability When all outcomes of an action are equally likely, $P(\text{event}) = \frac{\text{number of favourable outcomes}}{\text{number of possible outcomes}}$.

Probabilidad teórica Cuando todos los resultados de una acción son igualmente probables, $P(\text{evento}) = \frac{\text{número de resultados favorables}}{\text{número de resultados posibles}}$.

Third quartile For an ordered set of data, the third quartile is the median of the upper half of the data set.

Tercer cuartil Para un conjunto de datos ordenados, el tercer cuartil es la mediana de la mitad superior del conjunto de datos.

Thousandths One thousandth is one part of 1,000 equal parts of a whole.

Milésimas Una milésima es 1 de 1,000 partes iguales de un todo.

Three-dimensional figure A three-dimensional (3-D) figure is a figure that does not lie in a plane.

Figura tridimensional Una figura tridimensional es una figura que no está en un plano.

Total cost of a loan The total cost of a loan is the total amount spent to repay the loan. Total cost includes the principal and all interest paid over the length of the loan. Total cost also includes any fees charged.

El coste total de un préstamo El coste total de un préstamo es el cantidad total que es gastado para devolver el préstamo. El coste total incluye al director y todo el interés pagó sobre la longitud del préstamo. El coste total también incluye cualquier honorario cargado.

Transaction A banking transaction moves money into or out of a bank account.

Transacción Una transacción bancaria mueve dinero en o fuera de una cuenta bancaria.

English/Spanish Glossary

Transfer A transaction that moves money from one bank account to another is a transfer. The balance of one account increases by the same amount the other account decreases.

Transferencia Una transacción que mueve dinero de una cuenta bancaria a otro es una transferencia. El equilibrio de un aumentos de cuenta por la misma cantidad que la otra cuenta disminuye.

Transformation A transformation is a change in position, shape, or size of a figure. Three types of transformations that change position only are translations, reflections, and rotations.

Transformación Una transformación es un cambio en la posición, la forma o el tamaño de una figura. Tres tipos de transformaciones que cambian sólo la posición son las traslaciones, las reflexiones y las rotaciones.

Translation A translation, or slide, is a rigid motion that moves every point of a figure the same distance and in the same direction.

Traslación Una traslación, o deslizamiento, es un movimiento rígido que mueve cada punto de una figura a la misma distancia y en la misma dirección.

Transversal A transversal is a line that intersects two or more lines at different points.

Transversal o secante Una transversal o secante es una línea que interseca dos o más líneas en distintos puntos.

Trapezoid A trapezoid is a quadrilateral with exactly one pair of parallel sides.

Trapecio Un trapecio es un cuadrilátero que tiene exactamente un par de lados paralelos.

Trend line A trend line is a line on a scatter plot, drawn near the points, that approximates the association between the data sets.

Línea de tendencia Una línea de tendencia es una línea en un diagrama de dispersión, trazada cerca de los puntos, que se aproxima a la relación entre los conjuntos de datos.

Trial In a probability experiment, you carry out or observe an action repeatedly. Each observation of the action is a trial.

Prueba En un experimento de probabilidad, realizas u observas una acción varias veces. Cada observación de la acción es una prueba.

Triangle A triangle is a polygon with three sides.

Triángulo Un triángulo es un polígono de tres lados.

English/Spanish Glossary

Triangular prism A triangular prism is a prism with bases in the shape of a triangle.

Prisma triangular Un prisma triangular es un prisma cuyas bases tienen la forma de un triángulo.

True equation A true equation has equal values on each side of the equals sign.

Ecuación verdadera En una ecuación verdadera, los valores a ambos lados del signo igual son iguales.

Two-way frequency table A two-way frequency table displays the counts of the data in each group.

Tabla de frecuencia con dos variables Una tabla de frecuencia con dos variables muestra el conteo de los datos de cada grupo.

Two-way relative frequency table A two-way relative frequency table shows the ratio of the number of data in each group to the size of the population. The relative frequencies can be calculated with respect to the entire population, the row populations, or the column populations. The relative frequencies can be expressed as fractions, decimals, or percents.

Tabla de frecuencias relativas con dos variables Una tabla de frecuencias relativas con dos variables muestra la razón del número de datos de cada grupo al tamaño de la población. Las frecuencias relativas se pueden calcular respecto de la población entera, las poblaciones de las filas o las poblaciones de las columnas. Las frecuencias relativas se pueden expresar como fracciones, decimales o porcentajes.

Two-way table A two-way table shows bivariate categorical data for a population.

Tabla con dos variables Una tabla con dos variables muestra datos bivariados por categorías de una población.

U

Uniform probability model A uniform probability model is a probability model based on using the theoretical probability of equally likely outcomes.

Modelo de probabilidad uniforme Un modelo de probabilidad uniforme es un modelo de probabilidad que se basa en el uso de la probabilidad teórica de resultados igualmente probables.

Unit fraction A unit fraction is a fraction with a numerator of 1 and a denominator that is a whole number greater than 1.

Fracción unitaria Una fracción unitaria es una fracción con un numerador 1 y un denominador que es un número entero mayor que 1.

Unit price A unit price is a unit rate that gives the price of one item.

Precio por unidad El precio por unidad es una tasa por unidad que muestra el precio de un artículo.

Unit rate The rate for one unit of a given quantity is called the unit rate.

Tasa por unidad Se llama tasa por unidad a la tasa que corresponde a 1 unidad de una cantidad dada.

Use To use given information, draw on it to help you determine something else.

Usar Para usar una información dada, apóyate en ella para determinar otra cosa.

V

Valid inference A valid inference is an inference that is true about the population. Valid inferences can be made when they are based on data from a representative sample.

Inferencia válida Una inferencia válida es una inferencia verdadera acerca de una población. Se pueden hacer inferencias válidas si están basadas en los datos de una muestra representativa.

Variability Variability describes how much the items in a data set differ (or vary) from each other. On a data display, variability is shown by how much the data on the horizontal scale are spread out.

Variabilidad La variabilidad describe qué diferencia (o variación) existe entre los elementos de un conjunto de datos. Al exhibir datos, la variabilidad queda representada por la distancia que separa los datos en la escala horizontal.

Variable A variable is a letter that represents an unknown value.

Variable Una variable es una letra que representa un valor desconocido.

Variable expenses Variable expenses are expenses that change from one budget period to the next.

Gastos variables Los gastos variables son los gastos que cambian de un período económico al próximo.

Vertex of a cone The vertex of a cone is the point farthest from the base.

Vértice de un cono El vértice de un cono es el punto más alejado de la base.

Vertex of a polygon The vertex of a polygon is any point where two sides of a polygon meet.

Vértice de un polígono El vértice de un polígono es cualquier punto donde se encuentran dos lados de un polígono.

Vertex of a three-dimensional figure A vertex of a three-dimensional figure is a point where three or more edges meet.

Vértice de una figura tridimensional El vértice de una figura tridimensional es un punto donde se unen tres o más aristas.

Vertex of an angle The vertex of an angle is the point of intersection of the rays that make up the sides of the angle.

Vértice de un ángulo El vértice de un ángulo es el punto de intersección de las semirrectas que forman los lados del ángulo.

Vertical angles Vertical angles are formed by two intersecting lines and are opposite each other. Vertical angles have equal measures.

Ángulos opuestos por el vértice Los ángulos opuestos por el vértice están formados por dos rectas secantes y están uno frente a otro. Los ángulos opuestos por el vértice tienen la misma medida.

Vertical-line test The vertical-line test is a method used to determine if a relation is a function or not. If a vertical line passes through a graph more than once, the graph is not the graph of a function.

Prueba de recta vertical La prueba de recta vertical es un método que se usa para determinar si una relación es una función o no. Si una recta vertical atraviesa la gráfica más de una vez, la gráfica no es la gráfica de una función.

Volume Volume is the number of cubic units needed to fill a solid figure.

Volumen El volumen es el número de unidades cúbicas que se necesitan para llenar un cuerpo geométrico.

Volume of a cone The volume of a cone is the number of unit cubes, or cubic units, needed to fill the cone. The formula for the volume of a cone is $V = \frac{1}{3}Bh$, where B represents the area of the base and h represents the height of the cone.

Volumen de un cono El volumen de un cono es el número de bloques de unidades, o unidades cúbicas, que se necesitan para llenar el cono. La fórmula del volumen de un cono $V = \frac{1}{3}Bh$, donde B representa el área de la base y h representa la altura del cono.

Volume of a cube The volume of a cube is the number of unit cubes, or cubic units, needed to fill the cube. The formula for the volume V of a cube is $V = s^3$, where s represents the length of an edge of the cube.

Volumen de un cubo El volumen de un cubo es el número de bloques de unidades, o unidades cúbicas, que se necesitan para llenar el cubo. La fórmula del volumen, V, de un cubo es $V = s^3$, donde s representa la longitud de una arista del cubo.

Volume of a cylinder The volume of a cylinder is the number of unit cubes, or cubic units, needed to fill the cylinder. The formula for the volume of a cylinder is $V = \pi r^2 h$, where r represents the radius of a base and h represents the height of the cylinder.

Volumen de un cilindro El volumen de un cilindro es el número de bloques de unidades, o unidades cúbicas, que se necesitan para llenar el cilindro. La fórmula del volumen de un cilindro es $V = \pi r^2 h$, donde r representa el radio de una base y h representa la altura del cilindro.

Volume of a prism The volume of a prism is the number of unit cubes, or cubic units, needed to fill the prism. The formula for the volume V of a prism is $V = Bh$, where B represents the area of a base and h represents the height of the prism.

Volumen de un prisma El volumen de un prisma es el número de bloques de unidades, o unidades cúbicas, que se necesitan para llenar el prisma. La fórmula del volumen, V, de un prisma $V = Bh$, donde B representa el área de una base y h representa la altura del prisma.

Volume of a pyramid The volume of a pyramid is the number of unit cubes needed to fill the pyramid. The formula for the volume V of a pyramid is $V = \frac{1}{3}Bh$, where B represents the area of the base and h represents the height of the pyramid.

Volumen de una pirámide El volumen de una pirámide es el número de bloques de unidades, o unidades cúbicas, que se necesitan para llenar la pirámide. La fórmula del volumen, V, de una pirámide es $V = \frac{1}{3}Bh$, donde B representa el área de la base y h representa la altura de la pirámide.

Volume of a sphere The volume of a sphere is the number of unit cubes, or cubic units, needed to fill the sphere. The formula for the volume of a sphere is $V = \frac{4}{3}\pi r^3$.

Volumen de una esfera El volumen de una esfera es el número de bloques de unidades, o unidades cúbicas, que se necesitan para llenar la esfera. La fórmula del volumen de una esfera es $V = \frac{4}{3}\pi r^3$.

W

Whole numbers The whole numbers consist of the number 0 and all of the natural numbers.

Números enteros no negativos Los números enteros no negativos son el número 0 y todos los números naturales.

Withdrawal A transaction that takes money out of a bank account is a withdrawal.

Retirada Una transacción que toma dinero fuera de una cuenta bancaria es una retirada.

Withholding allowance You can exclude a portion of your earned wages, called a withholding allowance, from federal income tax. You can claim one withholding allowance for yourself and one for each person dependent upon your income.

Retener concesión Puede excluir una porción de sus sueldos ganados, llamó una concesión que retiene, del impuesto de renta federal. Puede reclamar una concesión que retiene para usted mismo y para uno para cada dependiente de persona sobre sus ingresos.

Word form of a number The word form of a number is the number written in words.

Número en palabras Un número en palabras es un número escrito con palabras en lugar de dígitos.

Work-Study Work-study is a type of need-based aid that schools might offer to a student. A student must earn work-study money by working certain jobs.

Práctica estudiantil La práctica estudiantil es un tipo de ayuda necesidad-basado que escuelas quizás ofrezcan a un estudiante. Un estudiante debe ganar dinero de práctica estudiantil por ciertos trabajos de trabajo.

X

x-axis The x-axis is the horizontal number line that, together with the y-axis, forms the coordinate plane.

Eje de las x El eje de las x es la recta numérica horizontal que, junto con el eje de las y, forma el plano de coordenadas.

x-coordinate The x-coordinate is the first number in an ordered pair. It tells the number of horizontal units a point is from 0.

Coordenada x La coordenada x (abscisa) es el primer número de un par ordenado. Indica cuántas unidades horizontales hay entre un punto y 0.

Y

y-axis The y-axis is the vertical number line that, together with the x-axis, forms the coordinate plane.

Eje de las y El eje de las y es la recta numérica vertical que, junto con el eje de las x, forma el plano de coordenadas.

y-coordinate The y-coordinate is the second number in an ordered pair. It tells the number of vertical units a point is from 0.

Coordenada y La coordenada y (ordenada) es el segundo número de un par ordenado. Indica cuántas unidades verticales hay entre un punto y 0.

y-intercept The y-intercept of a line is the y-coordinate of the point where the line crosses the y-axis.

Intercepto en y El intercepto en y de una recta es la coordenada y del punto por donde la recta cruza el eje de las y.

Z

Zero exponent property For any nonzero number a, $a^0 = 1$.

Propiedad del exponente cero Para cualquier número distinto de cero a, $a^0 = 1$.

Zero Property of Multiplication The product of 0 and any number is 0. For any number n, $n \cdot 0 = 0$ and $0 \cdot n = 0$.

Propiedad del cero en la multiplicación El producto de 0 y cualquier número es 0. Para cualquier número n, $n \cdot 0 = 0$ and $0 \cdot n = 0$.

Formulas

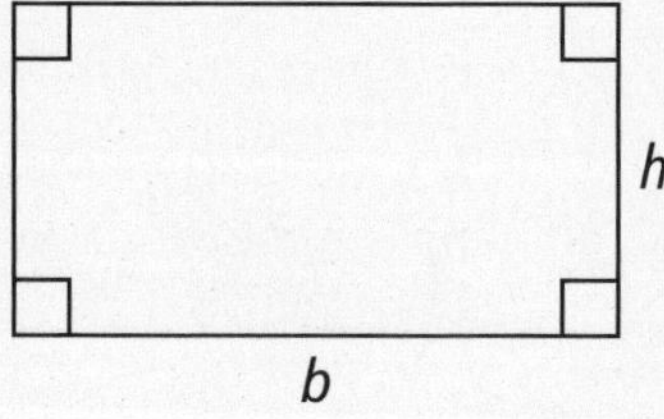

$P = 2b + 2h$

$A = bh$

Rectangle

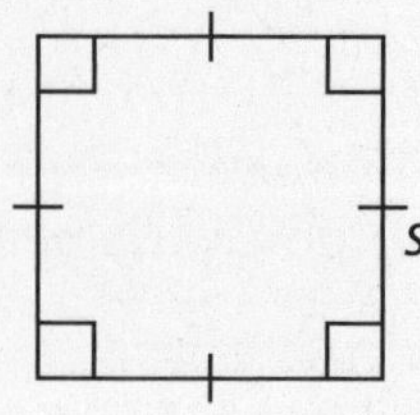

$P = 4s$

$A = s^2$

Square

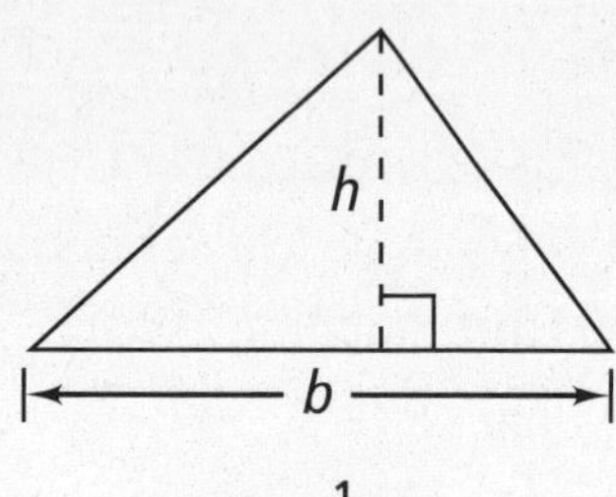

$A = \frac{1}{2}bh$

Triangle

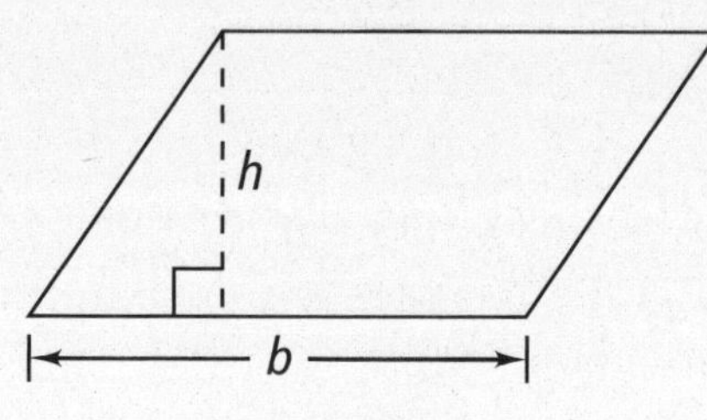

$A = bh$

Parallelogram

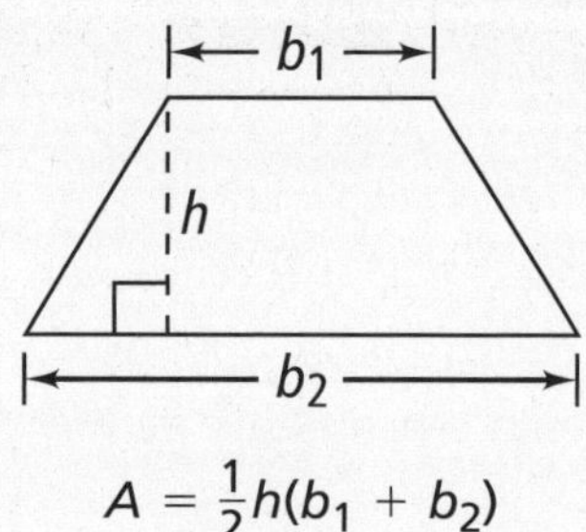

$A = \frac{1}{2}h(b_1 + b_2)$

Trapezoid

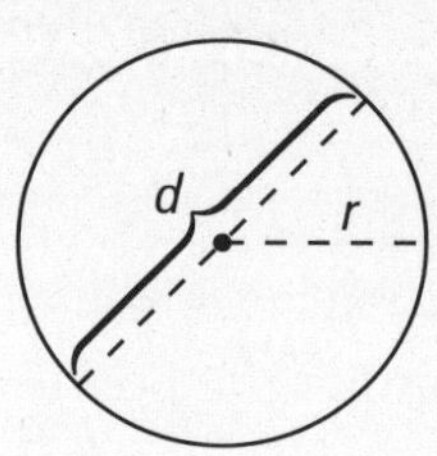

$C = 2\pi r$ or $C = \pi d$

$A = \pi r^2$

Circle

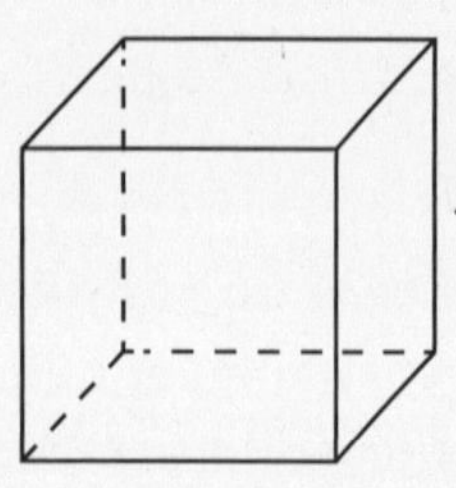

S.A. $= 6s^2$

$V = s^3$

Cube

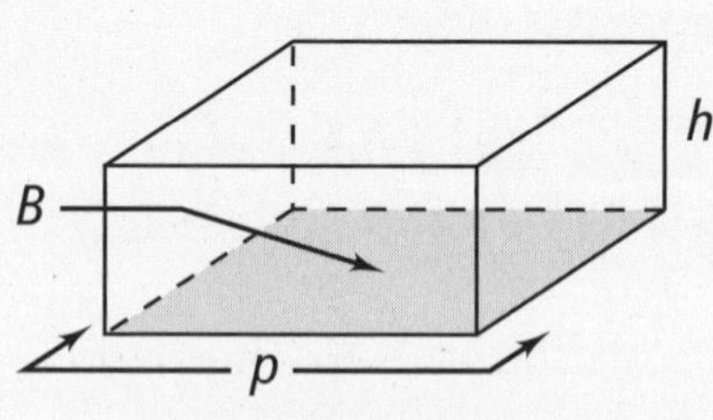

$V = Bh$

L.A. $= ph$

S.A. $=$ L.A. $+ 2B$

Rectangular Prism

Formulas

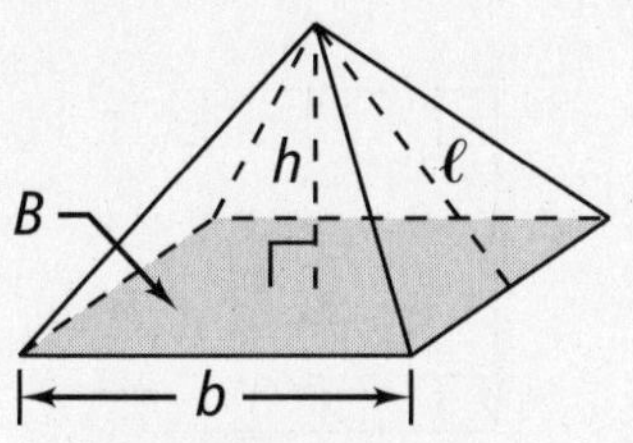

$V = \frac{1}{3}Bh$

L.A. $= 2b\ell$

S.A. $=$ L.A. $+ B$

Square Pyramid

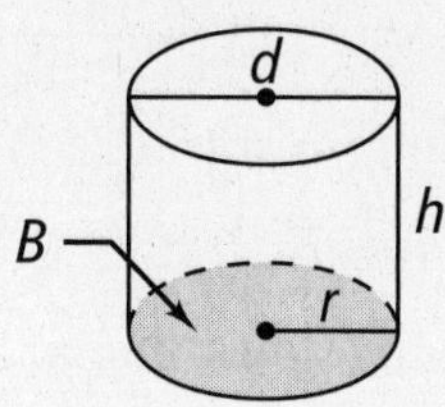

$V = Bh$

L.A. $= 2\pi rh$

S.A. $=$ L.A. $+ 2B$

Cylinder

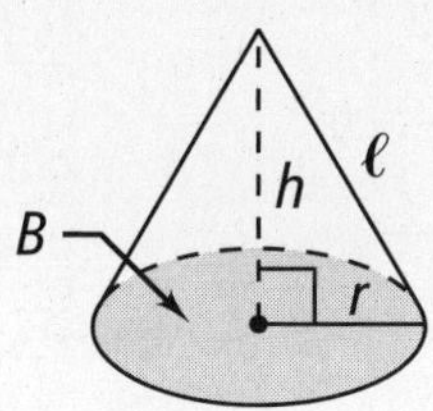

$V = \frac{1}{3}Bh$

L.A. $= \pi r\ell$

S.A. $=$ L.A. $+ B$

Cone

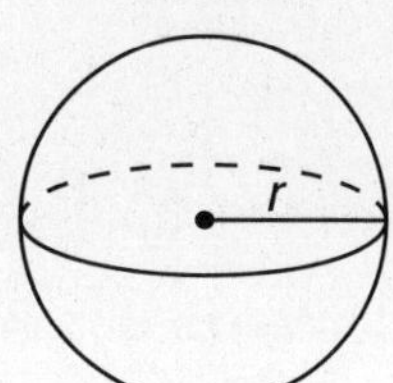

$V = \frac{4}{3}\pi r^3$

S.A. $= 4\pi r^2$

Sphere

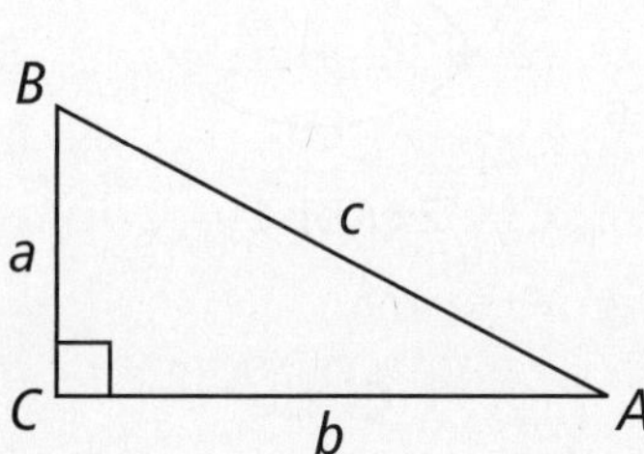

$a^2 + b^2 = c^2$

Pythagorean Theorem

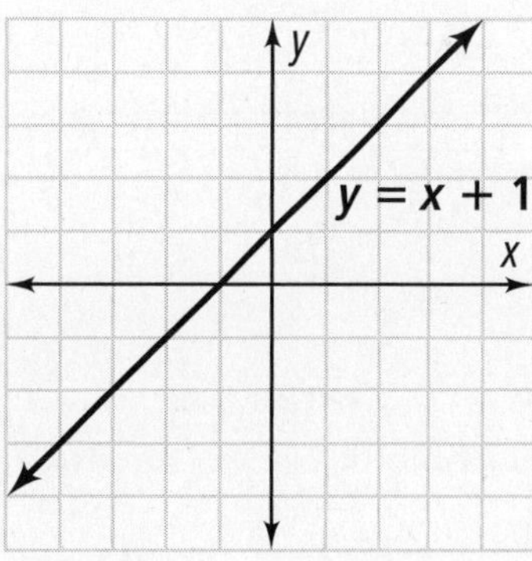

$y = mx + b$, where
$m =$ slope and
$b = y$-intercept

Equation of Line

Math Symbols

Symbol	Meaning
$+$	plus (addition)
$-$	minus (subtraction)
$\times$, $\cdot$	times (multiplication)
$\div$, $\overline{)\ }$, $\frac{a}{b}$	divide (division)
$=$	is equal to
$<$	is less than
$>$	is greater than
$\leq$	is less than or equal to
$\geq$	is greater than or equal to
$\neq$	is not equal to
$(\ )$	parentheses for grouping
$[\ ]$	brackets for grouping
$-a$	opposite of *a*
$\ldots$	and so on
$^\circ$	degrees
$\lvert a \rvert$	absolute value of *a*
$\stackrel{?}{=}$, $\stackrel{?}{<}$, $\stackrel{?}{>}$	Is the statement true?
$\approx$	is approximately equal to
$\frac{b}{a}$	reciprocal of $\frac{a}{b}$
A	area
ℓ	length
w	width
h	height
d	distance
r	rate
t	time
P	perimeter
b	base length
C	circumference
d	diameter

Symbol	Meaning
r	radius
S.A.	surface area
B	area of base
L.A.	lateral area
ℓ	slant height
V	volume
a^n	*n*th power of *a*
$\sqrt{x}$	nonnegative square root of *x*
π	pi, an irrational number approximately equal to 3.14
(a, b)	ordered pair with *x*-coordinate *a* and *y*-coordinate *b*
$\overline{AB}$	segment *AB*
A'	image of *A*, *A* prime
$\triangle ABC$	triangle with vertices *A*, *B*, and *C*
$\rightarrow$	arrow notation
$a : b$, $\frac{a}{b}$	ratio of a to *b*
$\cong$	is congruent to
$\sim$	is similar to
$\angle A$	angle with vertex *A*
AB	length of segment $\overline{AB}$
$\overrightarrow{AB}$	ray *AB*
$\angle ABC$	angle formed by $\overrightarrow{BA}$ and $\overrightarrow{BC}$
$m\angle ABC$	measure of angle *ABC*
$\perp$	is perpendicular to
$\overleftrightarrow{AB}$	line *AB*
$\parallel$	is parallel to
%	percent
P (event)	probability of an event

Measures

Customary	Metric
Length	**Length**
1 foot (ft) = 12 inches (in.) 1 yard (yd) = 36 in. 1 yd = 3 ft 1 mile (mi) = 5,280 ft 1 mi = 1,760 yd	1 centimeter (cm) = 10 millimeters (mm) 1 meter (m) = 100 cm 1 kilometer (km) = 1,000 m 1 mm = 0.001 m
Area	**Area**
1 square foot (ft^2) = 144 square inches ($in.^2$) 1 square yard (yd^2) = 9 ft^2 1 square mile (mi^2) = 640 acres	1 square centimeter (cm^2) = 100 square millimeters (mm^2) 1 square meter (m^2) = 10,000 cm^2
Volume	**Volume**
1 cubic foot (ft^3) = 1,728 cubic inches ($in.^3$) 1 cubic yard (yd^3) = 27 ft^3	1 cubic centimeter (cm^3) = 1,000 cubic millimeters (mm^3) 1 cubic meter (m^3) = 1,000,000 cm^3
Mass	**Mass**
1 pound (lb) = 16 ounces (oz) 1 ton (t) = 2,000 lb	1 gram (g) = 1,000 milligrams (mg) 1 kilogram (kg) = 1,000 g
Capacity	**Capacity**
1 cup (c) = 8 fluid ounces (fl oz) 1 pint (pt) = 2 c 1 quart (qt) = 2 pt 1 gallon (gal) = 4 qt	1 liter (L) = 1,000 milliliters (mL) 1000 liters = 1 kiloliter (kL)

Customary Units and Metric Units	
Length	1 in. = 2.54 cm 1 mi ≈ 1.61 km 1 ft ≈ 0.3 m
Capacity	1 qt ≈ 0.94 L
Weight and Mass	1 oz ≈ 28.3 g 1 lb ≈ 0.45 kg

Properties

Unless otherwise stated, the variables a, b, c, m, and n used in these properties can be replaced with any number represented on a number line.

Identity Properties

Addition $n + 0 = n$ and $0 + n = n$

Multiplication $n \cdot 1 = n$ and $1 \cdot n = n$

Commutative Properties

Addition $a + b = b + a$

Multiplication $a \cdot b = b \cdot a$

Associative Properties

Addition $(a + b) + c = a + (b + c)$

Multiplication $(a \cdot b) \cdot c = a \cdot (b \cdot c)$

Inverse Properties

Addition

$a + (-a) = 0$ and $-a + a = 0$

Multiplication

$a \cdot \frac{1}{a} = 1$ and $\frac{1}{a} \cdot a = 1, (a \neq 0)$

Distributive Properties

$a(b + c) = ab + ac$ $(b + c)a = ba + ca$

$a(b - c) = ab - ac$ $(b - c)a = ba - ca$

Properties of Equality

Addition If $a = b$, then $a + c = b + c$.

Subtraction If $a = b$, then $a - c = b - c$.

Multiplication If $a = b$, then $a \cdot c = b \cdot c$.

Division If $a = b$, and $c \neq 0$, then $\frac{a}{c} = \frac{b}{c}$.

Substitution If $a = b$, then b can replace a in any expression.

Zero Property

$a \cdot 0 = 0$ and $0 \cdot a = 0$.

Properties of Inequality

Addition If $a > b$, then $a + c > b + c$. If $a < b$, then $a + c < b + c$.

Subtraction If $a > b$, then $a - c > b - c$. If $a < b$, then $a - c < b - c$.

Multiplication

If $a > b$ and $c > 0$, then $ac > bc$.

If $a < b$ and $c > 0$, then $ac < bc$.

If $a > b$ and $c < 0$, then $ac < bc$.

If $a < b$ and $c < 0$, then $ac > bc$.

Division

If $a > b$ and $c > 0$, then $\frac{a}{c} > \frac{b}{c}$.

If $a < b$ and $c > 0$, then $\frac{a}{c} < \frac{b}{c}$.

If $a > b$ and $c < 0$, then $\frac{a}{c} < \frac{b}{c}$.

If $a < b$ and $c < 0$, then $\frac{a}{c} > \frac{b}{c}$.

Properties of Exponents

For any nonzero number n and any integers m and n:

Zero Exponent $a^0 = 1$

Negative Exponent $a^{-n} = \frac{1}{a^n}$

Product of Powers $a^m \cdot a^n = a^{m+n}$

Power of a Product $(ab)^n = a^n b^n$

Quotient of Powers $\frac{a^m}{a^n} = a^{m-n}$

Power of a Quotient $\left(\frac{a}{b}\right)^n = \frac{a^n}{b^n}$

Power of a Power $(a^m)^n = a^{mn}$